WHAT the KIDS SAID TODAY

Using Classroom Conversations to Become a Better Teacher

by Daniel Gartrell

Redleaf Press

Published by: Redleaf Press
   a division of Resources for Child Caring
   450 N. Syndicate, Suite 5
   St. Paul, MN 55104

Library of Congress Cataloging-in-Publication Data
Gartrell, Daniel.
   What the kids said today : using classroom conversations to become a
better teacher / by Dan Gartrell.
      p. cm.
   ISBN 1-884834-81-7
   1. Early childhood education—United States—Case studies. 2. Teacher
effectiveness—United States—Case studies. 3. Classroom environment—
United States—Case studies. 4. Communication in education—United States—
Case studies. I. Title.

LB1139.25 .G37 2000
372.1102—dc21

99-055727

*To the women in my life, who have taught me
most of what I know:*

*Dear Wife, Julie
Hip Mother, Beth Goff
Daughters of a blended family—
Kateri, Sara, and Angie
Our Granddaughters Julia and Claire
and
esteemed colleagues and students
over the years*

Acknowledgments

Acknowledgments are due to so many who helped with the book. First, as always, thanks to my wife, Dr. Julie Jochum, for her continual support. While other things were going on, she gave me the time, space, and encouragement I needed to work. She enjoyed the anecdotes as much as I did, and her responses were guiding and helpful.

Thanks to our friend Sharon Hoverson, who not only contributed anecdotes over time as a student, teacher, and mother, but did careful readings of the manuscript. Thanks to my student, Melissa Coleman, for her technical assistance and diligent reading of the material. Two students, now both teachers, contributed many anecdotes: Julie Curb, whose delightful observations grace all eight chapters, and Becki Pederson, whose forthright contributions invariably were perceptive and germane.

Gratitude is due to Pat Sanford, kindergarten teacher, both for her fresh and funny anecdotes and for her insightful statements about the purpose of early childhood education—which I seem to quote at least once in each piece that I write. Appreciation goes as well to Connie Grant, of Q-Net and the Child Development Training Program, for her caring write-ups and feedback, and to Leah Pigatti, Director of Mahube Head Start for, as always, sound logistical advice.

Thanks next go to the families whose children participated in the many encouraging classrooms from which the anecdotes come. By keeping confidential the identities of programs, centers, and schools, I have taken the steps necessary to ensure the children's privacy. Thank you for sharing their priceless experiences with us. I am also grateful to the staff of the many classrooms depicted in the book. Their willingness to have their actions and words both recorded and *published* has made this book possible.

Attention now turns to the 60 anecdote contributors. These university students, assistant teachers, teachers, professors, and administrators submitted anecdotes as student teaching journals, paper assignments in courses, and responses to my requests from the field. Thanks to them for contributing their observations and reflections. Without their willingness to share unguarded parts of theirs and their children's lives, there would be no book. In alphabetical order, they are:

Chris Abner	Trish Dinsha	Selma Needles
Christine Abrahamson	Dawn Eckdahl	Cynthia Ortloff
Kathleen Anderson	Sandy Fladland	Lori Paavola
Lisa Anderson	Michelle Gibson	Karen Palubicki
Sue Anderson	Connie Grant	Becki Pederson
Jessica Armstrong	Cynthia Hanson	Carol Pelton
Kathleen Arola	Sharon Hoverson	Jill Pirotta
Brenda Aslakson	Gretchen Irvine	Virgie Pikula
Jenny Bartz	Sandy Johnson	Suzanne Prom
Dawn Bergerson	Joe Koman	Laurie Rakow
Randy Berstrom	Molly Larson	Julie Rasmussen
Jo Ann Bueckers	Dawn Leesberg	Jodie Riewer
Nellie Cameron	Nicole LeDoux	Connie Stam
Kathy Cavanaugh	Joyce Larson	Arlene Swenson
Patricia Christlieb	Lee Siew Fang	Kathy Ulner
Tammy Christopherson	Kimberly Lord	Marta Underthun
Kelly Clafton	Wendy Love	Laura Vukmanich
Cindy Cronemiller	Jason Marshall	Beth Wallace
Stephen Derby	Pam Mertens	Sandra Weiland
Charissa Dimberio	Brea Musel	Carolyn Williams

The book includes 145 anecdotes from thirty-seven different programs, centers, and schools in Minnesota, North Dakota, New Mexico, California, Alaska, and Vermont. The majority of the Minnesotan programs are in rural northern Minnesota, but I have also included some from Minneapolis and St. Paul. Head Start classrooms were most frequently represented, but child care and kindergarten classrooms were plentiful too. Thanks to all of these programs for participating. Special appreciation is expressed to the staff of Bi-County Head Start in Bemidji and Blackduck, and to the campus child care centers at Bemidji State University and the University of Minnesota–Crookston, for hosting so many student teachers who contributed to the book. To all, your willingness, assistance, and support have been heartwarming.

Finally, appreciation is expressed to editor Beth Wallace, and the rest of the Redleaf Press staff, for forthright editing and capable technical production. You made what would have been a major chore into a learning experience. You made this book possible.

Dan Gartrell, Ed.D.
Director, Child Development Training Program
Professor, Early Childhood and Elementary Education
Bemidji State University, Bemidji, MN 56601
E-mail: dgartrell@vax1.bemidji.msus.edu

Contents

Introduction 1

CHAPTER ONE: SEPARATION AND ATTACHMENT 7

Beginnings 9
Problems 13
Progress 17
Attachment 21

CHAPTER TWO: FAMILY AND SCHOOL 25

It's All about Families 28
Building Connections with the Family 40
Bridging Differences 50

CHAPTER THREE: SAFETY AND LEARNING 54

Classic Ideas about Safety and Learning 56
Brain Research, Safety, and Growth 59
Significant Learning 68

CHAPTER FOUR: GUIDANCE AND MISTAKEN BEHAVIOR 87

Beyond Traditional Discipline 88
Mistaken Behavior 92

CHAPTER FIVE: CONFLICT AND RESOLUTION 112

Social Problem-Solving 112
Three Levels of Conflict Management 120
Putting It All Together 131

CHAPTER SIX: LOSS, LIBERATION, AND RESILIENCY 134

Helping Children Cope with the Death of a Family Member 136
Helping Children Cope with Loss Due to Family Discord 141

Helping Children Cope with Loss Due to Dislocation 143

Helping Children Rebound from a Loss of Personal Control 145

CHAPTER SEVEN: WONDER AND DELIGHT 151

Word Meanings 154

Colorful Language 155

Dealing with Emotions 157

Their Bodies, Themselves 159

Holidays, Holy Places, and Ceremonies 162

Wonder 164

Grandmas and Other Wondrous Things 167

CHAPTER EIGHT: THE ENCOURAGING CLASSROOM 171

Separation and Attachment 173

Identification with the Family 175

Initiative and Learning 176

Reducing the Need for Serious Mistaken Behavior 181

From Conflict to Consideration 184

Loss and Resiliency 187

Permission to Wonder 188

Appendix 196

Introduction

The Theme

Back in the 1960s Paul Goodman wrote that schools socialize our children (condition them for life in society) even more than they educate them (*Compulsory Miseducation,* New York: Horizon Press, 1964). Sixty years before Goodman, John Dewey held that the primary task of schools is to model and teach the processes of democratic living (*The School and Society,* Chicago: University of Chicago Press, 1900/1969). Progressive educators today build on the views of these social thinkers. Outcome attainment, successful test scores, functional literacy, and technological competence have meaning only if young people can use these skills to get along with one another, accept human differences, and solve problems in humane and creative ways. During the last five years of the century the glaring jolts of violence committed by students at school have sounded a clarion call for educators to build together with students a sense of community in our classrooms and schools. From preschool to university, this challenge to our socializing institutions continues to emerge.

The theme of *What the Kids Said Today* is that teachers need to build their classrooms into model caring communities, epitomized by what I call the *encouraging classroom.* In an encouraging classroom, where mutual acceptance is the priority, children learn the skills they need as citizens of larger communities to come: how to accept and cooperate with others, solve problems creatively and peaceably, and express emotions in ways that all can live with.

Adults and children together build encouraging classrooms. The intent of this book is to look directly and openly at how teachers and young children converse in this building process. The windows for the exploration are real life anecdotes, short observations of interactions between young children and with adults, graciously shared with me over recent years by my university students and colleagues. I sought to explore these classroom conversations—and the relationships behind them—for what they tell us about an emerging educational priority: the

1

empowerment of children to build and sustain a sense of community in their lives. I believe that in our increasing ability to teach children to care about and work with each other—despite differences in personality, gender, race, and culture—the path to the twenty-second century can be found.

The chapters in the book discuss real life issues that young children face, and how teachers respond if they are working with children to build an encouraging classroom. With this priority in mind, the eight chapters of the book discuss and illustrate the following issues:

1. Helping children make the separation from home and build attachments with teachers in the classroom
2. Responding to the child's total identification with the family, especially when values of teachers and families differ
3. Nudging children from a need for safety to growth—encouraging them to take the initiative in learning situations
4. Looking at what traditionally has been called *misbehavior* as *mistaken behavior* and using guidance instead of traditional discipline to help children learn from their mistakes
5. Teaching children to solve their problems by using the life skills of conflict management
6. Helping children to recover from loss and find resilience within themselves
7. Appreciating the humor and wonder that are natural parts of life in the encouraging classroom
8. Assessing children's progress in the encouraging classroom

The Method

What the Kids Said Today is written for practicing teachers and persons preparing to become teachers of young children. Sixty different university students, teachers, and other early childhood professionals, including the author, contributed the 145 anecdotes in the book. About 300 young children participated in the anecdotes, from twenty-five different communities ranging from Blackduck, in northern Minnesota, to Minneapolis–St. Paul, and five other states: North Dakota, New Mexico, California, Vermont, and Alaska. The book is written for present and future early childhood teachers by present and future early childhood teachers—with the help of one gnarly old "way-past" early childhood teacher—who believes in young kids and their teachers.

As most of us know, there is always much to learn about teaching young children. Even experienced teachers learn every day. In fact, the freshness of the life lessons that young children teach keeps many teachers rejuvenated and committed to the field. One hundred and forty "life lessons" are encapsuled in the anecdotes in these pages. My job was to piece the conversations together and give a connecting perspective to the story that each tells. Though I am a college professor, the book is not intended as a primary text because it is built around the anecdotes. Social scientists tell us that "anecdotal evidence" is not a strong research strategy. Over the millennia, however, anecdotes always have had educational value. They illustrate what is and what can be in ways that facts, figures, and empirical findings cannot. Whether it is used in classes or for general reading, my hope is that the book will be instructive but also fun to read.

I want the book to be like a conversation. Of course to the reader, the conversation will be somewhat one-way. So let's say that if the book is a *little* like a college lecture, but also a little like the David Letterman show—then I'm getting close to my objective. Oh, about the lecture part—have you ever heard a lecture from a professor who felt passionately about the topic and almost had a sense of humor? That's the kind of lecture I am aiming for.

The Technical Stuff

A few words might serve to introduce the people in the book. The children in the anecdotes are from prekindergarten through primary classrooms and range in age from two to seven years old. European-, African-, Asian-, and Native American children all are represented. Most of the children, however, are low- to middle-income European-American children, since that is the actual population of northern Minnesota. In the anecdotes, the names of children, teachers, centers, schools, and communities were changed or deleted to protect the privacy of participants. All anecdotes are used with permission. The community most represented by anecdotes is Bemidji, Minnesota, where many of the local university's prekindergarten student teachers are placed. Many of the anecdotes are by early childhood education students at Bemidji State University. Many as well are by assistant teachers, lead teachers, and an administrator and college professor or two.

Readers will notice that most of the anecdotes are in two parts: observations and reflections. For years I've encouraged students to separate in their minds what they see from how they interpret what they see. The two-part anecdote trains observers to make this distinction, a crucial one for reasons of perspective, objectivity, and professionalism. I edited the anecdotes only slightly, deleting or changing names for privacy, filling in logistical details, and correcting typos that students would want corrected before their writing appeared in a book. On a few occasions, after talking with the parties involved, I provided additional information about the anecdotes.

Monitoring more than 300 names in the anecdotes, both for privacy and to avoid duplication, was a challenge. (If people are searching for new baby names, I suggest reading this book before buying a "name" dictionary—names from Abby to Zoey appear, with stops for Collier, Voshon, Emily, and Janeen along the way!) I am continually impressed with the imagination shown in children's names these days. Going beyond traditional cultural ties in name selection, today's parents are offering eloquent testimony to the pluralism in American life. In name selection for the book, I tried to reflect this diversity.

Terms

Terms associated with my writing, such as *encouraging classroom, guidance, mistaken behavior, levels of mistaken behavior,* and *liberation teaching,* are defined adequately in the body of the book and the reprint of my article in the Appendix, "Beyond Discipline to Guidance." A few common terms, used a bit differently than usual, need to be explained:

- Classroom. This term is used broadly. It refers to the space used by young children and adults where there is learning going on. It includes playgrounds, activity rooms, lunch rooms, and even transporting vehicles, as well as the classroom itself. The term refers to spaces in homes used for family child care as well as to prekindergarten and primary grade classrooms.
- Early Childhood. The inclusive definition of the term is the period from birth to age eight. The specific age range addressed in the anecdotes is two to seven years. Contributors of anecdotes usually, but not always, identified the type of classroom depicted. When they didn't, I sometimes identified classroom level and program type if I thought that information was helpful to the anecdote. In selecting anecdotes for the book, I looked for the perceptive depiction of the lives of children and their teachers. Whether the anecdote depicted the life of young child in a child care center, versus a child care home, versus a Head Start program, versus a kindergarten classroom, was not important.
- He and She. I alternated the pronouns in each chapter. In odd chapters, the child receives a "he" pronoun, and a teacher receives a "she" pronoun. In even chapters, the sequence is reversed. (The alternative was to use the unreadable term s/he throughout, which some readers like, but editors generally do not.)
- Kid. Mostly, I used *child* or *children.* *Kid* in this book is an affectionate alternate to child, substituted in order to avoid overuse of the more formal designation.
- School. In this day and age a school might house both prekindergarten and kindergarten programs. *Center*—as opposed to in-room *learning centers*—is a common designation for a prekindergarten facility not located in a school. Where *school* got used to indicate *center,* I was using the term the way young children do, often referring to their center as "school."
- Student. Except when referring to someone at the university level, I avoided the term *student,* although some observers used this term in anecdotes. When people refer to a child as a student, they imply that "real learning" is primarily "academic," traditionally involving worksheets and symbol recognition activities. As the National Association for the Education of Young Children maintains, traditional academic

expectations in early childhood tend to be developmentally inappropriate for young children.

- Teacher. To children in an early childhood classroom, anyone bigger than they are is a teacher. In the book this term is loosely defined to include practicum students, student teachers, teacher aides, assistant teachers, lead teachers, and child care providers. Children learn from all caregivers, so in this book they are all teachers.

One Other Note

I know that many family child care providers grow uncomfortable reading words like "teacher" and "classroom" and "center" and (especially) "school," which don't apply to the in-home child care situation. Rather than prejudge the use of these terms in the book, I would encourage family child care providers to let the anecdotes speak for themselves. My guess is that you will do a lot of "been there, heard that" kind of reacting, in a positive kind of way. You are teachers too, in the best sense of the term.

In conclusion, I've been around long enough not to think of this book as showing the early childhood profession a better way. *What the Kids Said Today* is meant as a celebration of what is good and getting better in early childhood education—improvements that you practicing teachers are probably contributing to. I invite you to feel free to smile and nod about what you read in the book that you are doing already. Please consider the book a reinforcement of your life's work.

I hope that teachers-in-preparation find that these ideas have meaning for you in your personal and professional development. May the anecdotes stay with you as illustrations of what liberating (or just plain good) teaching can be.

For all readers, if you find this book about building encouraging classrooms educational, sometimes humorous, and maybe a bit moving, then its purpose is fulfilled.

Separation and Attachment

Outside of the home, the primary institution through which we initiate children to social life is the classroom. When young children leave home for the daily trip to a classroom, they are often making the first of a lifetime of major transitions. Transitions, abrupt and sometimes jolting changes to one's personal circumstances, seem to be part of modern life to an extent not seen in previous times. For most children in the recent past, the first major planned transition took place when they were five or six years old and started kindergarten. These days children who are only a few months old are required to make transitions. Pre-kindergarten classrooms in centers, homes, and elementary schools have become the new entry points for the out-of-home socialization process. More than in the past, many children make numerous transitions long before they begin elementary school.

With the increase of very young children in out-of-home programs, critics claim that the traditional role of the family is being given over to an early childhood "industry." Parents are losing contact with their children, they say, and in the long run society will pay the cost. On the contrary, as members of the early childhood profession well know, teachers work with the family to extend the child's social experience, so that he can bring together life at home and in the classroom, and feel a sense of belonging in both. Early childhood teachers recognize that through feeling valued as a member of family and peer group, the child begins healthy development as a member of an expanding community whose center is the home.

Children making the transition to early childhood programs face the same two challenges that children faced in the past when transitioning into kindergarten: separation from family members in the home and development of new relationships in the classroom. Early childhood teachers must not underestimate the dramatic nature of this transition. The child has little if any previous experience to help him understand the life change involved in going to an early childhood program. Even though it's for hours rather than days, the first separation from the family seems total. The child is bound to feel not only anxiety, but also a loss of connection with family members.

Given this predicament, developing an attachment to a caregiver in the new setting becomes crucial. Attachment—a reliable, warm relationship between child and caregiver—establishes trust in the child's mind that nurturing will occur in the new setting. Through the interactions that lead to attachment, the teacher helps the child make a connection to the classroom community. The child feels membership in both the family and this new group outside of the home. As the child accomplishes the transition to school, he gains vital experience that will be helpful in other transitions to come, into unknown future communities.

Through anecdotes and discussion, the four sections of chapter one show how teachers can respond to separation in ways that will guide children into attachment. "Beginnings" looks at how teachers respond to children as they begin the classroom experience. As the child enters the classroom, the teacher on occasion must set aside the usual program expectations to make the child feel welcome. "Problems" shows how adults can respond helpfully when children experience separation and attachment difficulties. "Progress" illustrates how adults recognize and support signs that the child is adjusting. "Attachment" shares the gratification and even exhilaration that teachers feel when children "have arrived," when they have formed attachments with caregivers and found membership in the classroom community.

Beginnings

When beginning in a program, something that the infant, toddler, or preschooler needs very much, but cannot easily express in ways acceptable to adults, is a supportive relationship with a caregiver. In the first anecdote, Annette observes a four year old's arrival at his child care classroom soon after starting the program. Her anecdote documents the active reassurance given by the teacher and reflects what Scott must be feeling.

OBSERVATION: *At 8 A.M. children and their parents were filing into the classroom. One little boy, Scott, and his dad came in. Scott is a young four-year-old and as he walked in he had to be guided by his father. Scott resisted entering the classroom, and his dad was saying things like, "Come on, Scott, it's just like the other day. Daddy has to go to class." It was five minutes after 8:00. Scott's dad looked at his watch and said, "Scott, give me a hug and then I have to go. I'm late for class." Scott gave his dad a hug and cried, holding on tightly to his dad.*

The teacher walked over, took Scott from his dad, and told dad, "We will be just fine." The dad left Scott crying and went to class. The teacher sat down on a chair with Scott and held him tight. She said, "Don't worry, Scott; your dad will be back after his classes." Another child came over to try to comfort him, and Scott hid his face. The teacher asked the other child in a friendly tone to find something to play with while she talked to Scott for a minute. She proceeded to tell Scott, "I know you're embarrassed about crying in front of your friends, but that's okay; everyone misses their mom and dad sometimes, even teachers. She was just trying to help and tell you that it was okay. It really is okay to be sad when your dad leaves, but you know that he will come back as soon as his classes are over." She paused, and Scott nodded. She said, "Would you like to sit here and cuddle for a little bit?" Scott nodded his head again. He sat there for about two minutes and then slid off of the teacher's lap and went to go play with the girl who had tried to comfort him.

REFLECTION: *Haim Ginott said, "To reach a child's mind a teacher must capture his heart. Only if a child feels right can he think right" (Teacher and Child, New York: Avon Books, 1972). If a teacher shows even the slightest bit of rejection toward a child, not only will the child have a hard time in the classroom, but the child will also have hard feelings toward the teacher. From my observation I actually saw and felt the acceptance of the teacher toward Scott. I think of myself as a sad little kid and missing my mommy. I would also just want to be held for a while. I think the way the teacher worked with Scott showed him that he was accepted and therefore made the transition from home to school a bit easier.*

When a young child leaves home and enters the classroom, he leaves a familiar world and enters a foreign one. The door to the classroom is a door to unknown social dynamics and personal challenges—this to a child with only months of life experience. Whether on the first day, or after a few weeks when reality has set in, the child realizes that he is in the midst of perhaps more children than he has seen before, and with adults who are strangers. Thinking of this situation, we might well agree with Annette's reflection about the perceptive way that the teacher made Scott feel accepted and eased his transition from home to school.

Most parents recognize teachers' efforts to help young children find a place in the classroom community. In the following anecdote, Jeri shares with us how she helps Carlos with a difficult transition. When a child starts a new program, the teacher must help him adapt not just to adults, but to the other children as well.

OBSERVATION: *Carlos, age three, was an only child. He had begun to attend the center five full days each week. On this particular day, I heard Carlos more than a few minutes before he entered our classroom. His mother lived on campus and had given him a sled ride to the center, as well as right into our classroom! I heard Carlos's exclamations, "No, no, no Mommy, no go today, no stay here Mommy." Upon Carlos's entrance, I noticed two of the staff members giving each other a look like, "Oh-oh, here comes trouble." Carlos's friends were* *anxious to say hello and greeted both him and his mother. Before taking his coat off, Carlos unzipped his backpack and started sorting out his tractors, loaders, graders, bulldozers, etc., all of which were toys from home. One toddler, Trish, immediately grabbed for the bulldozer, and Damien ran off with the tractor, which left Carlos with only two of his vehicles.*

I was engaged in conversation with Carlos's mother at the time, but noticed that another staff member stepped in and took control of Carlos's situation. She raised her voice and said, "Trish, Damien, and Carlos. Come here, all of you, over here!" The toddlers continued their play with Carlos's prized possessions. Carlos continued to be upset and began to cry. After a few more pleas, the staff member realized that Trish and Damien weren't going to give Carlos his belongings back. The staff member took Carlos aside and told him, "You're going to have to share, I guess, because your friends want to see them too, and you know you aren't supposed to have home toys in the class."

About then, I told Carlos's mother goodbye and stepped over to where Carlos was shaking and sobbing uncontrollably. He sat clutching the two toys that were left. I spoke in a calm voice as I put my arm around Carlos's shoulders, "Carlos, I know that these tractors are very special to you and they are your favorite. Sometimes you don't want to share with your friends and that is okay because they belong to you. I can walk with you over to your friends to tell them you'd like your toys back." Carlos looked me square in the eye and hollered, "NO!" I proceeded to approach the two children and explained that Carlos had brought these toys from home and that they weren't for sharing unless Carlos decided he'd like to share them. Trish and Damien were quick to understand this, as they both brought toys from home on occasion as well. The vehicles were returned to Carlos, and he quickly secured them in his backpack. He continued to sit by the door and grip his belongings for five minutes following this interaction. I eventually got him playing with the other children.

REFLECTION: *Carlos needs to be given due time to transition between home and school each morning. On this day, the other staff member didn't respond to Carlos's needs. Carlos certainly did not understand that bringing home toys was not okay in the room at this particular point in time. It is my view that a child shouldn't be forced to share something that is his or her very own personal belonging. How many adults share their favorite coffee mug with their colleagues? The* *child should be offered a choice whether to share or not. It is the center policy not to bring home toys into the classroom. Yet, there are certain situations where a teacher must adapt to the situation. Allowing Carlos the chance to hold on to a familiar object to comfort himself until he is ready to move on has proved beneficial.*

In building an encouraging classroom, teachers find ways to address problems without causing children to feel isolated from the group. Jeri showed this priority clearly in her responses. First, she helped Carlos through a transition made more difficult by the responses of another teacher. Jeri demonstrated that she appreciated his feelings and enabled him to get through the crisis of having both his mom and his toys leave at once. She took action to help Carlos retrieve his "security objects" and regain self-esteem.

Second, Jeri guided the other children to consider Carlos's feelings and facilitate his transition. As both anecdotes illustrate, separation situations impact other children in the class, not just the child experiencing strong feelings. Jeri helped Trish and Damien to be contributing community members—and recover from "being in trouble" with the other teacher.

Jeri made a solid point in her reflection about the no-toys-from-home rule. When children cannot understand rules, enforcing them "because children need to learn to follow rules" tends to make problems worse. Sometimes if emotions are high, an adult finds it easier to enforce the letter of the law than to make a professional judgment based on the whole picture. When teachers are being professionals rather than technicians, they do enforce established limits, but sensibly, in ways that guide toward the goals of the encouraging classroom. From the anecdote, it seems that the other teacher still is learning this high-level skill.

Ever since Carlos had begun at the center, both he and his mother had had difficulty with separations. Jeri spoke with the mother at pickup and reassured her that Carlos soon felt better and joined the other children. In this situation Jeri stayed focused on the issues that really mattered: She helped Carlos separate from his mom, recover control of his feelings, and transition into the classroom. Jeri also helped all three children—clearly at different points in the separation–attachment process—to feel that they were part of the classroom community. So much learning begins the first times a child walks through the door and is greeted by a teacher.

Problems

In my university classes I often say that the third most difficult job in the world is being a teacher; the second most difficult is a tie between being a substitute teacher and being a Head Start home visitor. The most difficult job in the world is being a parent. Think about it. For this most important vocation there is so little preparation: no license, degree, or certificate required. (I'd like to see a Child Development Associate credential for this job!) Once you become a parent, you work 24 hours a day, paying out more than you take in, and for most of us there aren't many days off, vacations, or sick leave. Usually, you have to hold down another job or two just to finance the first one! Even security for when you retire isn't assured. Oh, maybe once in a while you get a nice fringe benefit or two, but that's about it.

Sometimes one parent—or even a grandparent, aunt, or uncle—must raise a family alone. There are bills to pay, housing costs to cover, and food to buy. On top of this, one kid wants a battery-powered Space Wars vehicle to ride in, and another wants a computer. How do you make ends meet? Not to mention that a single parent lacks a tag-team partner for momentary relief in the ongoing wrestling match of family life.

There's no way around it. The psychological pressures on parents today are just plain heavy. In the face of modern life, the issue is not that some parents "don't care about their kids." It is that sometimes life is so hard, parents can't even care about themselves—and may seem preoccupied with this effort as a result. These parents don't have the psychological strength to give the nurturing to their children that all parents want to give. Such families need support and guidance, rather than blame. The reason is simple. The home situation, even if it is unreliable, is the only life the young child knows. Children identify with even the most marginally functioning family situations and develop strong attachments, if less secure ones, with their family members. By working with the child *and* the family, teachers strengthen the dynamics that will sustain the child in the future.

In the individual transition process, as in Kellie's story on the next page, teachers often see how family circumstances weigh on a child.

13

OBSERVATION: *There is a child in our class who has been a great challenge to me. I have talked to the teacher about Amber, and she comes from a difficult family life. She has six older brothers and sisters and her mother has not been around very much—she has been in treatment for drugs and alcohol. Her father has been raising the kids and recently he just tried to commit suicide by taking pills, but did make it to the hospital in time to be saved.*

Amber is very quiet verbally, but when she wants something, she will let you know physically. She is quite physical with the other children. There have been numerous situations where she has pulled things out of other children's hands or tugged back and forth things she wants. I have not witnessed her ever asking another child for an item. She has a hard time verbally expressing what she wants.

I will ask Amber to do something and all she will usually do is shake her head no, with half a smile on her face. She will listen to the other teachers usually pretty well, but there have been a couple of situations where they have had to get firm with her. The last couple of times I have been there, she has been warmer to me. She has been wanting to sit on my lap during circle and last Thursday she brought in a picture-letter she made for me at home. She was very shy about giving it to me. Amber told me in the morning she had something for me but didn't give it to me right away. At the end of the day, I was reading a story to the kids waiting for the bus to come. Just as I finished, she rushed over to me, threw the picture down and walked away real fast. She was almost embarrassed that she had something for me. I looked at it and asked her to read to me what it said and she said, "I don't know..." She took it back and returned it to me three different times, adding something to it each time. Each time I asked her to read it to me, she refused.

REFLECTION: *I feel that we must be moving forward. We are having positive contact between us, and that is definitely a step in the right direction. Maybe once Amber knows she can be my friend and trust me, then she will learn to respect me too. I will keep working on her friendship and hopefully the respect will come naturally.*

Long-term studies of *attachment* done by many researchers, including Marti Erickson and R. C. Pianta ("New Lunch Boxes, Old Feelings: What Kids Bring to School," *Early Education and Development* 1[1] 35–49), suggest that children gain from personally meaningful positive relationships with teachers and other significant adults as well as with parents. This is not to say that teachers should see themselves as substitute parents, but that through their relationships with both children and parents, teachers can and do make a difference in children's lives.

Attachment occurs when a child feels friendship, trust, identification with, and (sometimes later) respect toward an adult. Many adults believe that the order should be reversed, with respect for the adult coming first. But an adult cannot build a relationship with a child based on acts of discipline. The child has a difficult time with rules he cannot understand, and he looks to the adult for nurturance and seeks identification with, rather than obedience toward, significant adults. Children need attachments in order to make the initial transition to the classroom, especially when home conditions are difficult.

After a child has made initial connections within a classroom, events that are sometimes overlooked can re-aggravate separation anxieties. Two such events are the promotion of a child to an older group, with the new adjustments made necessary by this transition, and the promotion of a sibling, resulting in the separation of a relative on whom the other child has come to rely. Sometimes licensing laws and safety concerns cause the segregation of children by age groups, a practice that results in *institutional separation*. Family child care generally avoids institutional separation, due to its natural use of family groups (groups of children of different ages that do things together each day). Teachers in center-based programs would also do well to structure their programs on a family-group basis and to take steps to ease children's transitions across groups. Krista observed the consequences of institutional separation on Donny, who had been making progress in his transition to the center.

OBSERVATION: *When I first came into the toddler room, there was a little boy crying his eyes out. His name was Donny. When I went up to him, I picked him up, and he clung to me. The teacher had said that he was tired, but was also without his sister. His sister, Katya, is almost two years older and had gotten to go to the preschool room to be with the bigger kids this year. Donny has had a hard time adjusting to that. As I talked with him and got him to stop crying and took his mind off things, he settled right down and had a good time.*

When we went outside for playtime, the preschoolers were out there also. At the beginning of outside time the preschoolers were on the other side of the fence from the toddlers. After a while the preschoolers came into the fenced-in area, and Katya came right up to Donny and hugged and kissed him. After that, neither one did anything without the other while they were outside.

When it was time to come inside, Donny was upset. Katya was also upset because their mom hadn't been there yet. Mom usually came while they were outside. We got Donny settled down as we went in, and the preschool teacher got Katya settled down also. His mom did come a little while later. They were both very happy to see her. She looks to be an older mother and seemed very close with the kids.

To the child in an early childhood setting, just as there is no replacing parents, so there is no replacing sisters and brothers. A task of the teacher in the transition process is to help children keep in balance two connected human needs: the need for safety, and the need for growth (A. H. Maslow, *Toward a Psychology of Being*, Princeton, NJ: Van Norstrand Company, Inc., 1962). Parents often encourage children to look after each other outside the home. For young children, this may bring an initial sense of safety, but the related responsibilities in the task often become more than young children can handle. It is hard enough looking after yourself when you are 48 months old; looking after a "littler" brother or sister as well cannot be relaxing. In these circumstances, growth becomes difficult for both children.

By gradually nudging siblings toward separation, and helping them to adjust, the teacher in the long run empowers each to work on that all important need for growth. Helping parents adjust their expectations is often part of this task. Some-times you can almost see a parent's mind at work, thinking, "If I can't be there to care for my children, I can at least get Katya to look after Donny." Teachers need to assure parents that they will care for both children, and that the older child needs to enjoy being a child by having to look out only for himself.

The occasional need for planned separation of siblings was illustrated in the experience of Terry, a Head Start teacher from a small rural town. In a recent year, identical triplet four-year-old boys were in her class. When they began, the boys stuck to each other and held back from outside interactions. The staff worked hard to help each child build a unique identity, keeping them in the same large group but gently separating them for small groups and individual activities. The staff knew the children had become at ease in the program when by spring they began to switch names to trick other children and the teachers. Although the mother was reluctant, Terry counseled her that the triplets were ready for separate kindergarten placements. The next year they were in three separate kindergarten classes in the public school, and Terry was not surprised to hear that all agreed this had been the right decision.

Progress

Clearly, progress in transitioning shows itself in different ways for different children. The child's disposition, the family's dynamics, and the staff's human relations skills all influence the path and pace of acceptance by the child of the program. Sometimes a teacher knows that young children have come to feel safe in a classroom when they let themselves nap. Other times, a child may speak in a voice louder than a whisper for the first time—or speak at all. A child who begins to sing to himself, join others in play, or even act mischievously has probably grown comfortable with the program. The following two anecdotes, both by student teachers in Head Start classrooms, show children who are begin-ning to feel acceptance for and by the group.

OBSERVATION: *As Brenna arrived today, I was again greeted by an animal sound. Today she was a cat! She took on all the mannerisms and actions of the* *cat. She pretended to lick herself and had the aloof and haughty look of a cat. She came in, went to the other children, and meowed! Cassandra (another child) announced that Brenna was a kitty today. So the children played in the house-keeping area with Brenna as their pet cat.*

REFLECTION: *This behavior takes place almost every time Brenna arrives. There are numerous animals that she imitates quite well. She usually will not respond with oral language for at least 10 minutes. At the beginning of school it was longer and repeated at different times during the day. Now she is an animal only at the beginning of each session. She is an only child. Grandma is her baby sitter. Except for us, she has no social time with other children. They have a number of pets, including cats. Brenna is making progress, but I am glad she will have another year in Head Start before she starts kindergarten.*

Brenna's increasing comfort in the class shows in her growing willingness to leave the animal roles behind. At this point in the year (April), she used the roles to assist with the initial transition at the beginning of the day. The anecdote also shows another factor important for transition to occur: acceptance of the child by her peers. When comfortable in their own circumstances, young children have an adaptability to others' behaviors that adults can only wonder at. The children in this situation probably have an intuitive understanding of where Brenna is coming from. The children as much as the teachers are helping Brenna to adjust.

By their hard work, teachers help children accept, and be accepted by, the group even when a child's behavior puts him at risk for rejection. Modeling and teaching the values of an encouraging classroom is an ongoing task—beginning at start-up and with results sometimes not seen until the following spring. With the exception of a child who has serious problems, children tend to be friendly and accepting in an encouraging classroom—because they know that they are accepted.

In early childhood education, bringing children's home life into the classroom is a time-honored technique for encouraging their involvement. Frederich Froebel pioneered this practice in the early kindergartens of the 1800s through home visits, mothers' meetings, and the use of mothers as teachers. Carlos was working toward the same goal when he brought familiar toys to school in his backpack. Security blankets, and classic stories of how adults gently weaned children from them, are common in the early childhood field. Teachers also talk with families about customs, interests, and activities and use this information to make the classroom less foreign and more familiar to the child. Kellie's anecdote, below, illustrates this practice of including elements of a child's home life in the classroom to help bring a child around.

OBSERVATION: *Shelby is probably the quietest little girl in the class, and she has been hard for me to get to know. She is real shy with all of the other kids and all of the adults in the room. At the recent Head Start auction, her mother mentioned that she likes to line dance at home and does a great imitation of Steve Erkel. When Mom told me this I told her I was going to try to see if Shelby would show me this stuff at school. I told Shelby the next day that I heard from her mother that she can line dance and imitate Steve Erkel(!). She had a big smile on her face when I asked her to show me how to line dance. In the morning, she wanted no part of line dancing in front of me. By the end of the day, I asked her again and she did it. I couldn't believe it. I said to her, "Shelby, are you sure you don't want to teach me how to line dance? I would really like to learn and I bet you would be a great teacher." She looked at me a little hesitantly but started in on the dance. After she was done, I got up and tried to do it too, using her advice, of course.*

The idea of *emergent curriculum*—creating curriculum around the interests and experiences of children—relies heavily on knowing about children's lives outside of school. In an informal fashion Kellie practiced emergent curriculum with Shelby. When emergent curriculum includes warm teacher–child interaction, as Kellie demonstrated, children respond. Emergent curriculum abounds in early childhood education today. Examples range from the well-known emergent programs of Reggio Emilia in Italy, to the materials, activities, themes, and projects teachers build around ethnic celebrations, ceremonies, and customs that are a part of the children's community life.

Cultural connections between family and school make the classroom familiar and accepting for children. Such connections are easier when teachers and children share similar cultural backgrounds. When teachers differ in their ethnicity and heritage from children in the class, they need to work hard to be culturally responsive in their teaching. The preschool teacher in the following anecdote has gone on in her education and is now a successful superintendent in a rural community. She still regards the following event as a vital learning experience in her professional development.

OBSERVATION: *A teacher had been showing her preschoolers how to play rhythm sticks when two Ojibwe children joined her class. The teacher invited DJ and Tucker to either participate with the group or sit and watch. The two boys watched, then noticed two extra sticks on a chair behind the teacher. They crawled behind her and each picked up a stick. The boys each cupped one ear and began drumming the sticks on the chair in time to the music. The teacher became upset with them, took away the sticks, and told them to sit quietly for the rest of the activity.*

Afterwards, the teacher aide, who was also Ojibwe, explained that the children were using the sticks as their older relatives did, to "beat the drum and sing like at a pow-wow." Embarrassed, the teacher apologized to the boys and asked the aide to help organize a traditional Ojibwe dance for the preschool. The aide knew the boys' relatives and got them to visit the class, complete with drum and ceremonial dress (which they changed into from their street clothes only after meeting the children). DJ and Tucker were proud to sit with the singers and dance for and with the rest of the class. Pow-wows, with recorded music, drums and a new use for the rhythm sticks became a regular part of the preschool program. (Dan Gartrell, A Guidance Approach for the Encouraging Classroom, *Albany, NY: Delmar/ITP Publishers, 1998, 75).*

This anecdote shows a professional teacher's ability to learn from her colleague and take steps to redress a mistake that could have alienated a new family. It also demonstrates that emergent activities, even if they come directly from the experience of only some of the children, can have benefits for all. To help children find a place in the classroom community, however, events must be interactive experiences with personal meaning for the children rather than performances for the benefit of adults. In the encouraging classroom, *emergent curriculum* requires culturally relevant learning experiences that children are developmentally ready for and can actively engage in. When teachers engage a child in activity that grows from her life outside of school, they have made real progress in helping the child find membership in the class. Clearly, the success of emergent curriculum depends on the school's relationship with family as well as with the child.

Attachment

The teacher knows when the child has successfully made the transition: accepted regular separation from the family, accepted the children in the early childhood program, and accepted as a positive his relationship with the teacher. The signs are clear. The child shows less-frequent anxious behavior and more behavior that is confident and indicates growth. In the following anecdote, Swoosie, a student teacher in a child care center, is amazed when Jake comes and sits by her at the art center. Jake has kept to himself, rarely initiating conversations with children or adults since he began in the program. His family has recently moved to the community, and with the move, the four year old has left family and friends behind. Swoosie recorded the anecdote two months after Jake had first come into the class.

OBSERVATION: *I was sitting at the table with our home-made goop during free choice. Jake came over and started to play with the goop. The first thing he said was, "This feels like an egg!" I agreed with him and he went on to say, "Guess what? I know how to bake!"*

I said, "Wow, you know how to bake?"

Jake said, "For real! I bake pancakes, and eggs, and bacon! I'm good at it. My Mom showed me how."

REFLECTION: *Jake was so excited when he talked about baking! He thought it was the greatest thing! It's obviously something he really takes pride in. I thought the conversation was fun because it came out of nowhere! When I asked him if he baked, he said "For real!" I was really amused at his answer and just the way he said it. I can still picture him saying that and exactly how it sounded. He was so thrilled with himself!*

Children show acceptance of the program when they productively engage in activities, initiate conversations, and share spontaneous expressions of happiness. Jake demonstrated all of these behaviors in his interaction with Swoosie. The delight of the child in such situations is often matched by the feelings of the teacher that the child has found a place in the classroom community. A common experience of teachers is that when a child comes around, as Jake did, it is as though he has decided the setting is safe. Barring outside circumstances, these children regress to previous behaviors only on occasion, often as a result of a temporary upset that they get over. The feeling among the staff on this day was, "Jake has arrived."

At a different place in her transition process, Jinada, the child in the next anecdote, had shown a need to control situations as a way of establishing her presence. Rather than fight Jinada's social needs, the staff worked with her to increase social responsiveness in her play. On this day, Jinada responded. Notice her invitation to the teacher to participate, an expression of attachment that the staff had not seen before.

OBSERVATION: *Jinada came over to me from the house area and told me about the "dancing party" they were having and said she would like me to come. Of course, I accepted the invitation. I asked her what her dancing party was all about and she told me that they slow danced and ate food. I asked what kind of food, and she replied, "Oh, you know, dance food stuff. Like cookies and cake and, um...oranges!" "Oh," I replied, "I will come for sure! Sounds like a wonderful time!" She grabbed my hand and drug me to the "dance floor." We danced and spun until we could dance no more! We had a blast. Then, of course we sat down for some cookies and oranges.*

REFLECTION: *Jinada is a great one for pretending. She was trying to recruit everyone to her dancing party. And it worked pretty well. I think she is quite comfortable in our class now, and that makes me feel good. I feel the other kids are pretty comfortable now too, because when we got out there dancing, some other kids joined us and soon we had a circle of four or five dancing.*

When children come to feel a sense of community in the encouraging classroom, their behaviors become more spontaneous and sociable. Busy in the activities of the day, class members are just plain having a good time. Even toddlers and young preschoolers find these behaviors "catchy" and show a sociability surprising to many adults. These are the days teachers thoroughly enjoy. They work hard to set the scene and to nurture the development of community in the classroom. They deserve to feel gratification, and even amazement, when their efforts are rewarded, sometimes beyond their expectations. Sherry, a kindergarten teacher, describes an exchange toward the end of her second year of teaching that she won't soon forget.

> **OBSERVATION:** *After I had talked with my class about graduating and going on to first grade next year, one little boy came up to me, looked me in the eye and said, "I want to keep you!" Thinking that Dillon was worried about next year, I tried to reassure him that the first grade teachers were great and that first grade would be another great adventure. He looked at me in frustration and said, "NO, teacher, I want to KEEP you! You know, at my house—you could be mine!"*

With an expression of affection like this, many teachers would find it hard to hide a big grin. But should a teacher feel guilty? Has Sherry replaced Dillon's parent, as some parents might fear? Of course not. Sherry has achieved an attachment that will have lasting value for Dillon, who experienced adjustment difficulties during the year. Through her relationship with him, she has helped Dillon extend his social world from home to school.

Later the same day, Sherry talked with Dillon's mom, who enjoyed the story and joked to Sherry that she could come stay in a spare room in their house. Parent and teacher agreed that Dillon had come a long way during the year—and was ready for first grade. When teachers and parents share in the effort to help a child find a place in the classroom, more often than not a successful transition will occur.

Suggested Readings

Armstrong, Jeanne. "Mad, Sad, or Glad: Children Speak Out about Child Care." *Young Children* 49, no. 2 (January 1994): 22–23.

Bakley, Sue. "Love a Little More, Accept a Little More." *Young Children* 52, no. 2 (January 1997): 21.

Blecher-Sass, Hope. "Good-byes Can Build Trust." *Young Children 52,* no. 7 (November 1997): 12–14.

Elicker, James, and Cheryl Fortner-Wood. "Adult–Child Relationships in Early Childhood Programs." *Young Children 51,* no. 1 (November 1995): 69–78.

McCormick, Linda, and Rita Holden. "Homeless Children: A Special Challenge." *Young Children* 47, no. 6 (September 1992): 61–67.

Raikes, Helen. "A Secure Base for Babies: Applying Attachment Concepts to the Infant Care Setting." *Young Children* 51, no. 5 (July 1996): 59–67.

Warren, Rita. "Letter from Child Care Provider to Mother on Baby's First Day." *Young Children* 53, no. 1 (January 1998): 27.

Discussion Activities

For reasons of professionalism, as you respond to these discussion activities, please respect the privacy of all children, adults, programs, and schools.

1. Think back to your first experience in a classroom: prekindergarten, kindergarten, or elementary school. What do you recall? What were your feelings at the time? As you look back on the experience, what made the transition into the classroom easier? More difficult?

2. Generate a list of three ideas that you might use to help children become comfortable in a classroom. What might be the roadblocks to using each idea? How might you overcome them?

3. Many teachers use multiple methods for building relations with parents at the beginning of the year. (This is discussed further in the next chapter.) Which of the following ideas are you comfortable with? Which would be uncomfortable for you? Why?

- letters to the child and family before school begins

- home visits to families before or just after start-up

- phone calls to families before school and/or on the evening of the first day of school

- "greeting meetings" to orient parents to the program

- giving out your school phone number

- giving out your home phone number

Family and School

A common mistake in education is to consider the child in the classroom as separate from the child in the family. Teachers make this error, often without thinking about it, when they consider life in the classroom as a partial replacement for the child's life at home. Examples of this attitude can be seen in such statements as, "You are a big child at school now and not a baby at home anymore," or, "You may act this way at home, but you do not act this way here at school." These statements indicate that the teacher is giving inflated importance to the socializing influence of the school and diminishing the importance of the family.

The teacher's error in judgment undermines the young child's natural identification with the family, as well as her personal identity as a family member. It tends to split school influence from family influence in the child's mind, putting her in the difficult position of having to choose between competing cultures. For children whose family backgrounds and values are similar to the teacher's, this dilemma of being caught between two cultures is less extreme, but it is still real. For children whose home culture is noticeably different from the school's—a different language is spoken, for instance—the child's cultural dilemma is extreme, indeed.

This unfortunate attitude—that the school replaces the home as socializing institution—is a remnant of the historical melting-pot function of American schools. Between the end of the Civil War and the beginning of World War II, the population of the United States was greatly increased by immigrants, many of whom spoke little English and knew little of American life. During this time, for political as well as educational reasons, schools were charged with "Americanizing the aliens." For example, a common practice was to punish children, sometimes physically, if they spoke a language other than English at school, even if the family wanted them to retain the home language.

As a result of the melting-pot theory, many immigrant parents, as well as parents from native minority groups, felt that they were giving their children over to the school and thus giving up the right to raise their children as they saw fit. For much of the twentieth century, especially in public schools, educators did little to change this view and regarded parents not as partners, but as clients.

RECOLLECTION: *"Say, Dan," Big Bud said, "You know what comes after Indian Summer, don't you?" When I taught Head Start for the Red Lake Ojibwe in northern Minnesota, Bud was janitor. The children were drawn to Big Bud, and he teased them gently in ways that made them smile. I knew I was in for it with his question, and shaking my head I told him I didn't know. "White man winter!" Bud boomed with a wide grin.*

Bud is gone now, but I got to know him well enough at Head Start to admire his quick mind, and the fact that this sixth-grade–educated janitor spoke four languages. At home in his early childhood, Bud spoke Ojibwe, the language of his family. At age six, he was taken to the reservation boarding school, less than ten miles away from his home. At the school, where he was required to live 364 days a year, Bud was whipped if he spoke his native language. Bud learned English quickly enough, but still spoke Ojibwe to his friends when he thought he wouldn't get caught. At age twelve, Bud was allowed to leave the boarding school and return home. He found work with a German American farmer in the area and soon learned German. Stationed in France during World War II, Bud picked up conversational French. I sometimes heard him sharing his linguistic gift with those around him.

When I talked about Bud in one of my university classes, a student commented that Bud could have been a one-man language department at a high school or college. I agreed that with support he could have been, but instead Bud was the victim of an almost-400-year cultural war waged against indigenous families. Two students in the class then spoke. One mentioned that her grand-mother had not been allowed to start school in northeastern Minnesota until she spoke English instead of Lithuanian. Another mentioned that his grandfather had been paddled by a teacher when he spoke Finnish at school.

Much of the rest of the world speaks two or more languages. Despite changes in our educational priorities, our schools have been too effective over the years at getting Americans to speak only one—with victims like Bud along the way.

In contrast to this public school melting-pot ideology, early childhood teachers have long seen the importance of home and school working together. They pride themselves on building and maintaining close ties with parents. The complaint of "too much institutional control over children's lives" is certainly not the fault of prekindergarten programs, which are not required and are there to serve families' needs. In fact, the relative success of early childhood teachers at forging home–school partnerships is undoubtedly due to teachers' recognition that the family is so important to young children. Early childhood programs provide a clear American model for how the home–versus–school issue can be made obsolete. The early childhood model points instead to a child's growing sense of community including both home and school.

The encouraging classroom expands home life for the child without trying to replace it. Through the anecdotes in this chapter, two priorities for the teacher emerge. First, the teacher supports each child's ties to the family as an important foundation on which the child builds a life. The anecdotes related to the first priority offer a detailed picture of how much family means to children and how teachers reinforce these bonds. In the classroom, teachers gain understanding about child–family connections largely through observations and conversations. These are basic strategies for learning about children in general and are the cornerstone skills modeled throughout this book.

Second, teachers build partnerships with parents in order to bridge differences between home and school and to cultivate connections between them. Anecdotes pertaining to this priority focus on four kinds of parent–teacher communication used in early childhood education: telephone contact, conferences, home visits, and contact with volunteers in the classroom. My intent is to share anecdotes of successful contacts in these four areas, and for readers to think about their own professional priorities and development in this area.

It's All about Families

Family life is never far from the mind of the young child. Family life is the experience that the child knows best. If the child is able to feel that thoughts about family are natural and completely acceptable in the classroom, she will extend her sense of community to include both home and school. She will see herself as an accepted and productive member of each group.

Most teachers have less trouble accepting a child's family life when the family's culture (all that the family believes, values, knows, and does) is familiar and acceptable to the teacher. Problems arise when the teacher detects differences that cause negative judgments about the family and so make productive communication with the child and family difficult.

The anecdotes that follow trace some ways that teachers work to help children extend family life into the classroom and make sense of each. As you read the anecdotes, notice the importance of family in the words and actions of these prekindergarten and kindergarten children. I have organized the anecdotes around *observations* and *conversations,* the two main strategies that teachers use to gain understanding about their children.

OBSERVATIONS

Teachers often say that they learn so much from observing children in the classroom. If the knowledge helps the teacher to understand and accept child and family, then observation is an important skill indeed. Observation is a way to illustrate the ideas one has read and discussed in abstract terms. Teachers who are open enough to observe children carefully and non-judgmentally tend to be responsive and fundamentally helpful to children—and to their families.

When students in my classes record observations, I ask them to separate *what* they see from *how they interpret* what they see: to separate observations from reflections. Teachers sometimes process information amazingly fast. In the time crunch of the classroom, we tend to take shortcuts, blending our perceptions and reactions together. It is important to pause and think about what we see, delaying interpretation until we get the whole picture.

For example, we walk past the dramatic play area, and Jericho, who is using the dramatic play blender, says, "Teacher, do you want a daiquiri?" If you're a non-drinker, your first reaction might be to call the social services coordinator for your program! Then you remember Jericho's mom mentioning that her older sister is going to school to learn to be a bartender. Maybe Jericho saw her sister (whom she talks about a lot) practicing at home. We need to delay that first reaction, pause a bit, and figure out what is really going on. The *two-part anecdote* demonstrated throughout this book in the observation/reflection format gives teachers practice at separating our observations from our thoughts and feelings about the observations. This pause gives us time to reflect, an important discipline for us American teachers who are geared to reacting fast and often. In this situation, with our knowledge about Jericho, we understand that Jericho's sister is important. We want our comments to support, rather than undermine, this important part of Jericho's relationship to her family.

I recall an incident that required me to contain my own first reaction to an observed situation. Four members of my Head Start class were sitting around the kitchen table in our dramatic play area. As I walked by, thinking they were having a tea party, one said, "Here's Dan. Sit down, Dan. Someone get him a beer!" I did not offer my first reaction which was, "Would that be a Grain Belt?" What I did say was, "Thanks, guys, but I'm teaching right now." I weighed my observation of four boys sitting at the kitchen table like their family members might, versus the issue of drinking inappropriate make-believe beverages in Head Start. I settled for modeling that there is a time to drink beer and a time not to, and let it go at that.

You never know what you are going to observe in a dramatic play situation! Situations of all kinds involving family and friends form the foundation of dramatic play, and the "housekeeping" or dramatic play center is often the hub of this activity. At an early age, children have already begun learning about the roles and activities of adults. They learn even more as they act out family situations daily in their play. The social give-and-take by children playing these roles clearly indicates the importance of family in children's lives. In fact, most children in early childhood programs could be considered Family Studies majors.

OBSERVATION: *During my observation of play in a kindergarten class, I saw three children, Rachel, Jeremiah (Mia), and Sarah, working hard at playing house. Rachel was preparing a meal in the kitchen. She was wearing an apron and cooking on the stove with a frying pan. "Good morning, Honey," said Rachel as she smiled at Mia and continued to cook.*

"Good morning to you, Cupcake," said Mia as he walked up to Sarah. Mia asked, "How is our big girl doing today?"

"Fine, Daddy," said Sarah as she held her baby doll.

"Breakfast is ready, have Sarah sit down and it is time to eat," said Rachel. Rachel made a motion to have them sit and they did. I noticed that Sarah dropped her baby doll and started drinking from a glass instead of from the sipper cup that was on the table. Both Mia and Sarah were sitting at the kitchen table being served by Mom. Then they all said a prayer and began to eat.

"I'm filled," said Mia. "I am late for work." Mia grabbed a hard hat out of the toy box and he also gave Rachel a kiss good-bye (which was promptly wiped off). When Mia was gone, Rachel started to clear the table, putting the dishes in the sink. Sarah walked over to the baby doll she had dropped and picked it up. She held the doll in her arms and said she wanted Mommy (Rachel) to play with her.

"I have to finish the dishes before I can go out and play," said Rachel.

"I want to play with you now," demanded Sarah.

"Barney is on now, go and watch him," said Rachel. She continued to wash the dishes, and Sarah went over to the TV and watched Barney. Mia, who had been wandering around and fixing things in the playroom, headed into the kitchen area. "Honey, I'm home," said Mia.

"You're home early," said Rachel. "Go back to work, I'm not done yet."

"I'm bored. I'm going to play with something different now," said Mia.

This anecdote is notable for the realistic detail these children brought to the family situation—so much language, social, personal, and even physical development comes from dramatic play like this. The observation is also notable because Arnetta, the observing student, informed me that none of the children came from a traditional two-parent family. The prevalence of the image of the traditional two-parent family in media means that this image often permeates the play of even young children. Because children depend so completely on their families, it's important for them to learn that families can take many shapes and forms—by looking at the actual families represented by the class. If teachers perpetuate the image of the traditional family, some children in virtually any class are going to feel that their family doesn't fit or isn't okay.

A Case in Point: Marriage in Dramatic Play

Whatever our own feelings, we need to respect the fact that for some families, marriage and the marriage ceremony are a big deal, and for other families, they're not a big deal at all. Many teachers comment that of all the dramatic play activities that take place in the classroom, the wedding is a favorite. The wedding pageant provides so much material for children's dramatic play. Teachers who set out wedding paraphernalia are invariably rewarded by the role play that results. (A local Head Start staff's favorite anecdote is about the "preacher," using a favorite story book as a bible, who asked the "groom," "Will you take her for your awfully wedded wife?")

> **OBSERVATION:** *Shante, age three, was playing in her favorite area, the house area. She quickly found a white slip to wear, a pink scarf which she draped over her face, a bouquet of flowers, and a purse. She was now transformed into a beautiful, beaming bride. The only thing she needed was a groom.*
>
> *After several boys turned her down, she assertively locked arms with another girl and directed her to be the husband. The couple was about to leave the house area and march around the room when Shante suddenly stopped. She realized she was missing something important before the wedding could begin. She threw up her arms and loudly proclaimed, "Where the hell is the baby?"*

> **REFLECTION:** *This gave me a lot of insight into Shante's life experiences and her family situation. I'm so glad that all families are not the same, celebrate diversity! Shante's wedding was fun for the children—not to mention the teachers!*

Kaitlin, the teacher, had made home visits to Shante and her family and knew the mother well enough to be able to enjoy the story with her. The diversity in modern family life, combined with the unique perspectives of young children, means that teaching young children should be fun. We cannot force moral codes on children or families. If we attempt to do so, we only separate the family from the program and put the young child in a terrible bind. By accepting the meaning of the family for the child—people who are mostly together and love and care for each other—we build an encouraging classroom that includes all, and nurtures all members to learn and grow.

In most dramatic play of real value, including the wedding, the teacher is an onlooker (observer), or at most a bit player. He is not the star. The importance of dramatic play lies in the experience children gain from taking on roles and solving social problems cooperatively. When participating in what is essentially the children's activity, the teacher becomes a participant observer, playing a supportive role while at the same time observing—as Kellie's anecdote illustrates.

OBSERVATION: *I observed Samarra, age four, getting everyone into a "pickup truck" in the active play area to go to her wedding. Samarra ordered the other nine children to get their chairs in order (side-by-side) and behind one another to form their truck. The children were cooperating tremendously and were very willing to take part in her journey to Nebraska, which was where they were getting married. They all had hats, scarves and/or coats on from the dramatic play center. She said to me as I observed them "traveling," "Shh! It's a secret! We're going to Nebraska to get married! Don't tell anyone!" She said it as if I should have known not to tell (ha!). They got to Nebraska in a matter of seconds, and that is where I married them!*

In her reflection, Kellie commented, "I was not so surprised that Samarra organized the bulk of this, but I was surprised that the other kids (nine!) were so willing to follow her ideas and plans." They all "had a blast pretending and making-believe." For many children, the wedding has personal meaning in the context of the home. When they can integrate this experience with classroom activity, they are able to build a bond between home and school. By practicing the roles and functions of adults in enjoyable ways, children are rehearsing to take part in the greater community when they are older. In the wedding, as in any role-play situation, there are organizers and there are followers. Through the cooperative exchanges of social play, children gain the opportunity to experience both.

OBSERVATION WHEN CHILDREN ARE HURTING

Through self-expression in dramatic play, art, and conversation, children cele-brate happy moments in family life, but also attempt to understand and grieve other moments that are not so happy. Teachers observe the sadder aspects of child expression as well, for it is a mistake to conclude that childhood is always a happy time and that children are oblivious to difficulty. The information gained from observation when children are hurting allows the teacher to be effectively supportive.

OBSERVATION: *Three preschool children were building a structure with blocks. It was really fancy and had a road leading up to it and even a park-ing lot. I noticed that some of the play cars were police cars, and I asked Jackson what they were building. He said, "The law enforcement complex." A few minutes later Jackson took his miniature figure out of a car and approached another child by the building holding a second figure. "Excuse me, sir," he said, "Can you tell me where the juvenile training center is?"*

REFLECTION: *I knew from talking with Jackson's mom that morning that his brother had gone into the juvenile detention center the day before. His mom hadn't taken Jackson, but had told him they could visit his brother on the weekend. Jackson later talked with me about his brother, and I showed him on the calendar how many days until Saturday and Sunday and helped him count the days on his fingers. He seemed relieved to know that the weekend was com-ing in three days.*

Whatever problems family members encounter, children may express those situations in their play. Like Abby, the teacher in the anecdote, teachers can help children make sense of life when they observe carefully and communicate with parents about the meaning of the child's play. Observation in itself does not resolve children's problems. When a teacher observes and understands how

33

family events affect a child at play, he is in a position to take steps—like listening, providing information, and offering non-sentimental comfort—that can help.

CONVERSATIONS

In the encouraging classroom, a teacher learns from children in two principal ways: by observing them, and by conversing with them directly. Conversations typically occur during play situations, informal activities, and meals or snack. The effective conversation with a child might be called a *contact* talk. In a contact talk, the adult makes a conscious decision to have the conversation, listens and attempts to follow the child's lead, and shares a quality moment with the child (rather than using the conversation to "teach, preach, or screech").

Teachers describe three characteristics of contact talks that make them worthwhile.

First, with the adult's undivided attention, children develop their thoughts, use rich language, share their feelings, and register the adult's responses. These qualities make contact talks, which do not have to be long, sources of significant learning for the child.

Second, after a contact talk, the adult and child will feel more attachment—mutual acceptance and trust have increased.

Third, through contact talks, teachers learn about children's joys and concerns and see particular ways in which a child's world is bound up with family.

> **OBSERVATION:** *While sitting at the lunch table during Head Start, we were talking about families. One child chimed, "I have a sister." Several other children began talking about their siblings as well.*
>
> *One little boy said, "I have a half-sister."*
>
> *I replied, "You have a half-sister, Daniel?"*
>
> *He looked at me, nodding, and said, "Yep, and when she grows up, she's gonna be a whole sister." Daniel and I looked at each other and smiled.*

Nedra, the teacher, indicated that she did not know if Daniel had thought this idea up himself or if it was "a happy family joke." She did see, though, that Daniel was pleased about his half-sister, and she affirmed his feeling by reflecting his comment back to him and sharing a smile. When a teacher reflects back the child's thoughts and feelings, he is practicing *reflective listening,* sometimes also called *active listening.* He actively supports the child's comments during contact talks.

Strengthening Family Ties

While they emulate mothers, fathers, and other family members, children also have their own identities to forge, their separate lives to live. Imagination helps a child to express and find meaning in this childhood predicament. By using imagination to momentarily take on the actions, roles, toils, and triumphs of family members, the child makes meaning out of the adult's life, and also out of her own. As Megan's anecdote shows, the adult must be tuned in so that the child can express the complicated circumstances of human life.

OBSERVATION: *I chose to converse with a five-year-old boy who was playing with the blocks by himself in the corner. I was somewhat hesitant to approach him, simply because I didn't want to bother him; he looked as if he was concentrating very hard on what he was doing. However, I decided to mosey on over and see what happened.*

Megan: Do you mind if I sit down and play blocks with you?

Ean: You can help me try and get this roof on my garage. I've been trying to get this thing on for a while now, and it keeps on falling. (He took all of the blocks off of the top of his garage and laid them on the floor in a perfect row.)

Megan: So you want me to help you put your roof on your garage?

Ean: Yep, this ain't a one-man job no more. I built this thing up all by myself, but now I need some help, do you think you can help me out?

Megan: I would love to help you; just tell me what to do.

Ean: (He grabbed two long narrow blocks and handed them to me.) You take these and hang on to them until I need them....ok? (He had a frustrated look on his face; he was concentrating very hard.)

Megan: Okay, I will hang on to these for you. So why are you building a garage?

Ean: I building one for my new Harley! (Big smile). You see...I bought it, and I have no place to keep it safe. I don't want no one to wreck it, so I got to build me a garage.

Megan: Why did you buy a Harley?

Ean: My dad just got one, so I decided I needed a new bike too, just like his!

You know...my dad is building a new garage too, so we can both keep our bikes safe. I never knew how hard it is to build a garage; it's like building a new house. That's why my dad is always tired at suppertime, building a garage is hard work. (He wiped his forehead off like he was sweating.) Okay, I'm ready for that red piece now.

Megan: Here you go.

Ean: Thanks. You know, if my dad had a good helper like you, he would get done a lot faster. Maybe I'll tell my dad when I get home that I can help him out if he needs someone to hold the wood. You know what...I'm getting pretty hungry. Let's leave this for now, we can come back and finish it after snack. (He stood up and took the other piece of wood from my hand and set it down by the other pieces.)

Megan: You know, I'm getting pretty hungry myself, maybe we should go have a snack.

Ean: Yeah, come on! (He took my hand and we walked over to the table where they were getting ready to have snack.)

Megan's conversation with Ean showed how the boy was emulating his father's interests—in the Harley, and in keeping it safe so no one would "wreck it." But even more, Ean was understanding his dad's sweat, his hard effort, and his tiredness from building the garage by himself. The empathy Ean felt for his dad, and the respect for his efforts, really came through in Megan's conversation with him. The statement is often made, "Play is the child's work." Play is a way of empathizing with loved ones and learning more about their lives through the power of imagination. When an adult has contact talks with children—caring conversations—she helps them understand the complicated world of thoughts and feelings in which each of us lives. Ean's taking Megan's hand as they walked to snack indicates the appreciation children feel when we talk with them about what is on their minds.

Right from the beginning of the year, teachers in the encouraging classroom work to build and maintain positive relations with families. The teacher who has built partnerships can often provide support sensitively and effectively when the child is in need. In the next anecdote, notice how seamlessly Carrie, the teacher, goes from child, to mother, to child again in order to assess the child's problem and find a solution.

OBSERVATION: *We had visitors in the Head Start center today, a psychologist and a Health Services nurse. We heard the children enter the classroom and greet us after a long weekend at home.*

> *Chad: Teacher, I hate you.*
>
> *Me: Can you tell me about why you hate me?*
>
> *Chad: No.*
>
> *Chad walked away with his head down.*
>
> *I called Chad's mom to find out what she knew. I found out that Chad's dad had been visiting from Alaska and was leaving today while Chad was at the center. His mom and I agreed that he was probably upset about his dad leaving and Chad having to be at class. I ask Chad's mom how she felt about Chad missing time at the center. She said she thought it best he not miss out on center. I gave her the option of rethinking. She decided to drive in and pick up her child, who was still standing in his coat and boots.*
>
> *Me: I talked to your mom and she has decided that this is a special day for you, she will come and pick you up.*
>
> *Chad: Can I go eat and play?*
>
> *Me: How about you get your coat and boots off, wash your hands, eat breakfast, brush your teeth, and if there is time, play.*
>
> *Chad: Carrie, I love you.*

The words, "I hate you," are so powerful that they frequently make teachers feel hurt, and maybe even hateful too. Carrie did not listen to the literal meaning of Chad's words, but heard instead something like this: "Carrie, I am dying here! I don't want to be at Center today, and it's maybe your fault that I am, and I don't know how to ask for help, but I need it." Carrie took Chad's words seriously, but not personally. Carrie's responsiveness allowed her not only to listen openly, but to call the parent and figure out a way to get help in a time of need.

Conversation When Children Are Hurting

Not all of the messages that children share about families are positive, of course. Sometimes teachers need to listen, acknowledge what a child has said, and then politely disagree—for the sake of the child.

OBSERVATION: *I was sitting on the rug helping some Head Start children put together puzzles when Kiko came up to me and said, "I think he's an idiot." I asked him who. He said, "Kiko is an idiot." I asked him if he was talking about himself. He said, "Yes, they told me I was the village idiot."*

I said, "Who told you that, Kiko?"

He pointed to his head and said, "The people up here in my dreams."

I said, "Sometimes people have strange dreams, I don't think you're an idiot."

He replied, "Yup, that's what they always tell me." Then he turned and walked away.

REFLECTION: *The same child told me later in the day that his uncle was not going to help him make a tree house because his uncle thinks he's a moron. I think this is something that he hears at home from his family on a regular basis. It is probably something he hears so often that he doesn't think anything is wrong with telling others that he is the village idiot because he believes it to be true. I told the teacher about the conversation. She has a meeting scheduled with the parent, and the teacher and I have decided to work with Kiko to help him change this idea about himself.*

What Janeen, the student teacher, told Kiko was appropriate—the fact that the child came and spoke with her later confirms this. What Kiko was doing here through the self-labeling was really asking for help. Though his words were different, he seemed to be asking Janeen, "Important people are saying that I am an idiot, I guess I am, right?" (It is unfortunate that children are forced to learn the message behind such words as "idiot" or "moron" so early.) Negative self-labels should not be ignored by teachers; the child using them is feeling frustration, despair, or depression. In this event, teachers need to build positive relationships with the child and educate the parent before the negative self-label takes permanent hold.

Notice also Kiko's initial reluctance to come out and say, "My uncle thinks I'm a moron." A child is attached to family members and to protect both them and herself, the child may be wary about what she says to a teacher. A trusting relationship and sensitive listening are important. A child may approach a sensitive topic indirectly the first time, and if the teacher is trusted, return to it more directly later.

The effects of families on children can be supportive and even uplifting, or they can constitute abuse. Coming upon clear signs of psychological, physical, or sexual abuse is a point of anxiety for many teachers, especially when they are starting out.

OBSERVATION: *Marsha was sitting at the breakfast table and tapped Lois (the teacher) on the arm. Lois turned to her and said, "Yes?"*

Marsha said, "My privates hurt." Lois asked her if she had to go potty. Marsha said, "No, they always hurt when I go to my daddy's." Lois did not pursue the conversation any further at that point. She talked to Marsha later and then did a report on possible child abuse.

REFLECTION: *I was glad she said it to Lois and not me. I'm glad Lois stopped the conversation, because all the other children were listening intently, and that she took Marsha aside later.*

Every school and center should have a well-understood, working policy for reporting suspected abuse, which is required of teachers in all fifty states. In the previous anecdote with Kiko, the teacher decided to speak directly to the parent about family members possibly berating the child. In the anecdote about Marsha, the teacher followed the program's established policy for suspected child abuse. Extreme family situations require a planned response by the team of educators, sometimes including outside professionals. Teachers do not intervene on their own in these situations, but work as part of the team. The individual teacher continues to report observations and advocate for the child, using the program's policy. Classroom teachers may even be an active part of an abuse intervention program, but in conjuction with an investigation by the appropriate county or city agencies.

Apparent abuse raises a difficult challenge for teachers: Should the teacher maintain a connection with the family when abuse is suspected? Upon discovery of abuse or neglect, a teacher frequently feels negative about the family and desires distance from them. He may also feel concern that the family will blame the teacher for the initial report. Rather than give in to these feelings, the teacher works from the understanding that the child is of central importance and that the child still depends on the family. In the situation just described, Lois and another teacher discussed the child's comments with the mother. The two teachers and the mother then met with the social worker, who conducted an investigation. Lois said later that, if anything, the mother got closer to the the staff, relying on the teachers for support.

When one family member has a problem that affects a child, the teacher should not assume that the whole family will rally round the offending adult and neglect the child's needs. A trusting relationship, built with the family over time, is essential. With a firm but friendly approach by teachers, the parent will often choose to work with teachers and face the problem. The encouraging classroom includes family members as well as the child.

Building Connections with the Family

In the encouraging classroom teachers work actively to build partnerships with parents in order to bridge differences between home and school and to empower the home–school connection. This section looks at four kinds of parent–teacher communication used in early childhood education: telephone calls, home visits, conferences, and contacts with volunteers in the classroom. The anecdotes about successful contacts in these four areas can help readers think about these strategies in relation to their own professional priorities and development.

Here's a story about a teacher in northern Minnesota, Pat Sanford, who uses a combination of several methods to start the school year out with strong communication with parents.

Pat takes a four-step approach to make connections with parents and children at the beginning of the year. A week or two before school starts, she sends a note to each child on Garfield the Cat stationery saying how happy she is that the child is in her class. She tells the child to watch for the Garfield picture outside of her room. She also writes to the parents, introducing herself and giving some guidelines for her classroom to help the year start off right. In her parent letter, she includes both her school and home phone numbers. (Giving out a home phone number is something not every teacher is comfortable with. Pat says that in her 20-plus years, she has never had a parent abuse this information.) A day or two before start-up, Pat calls every child. She tells them again that she is happy to be their teacher and reassures them that they will have a great time in her class.

Pat says the single most productive step she takes in building relations each year is to call each family on the evening of the first day of school. She talks with the parents about any problems with bus rides, during the day, etc., and gives the child any needed reassurance. Once when a child had a particularly difficult first day, Pat asked the parent if there were a jar of peanut butter in the house that he could bring in the next day, because "we could really use that peanut butter to put on crackers for snack." The child proudly presented the peanut butter the next morning, and Pat expressed her appreciation—and felt relief when the child had a much better day.

Pat says she would much rather drink a beverage of her choice and hit the sack early on that first night of the school year. However, given the responsiveness she sees in the parents over the next few weeks, Pat knows she needs to make those calls each year instead.

PHONE CALLS

A clear example of the effective use of the phone call was Carrie's call to Chad's mom to figure out what might make Chad say he hated his teacher. Carrie used the telephone to maintain positive teacher–parent–child relations. Another use of the phone is at the beginning of the school year to build relationships. Pat Sanford's story (above) gives several good examples of using the phone *before* there is a problem.

Phone calls are helpful for many types of communication between teacher and parent. The exception is a discussion of a serious problem. If it's serious, the talk should be face to face. When both teacher and parent have access to phones, and speak a common language, the value of phone calls to forge and maintain parent–teacher partnerships is pretty much granted. But not all teachers have telephones, at least in their classrooms, and not all parents have phones in their homes, or speak the teacher's language. When phone calls are not an option, teachers may turn to making home visits, depending on the circumstances.

HOME VISITS

Home visits by early childhood teachers are not new. In the nineteenth century, Froebel's kindergartens in Germany and the United States included home visits. During the first half of the twentieth century, both federal and state governments encouraged home visits by kindergarten teachers as a way to reach immigrant families.

Progressive early childhood programs, especially Head Start, have always included home visits as a strategy to reach the family. Head Start home visitors work with both parent and child and are known for being part social worker and part early childhood teacher. In this day and age, home visitors usually have connections to classes that the children attend. Home visits by teachers help them to learn about family dynamics and children's response styles in ways they cannot within the confines of the classroom alone. In the following anecdote, Kellie, a student teacher in a Head Start program, accompanied the teacher to Marsha's home. Note the understanding that Kellie gains about Marsha from the experience.

OBSERVATION: *During a visit to Marsha's home we did several things. Mainly, while the teacher talked with Marsha's mom about recipes and getting fuel assistance, Marsha and I made playdough. Marsha mixed it all herself, then began playing with it. She put her ring in the dough, then used another piece to make a treasure map. When her mom and the teacher got done, she asked her mom to use the map and try to find the ring. She did this over and over while we were there. Every time, she would giggle and laugh, then start over after the ring had been found. After this, her mom read Marsha a book we had brought; we had a snack, and said good-bye.*

REFLECTION: *Marsha has never laughed at school the way she did at home. I think this is because she is more comfortable at home. I saw a side of her that I had not previously seen. Her attention span was also longer than any of the adults at the table. She would have continued to hide the ring all day if the home visit had not come to an end.*

Another Head Start teacher, Diane, said that before she made home visits, she encountered a few children each year who were hard for her to understand and work with. Sometimes this problem lasted all year. She said that after she began making home visits, she did not have this problem. She understood the children more fully, and whatever they had learned about her, they seemed to be more accepting of her leadership in the classroom. Healthy, mutual attachments became easier to make and keep.

When difficult circumstances are suspected, home visits can be challenging for teachers, but they are important. The information gained helps the home visitor work with both parent and child. Depending on the program and the circumstances, the home visitor can also make referrals to other helping agencies. The relationship that the home visitor builds with the parents makes the referral process less threatening for all concerned.

OBSERVATION: *I went on a home visit with Shandra, my cooperating teacher, to see Samantha and her mother, Effie. Shandra told me that she has had a few hard situations throughout the year with this family, even reporting Effie for suspected abuse. Effie is still letting us visit their home, though, which says a lot about how Shandra gets along with them.*

We got there and I started an activity with Samantha while Shandra spoke with Effie. Samantha wanted to get her rocking chair pulled over to the couch so she could sit in it while we read a book. She said to me in a timid, quiet manner, "I want my rocking chair over here." She looked at me as though she was requesting something impossible.

I said, "Okay, go get it and pull it over if you would like."

"Only if it's okay with my mom," Samantha said.

"Okay. Go ahead and ask her," I said.

Samantha asked her mother, almost whispering, "Mom, can I bring my rocking chair over there?"

Effie said, "Yes, go ahead." Effie said it in a way that seemed like Samantha was asking a huge favor or asking for something totally unreasonable. The whole home visit, Samantha was walking on eggshells.

REFLECTION: *I feel it is obvious what is going on here. Samantha has no room to move or grow without hearing something from Effie. I discussed this with the teachers and they said that Effie has come a long way since the beginning of the year, so I am happy to hear that. We do feel she is trying, she just doesn't know appropriate techniques as a mother and how Samantha is as a child. I think she forgets Samantha is only five years old. I was relieved to learn that there are two counselors coming into their home to help them. I just want Samantha to know that what she has experienced is not typical. But there is no way to let her know that. She will hopefully learn through time.*

The student teacher's concerns are natural. They speak to an age-old dilemma of the teaching profession: The teacher cannot fix all situations and all kids. This observation, though, despite the element of frustration, also gives hope—found in the word *collaboration*. The teaching staff at this Head Start center valued the student teacher's observations and input; this is why they shared confidential information with her. She had the unified support of an entire teaching staff to help her understand and cope. The staff had built positive relations with the family, and with the local social service agency, and the family accepted the recommended services. The parent "had come a long way since the beginning of the year," and the child had an improved chance to grow up whole. Through collaboration, professionals in the encouraging classroom accomplish together what they cannot accomplish alone.

PARENT–TEACHER–CHILD CONFERENCES

Family conferences offer the teacher unique information that promotes teacher effectiveness. When done in a positive, non-threatening manner, conferences also increase parent interest and involvement in their child's education. An important trend in conferencing at all levels is to include the learner along with the parents. Teachers' first reactions to this prospect are guarded; they find they have to approach both the material and the communication process differently with the learner there. A common reflection after teachers get used to this format is that under most circumstances, they wouldn't have conferences any other way. Often a child will sit in for part of the conference, then be free to play in the classroom if the conference gets too involved.

The following write-up by a student teacher, Marchale, is a primer on the purpose and the conduct of parent–teacher–child conferences. Marchale's role in some of the conferences was to read a book or do a puzzle with the children while their parents continued to talk with the teacher.

OBSERVATION: *As a student teacher I was invited to sit in on the conferences for spring quarter. When my cooperating teacher first asked me to do this, I was surprised, because I had not taught enough of the class to really have a valuable insight into the children's performance. I realized later that it was a great learning experience for me, more than my benefiting the parent and child.*

Juanita had prepared an individual folder for each of the children. It contained samples of their work since the last conference as well as some of their previous work so she could show each parent and child their improvements. She also included some checklists and other assessment material that went along with the school's curriculum. She included in the folders a sheet so she could record parents' comments and refer back to them in the future.

At the beginning of each conference Juanita would greet the parent and the child and invite them to take seats next to her. She would tell them how much she enjoyed having the child in her class. She had something positive to say about each child. Juanita would then move on to showing the parents their children's work, asking the children to explain their pictures, journal entries, etc. With the children's help she would point out improvements and also showed the parent how they could help their children at home. She would always have inexpensive resources on hand, such as library books and a jar of counting-beans, and she would show the parents how to play the Bean Game.

If a child was in the Chapter program or receiving extra help in the classroom, she would also go over these assessments and tell the parent how the child was doing in relation to the Chapter program. Juanita ended each conference by going over her notes with the parent, and pointing out what more she and the parent could do to help the child continue to make progress. She always seemed to end the conferences on a positive note.

During one conference, Juanita was speaking with a father of one of the girls in the class who was receiving Chapter assistance. Cheyenne (the daughter) and I had gone over to the puzzles, but I couldn't help but hear the rest of the conference because the father was really upset. He was Native American and had a very bad experience when he was in school in the special education program. He was adamant that he did not want his daughter in the Chapter program. (She had been placed in the program by the mother.) I was uncomfortable sitting there, but the teacher stayed very calm.

Juanita acknowledged the pain he felt and expressed understanding. Then she explained how the Chapter program works today. The children are not removed from the class, they are not treated like outcasts, and the other children treat them no differently. She showed the father how much his daughter had improved and told him if he would be more comfortable, she would decrease his daughter's aid because she had come so far. Juanita asked him if he had any suggestions for her about how she could better help their child. She took notes and they agreed on a plan for Cheyenne. When the father left, he was happy with how the conference had gone. I don't think Cheyenne had caught the more serious parts of the conference, and her smile at the end when I said good-bye told me that she was happy about it too.

REFLECTION: *I thought that Juanita did a wonderful job with the conferences. She started every conference on a positive note. When she went over the child's work, she inquired about any issues the parents may have wished to discuss. When the teacher was dealing with the father who was upset, if she had invited him to sit across from her desk, he may have felt intimidated, which probably would have put him more on edge. When the teacher sat next to him, I think he felt more comfortable. In addition, she used reflective listening with him, responding to his complaint about his own problems with the special education program. Juanita used "compliment sandwiches," too, mentioning that while Cheyenne still needed Chapter aid, she was making progress.*

After all the conferences were done, the teacher reviewed her notes and made a list of things that she needed to do with each child or watch for in a child. I thought they were very productive conferences and I thought Juanita had developed good relationships with these parents over the course of the school year. I can say that I really learned a great deal about parent–teacher relations in those two nights and one day.

In early childhood, if a teacher can help a parent see children's education positively, he can make a difference in the life of the child and in the life of the family. When a teacher encourages and supports a parent's involvement in his child's schooling, the parent as well as the child stands to gain.

PARENTS IN THE CLASSROOM

Early childhood education includes child care in centers and homes, Head Start, nursery school, public and private "readiness" programs, and a new generation of parent–child programs, known in Minnesota as Early Childhood Family Education. Increasingly, kindergarten and the primary grades are also being considered part of early childhood education. In child care, the regular involvement of parents in the classroom is difficult, as parents typically work or are in classes while children are in care. Child care on the premises of the work-place or postsecondary institution makes it easier for parents to volunteer with activities or join a child for a meal or snack. Child care programs often schedule meetings, potluck suppers, open houses, and conferences in the evening, so parents can attend.

Nationally, Head Start has an enviable record of involving low-income, often minority-group, parents in their children's education. Through home visits, support services, parents' meetings, advisory councils, and classroom volunteering, parents find new potential in themselves personally, as parents, and even on occasion professionally. As a result of the Head Start experience, many parents begin career directions that simply had not occurred to them before. Often the whole family, not just the child in Head Start, benefits. Teachers in other kinds of early childhood programs can learn from the many strategies Head Start uses to engage parents in the program.

OBSERVATION: *On Wednesday, I had the opportunity to observe one of the Head Start parents volunteering in the classroom. It was ten o'clock in the morning, during the children's free play time. The mother who was volunteering decided that she would work with the kids at the worm center. The worm center had black dirt with live earthworms and plastic earthworms. The children could work at the center if they wanted to, but they were not required to. Once the children saw there were living worms in the center, they were soon digging in the dirt.*

For the first five or ten minutes, Angela (the mother) just watched the children. This did not last long, however. Adam quickly got Angela involved when he put an earthworm in her hand and said, "Here's your worm."

Angela said, "Why thank you, Adam."

Nea looked at Angela and asked, "Do these worms live all over in the ground?"

Angela responded, "Yes they do, Nea, although they don't live in hot sandy places like the desert."

Nea then said, "Is that because it's too hot for them there?"

Angela responded, "Yep."

Adam then jumped in and said, "Know what, me and my Daddy go fishing with these, and we catch lots of big fish too."

Angela responded, "I'll bet you do, Adam, fish like to eat worms, don't they?"

Morgan came over to the table to see what was going on; she picked up a plastic worm and said, "This one's not moving."

Angela responded to Morgan's statement by asking her, "Is that a real worm, Morgan?"

Morgan looked at Angela with a confused look on her face. Angela waited a few moments so Morgan had some time to really think about what she asked. After a while Angela directed a second question at Morgan. "Do you know the difference between what is real and what isn't?"

Morgan looked at her and shook her head no. Angela then moved to the other end of the table so she could be by Morgan. Angela put a real worm in Morgan's right hand and a plastic worm in her left hand. She asked Morgan to look at the real worm and tell her what she saw. Morgan said, "The worm is moving."

Angela then told Morgan, "Now look at the worm in your other hand and tell me what you see."

Morgan said, "That worm doesn't move at all, not even when I touch it."

Angela then picked up an earthworm that had died and said, "Morgan, is this a real worm?"

Morgan looked at it and touched it and then she replied, "Yeah, he's just dead." Angela looked at me and we both began to chuckle to ourselves.

REFLECTION: *At the worm table Angela was able to observe first hand the learning that goes on during play time. The children learned that worms live* *under the ground, but not in the desert. They also learned that worms are a food source for fish, and they worked on the concept of differentiating between what is real and what is not. Angela gained satisfaction from being able to help educate the children about worms. The children enjoyed her being there, and she showed some real teaching skills.*

This was my third time observing Angela in the classroom. I feel that she is participating at a very high level for two reasons. First is the comfort level that Angela displays when she is involved with the children. She interacts with them and directs stations without any hesitation. The second reason is that her son, Damien, is no longer by her side every waking moment that Angela is there, like he was the first time I observed her volunteering. I feel that her volunteering has helped both Damien and Angela grow in many ways.

In my university classes over the years, some of the most dedicated and responsive students have been parents of young children who chose teaching careers after finding their niche by volunteering in classrooms. In these encouraging classrooms, teachers were friendly enough to welcome them, help them find activities to do, thank them for volunteering, and invite them back. Finding the experience exhilarating, the parents returned. It does not take a college degree to talk with a child, read a story, help with an interest center, present an activity, or assist with a trip. Parents who come into the classroom benefit the program in all of these ways. The teacher whose goal is to bridge home and school knows that the children, the educational program, and the teacher himself all gain when a parent comes to school.

Most especially, the child whose parent comes into the classroom benefits. There is a well-known story about an unemployed dad who accompanied his daughter to preschool one day. He felt unsure as he entered the classroom, but the teacher welcomed him, introduced him to the children, and got him started reading stories. As he was reading, he overheard three children, including his daughter, talking about what their parents did. One child said his dad was a doctor. Another said her mom was a dentist. The man's daughter said with a big grin, "My dad's *here!*"

Bridging Differences

In building connections with families, teachers face the uncertainty that comes with cultural differences. Whether due to ethnic, religious, or lifestyle factors, differences can and sometimes do make building teacher–parent relations difficult. The teacher's ability to become a learner in such situations, to be open to the experience of the parent, is essential. Mary Beth, an experienced kindergarten teacher, recalls her experience with a family that other teachers found difficult to work with due to the family's religious beliefs.

RECOLLECTION: *In my first year, a veteran teacher told me to "watch out" for a certain family. Their younger child was to be in my kindergarten class. The family were Jehovah's Witnesses. As part of their faith, the family taught their children not to salute the flag or celebrate birthdays and holidays. This teacher told me that in the previous year the parents had become irate when they were not told of a Halloween party in the classroom of the older child, even though their child had not participated. The teacher then tried to let the family know of upcoming events, but she felt they remained distant and uncooperative. There were instances when the older child, now a third grader, had been made fun of by classmates. The parents had reported these incidents, but the teacher apparently told the family there was not much she could do.*

I remembered going to school, when I was in fourth grade, with a child of this faith. I remembered thinking how hard it must be for him to be left out of important school events. I took this teacher's comments as a personal challenge, and decided to work hard to get along with this family. It was my practice to send home notes of introduction to each family before school began and then continue with "happy-grams" home on a rotating basis for each member of my class. I made sure this child went home with at least one complimentary note every week. This was not a hard task. I enjoyed the child's pluckiness. (I read each note to her just to make sure it would get delivered.) I called the home a few times as well, but always got an answering machine. I left messages that I hoped the parents would find friendly.

Other teachers told me not to expect this family to attend the fall parent conference, but the mother did come. I was very pleased to see her, and she seemed rather surprised at my reaction. I decided to let her bring up the religion issue.

My job was to let her know how well her daughter was doing in my class. Well, she did bring it up. I told her I was interested to hear about her faith (because I was). She told me about the flag salute, and I said not to worry—we wouldn't be doing the flag salute until close to the end of the year because I didn't think the children could understand it. She smiled at this. About birthdays, I told her what I told all the parents: I preferred that the children had parties at home, but we let the children wear a "birthday crown" for the day if that was okay with the parents. She said no crown for Wilma, but otherwise she liked what I did. About holiday activities, I asked her what she would like me to do, and we had quite a conversation about that. I was very surprised when she said Wilma could stay in the classroom if I could figure out a way to have her fit in without participating. That year, I kind of downplayed the holidays, explaining to parents who asked that not all of the children in the class celebrate all holidays. I did more with the ideas behind the holidays—for instance, why should we be thankful?—rather than do pageants and crafts, a practice I still use today.

What I am still the proudest about with this family had to do with the flag salute. Before we started doing the flag salute in April, I had three parents come in to discuss with the class what saluting the flag meant to them. One was Wilma's mom, and she did a fine job of explaining why Wilma would stand up (out of respect for the class), but wouldn't be doing the rest. (I had previously told the other two parents what Wilma's mom would say and they were okay with this.) That whole year, I never remember any of the children making fun of Wilma—they liked her, just as I did.

As Mary Beth so bravely modeled in this anecdote, teachers can regard family cultural differences not as obstacles or burdens, but as sources of learning and mutual appreciation. In the encouraging classroom, all children feel they have a place, because they know that their families have a place as well.

This chapter has looked at ways that teachers can make the family ties that are so real for children a natural and accepted part of the encouraging classroom. As they mature, there will be time enough for children to separate more fully from the family—for the purposes of education, work, starting families of their own, or other life circumstances. While they are young, their connection with their families should be celebrated in the classroom, so that each child feels full and healthy membership in school and at home.

Suggested Readings

Bernal, Gilda Rios. "How to Calm Children through Massage." *Childhood Education* 71(1) (Fall 1997): 9–14.

Brewer, Jo Ann, and Judith Kieff. "Fostering Mutual Respect for Play at Home and School." *Childhood Education* 73 (2) (Winter 1996): 92–96.

Coleman, Mick. "Families and Schools: In Search of Common Ground." *Young Children* 52, no. 5 (July 1997): 14–21.

DeJong, Lorraine, and Barbara Cottrell. "Designing Infant Child Care Programs to Meet the Needs of Children Born to Teenage Parents." *Young Children* 54, no. 1 (January 1999): 37–45.

Gorham, Peter, and Pamela Nason. "Why Make Teachers' Work More Visible to Parents?" *Young Children* 52, no. 5 (July 1997): 22–26.

Greenwood, Deborah. "Home–School Communications via Video." *Young Children* 50, no. 6 (September 1995): 66.

Gutwirth, Valerie. "A Multicultural Family Study Project for Primary." *Young Children* 52, no. 2 (January 1997): 72–78.

Harding, Nadine. "Family Journals: The Bridge from School to Home and Back Again." *Young Children* 51, no. 2 (January 1996): 27–30.

Heath, Harriet. "Dealing with Difficult Behaviors—Teachers Plan with Parents. *Young Children* 49, no. 5 (July 1994): 20–24.

Howard, Sandy, Anne Shaughnessy, Dixie Sanger, and Karen Hux. "Let's Talk! Facilitating Language in Early Elementary Classrooms." *Young Children* 53, no. 3 (May 1998): 34–39.

Johnston, Lynne, and Joy Mermin. "Easing Children's Entry to School: Home Visits Help." *Young Children* 49, no. 5 (July 1994): 62–68.

Koch, Patricia, and Marsha McDonough. "Improving Parent-Teacher Conferences through Collaborative Conversations." *Young Children* 54, no. 2 (March 1999): 11–15.

Kratcoski, Annette, and Karen Katz. "Conversing with Young Language Learners in the Classroom." *Young Children* 53, no. 3 (May 1998): 30–33.

Lakey, Jennifer. "Teachers and Parents Define Diversity in an Oregon Preschool Cooperative—Democracy at Work." *Young Children* 52, no. 4 (May 1997): 20–28.

Lewis, Eleanore. "What Mother? What Father?" *Young Children* 51, no. 3 (March 1996): 27.

Murphy, Dana. "Parent and Teacher Plan for the Child." *Young Children* 52, no. 4 (May 1997): 32–36.

Nunnelley, Jeannette, and Teesue Fields. "Anger, Dismay, Guilt, Anxiety—The Realities and Roles in Reporting Child Abuse." *Young Children* 54, no. 5 (September 1999): 74–80.

Workman, Susan, and Jim Gage. "Family–School Partnerships: A Family Strengths Approach." *Young Children* 52, no. 4 (May 1997): 10–14.

Discussion Activities

For reasons of professionalism, as you respond to these discussion questions, please respect the privacy of all children, adults, programs, and schools.

1. Think about a time when you were in school and a family member visited to volunteer in a classroom or to attend a conference. Was the experience positive or negative for you? Why? What was the teacher's role? As a developing teacher, what did this experience teach you about working with families?

2. Ask a family member about their contacts with your teachers when you were in school. What were some positive experiences they remember? Some negative experiences? What have you learned from this talk that will help you as a teacher when working with parents?

3. Think about an experience when a teacher clearly either included or excluded something from your home life. How do you feel about the teacher's action? Why?

Safety and Learning

We are now ready to look at the single most important act in the child's life at school: The decision to engage in learning.

At one time or another we all have felt forced to study, and to demonstrate certain skills. Although most of the time we survive such episodes and perhaps build a bit of character in the process, embarrassment at "failing to learn" is a common experience. Most of us remember being dropped early in a spelling bee, reading out loud and being corrected, putting an incorrect example on the board, giving an answer in class that was not what the teacher had in mind, getting low test scores, or receiving a low grade. For some of us, the humiliation we experienced in class was echoed or even magnified by the reaction at home.

If we were lucky, we possessed the personal resources and the support from others to get past these failures. We found them hurtful but not devastating. Yet, how many people do you know who finished school and learned the basic academic skills, but who do not care to use those skills as adults?

- They can read but hardly ever do.
- They hate to use math for anything (and especially balancing checkbooks).
- They write only infrequently, and maybe only by e-mail.
- They think science is for better-educated folks.

- They won't sing, won't draw, won't do drama, won't do recreational activity.

They probably do watch television, though, and may use computers, at least to play video games and hit Web sites. I heard a lecture once in which the speaker joked that if we want to reduce TV viewing in our population (from an average of about four hours a day), we should make it a regular subject of study in our schools: teach courses in it, give tests in it, and organize ability groups around it.

There are two components to the learning process: the cognitive component, and the emotional component (the thinking we do about a subject, and our feelings about our thinking). If we are forced to study something in a way that makes us feel bad about our efforts, we lose interest in that subject and want to have as little to do with it as possible. Most of us have probably gone along with the rewards and punishments that teachers have traditionally used to make us accountable for our efforts—while we were in the classroom. As soon as we were out, however, we attempted to leave behind as much of the unpleasantness surrounding that subject as we could. Some never do put these frustrations behind, and they miss opportunities as a result.

The central job of the early childhood teacher is to nudge children toward a decision to engage in learning. We are going to explore this issue by looking first at two simple but elegant theories about learning that have stood the test of time, Abraham Maslow's landmark ideas about safety and growth, and the lesser known work on social relations by Steven Harlow. Then, we will look at an important finding from recent brain research, that brain development is affected by the positive and negative experiences in young children's lives. We will explore two ideas for moving children from safety to learning: *encouragement,* and *significant learning.* We will look at anecdotes of typical early childhood activities to explore how developmentally appropriate practice is actually significant learning at work. Finally, we will explore early childhood "social studies" as the study of human differences.

In the anecdotes, watch for the perceptive and supportive nature of the adults' comments, which reduce children's anxieties about trying new things and make the willingness to try a natural and comfortable disposition. The decision to try something new is really the decision to learn. In choosing to learn, the child engages the developmental dynamic that can make him a healthy and responsive adult.

Classic Ideas about Safety and Learning

In his landmark little book, *The Psychology of Being,* published in 1962, Abraham Maslow gave us a psychological explanation for personal development that is still much cited today, his *hierarchy of needs.* Maslow wrote that children, like all of us, have two sets of needs: one set for safety, and one set for growth. When children lack security, the need for safety is very strong, and they are likely to show reactions based on safety needs. For example, when children frequently tell us (with words or with their bodies), "Teacher, I can't," they are feeling the need for safety. Kids who always seem to cling to us and get us to do things for them are also feeling the need for safety. So are children who throw tantrums when a block tower falls over, glue is spilled, or it's time to clean up. They are expressing frustration because they were feeling insecure or conflicted in the situation. There is no doubt that family and personal circumstances affect children's reactions to challenging situations in the classroom. But how the teacher responds makes a great difference in the child's ability to meet the need for safety and progress toward growth.

OBSERVATION: *There were minnows in the water table today! [A common event around the time of "fishing opener" in northern Minnesota.] One little girl, Melissa, wanted to be in the first group of children to play in the table. After she got her smock on, she went to the table and would not put her hands in. I was standing at the table and I reached in and picked up a minnow. I asked her if she wanted to touch it and she said, "No, I want to touch a small one." I asked her if she wanted me to pick one up that was smaller and pointed out that they were almost all the same size. She said, "Get a smaller one I think," with a very serious look on her face. I found a much smaller one and asked her if she wanted to touch that one. She said yes, and then held out her hand. I tipped my hand to drop it into her hand and she pulled her hand back so the minnow fell into the water. I asked her if she* *was afraid to touch them and she said yes. For the rest of the time, she stood at the edge of the table watching the other children playing with the minnows, but never touched one. She laughed with the other children, and seemed to be having fun. She didn't want to give her smock up so the next child could have a turn, but she didn't want to touch the fish either!*

REFLECTION: *I think the activity was developmentally appropriate for Melissa. She enjoyed it at her own level. She was uncomfortable touching the fish and was not forced to. Yet, she clearly was not ready to be done when her turn was over. I did not force her to touch the fish, but just let her enjoy them at her comfort level.*

In this anecdote, Janeen allowed a child to find her own balance of safety and growth by engaging in the activity in her own way. Melissa was almost ready to abandon her concerns and touch the minnows—almost but (this time) not quite. Janeen found a way to allow Melissa to experience the minnows at a level she was ready for. Next time—and repeating popular activities always is a good idea in early childhood classrooms—Melissa may progress to handling a "small one."

In 1972, Steven Harlow provided a theory that complements Maslow's and gives a bit more explanation of human needs in his three *levels of social relations* (*Special Education: The Meeting of Differences,* Grand Forks, ND: University of North Dakota Press, 1975). Harlow said that children who live in threatening circumstances are at a *survival level* of social relations. By this he meant that they react in rigid and exaggerated ways to typical classroom situations. They fear classroom experiences, just as they fear many situations in life, and react defensively to them. These children are barely surviving life in the classroom. In Maslow's terms, these kids are totally consumed by unmet safety needs. In *A Guidance Approach for the Encouraging Classroom,* I described these kids as showing *strong-needs mistaken behavior* (Albany, NY: Delmar/ITP Publishers, 1998). These are the kids who have serious problems in the classroom, often on a daily basis. Fortunately, young children at the survival level of social relations are a small minority in most classrooms.

A larger number of children are at Harlow's *adjustment level.* These children have enough security to get by in most situations. In fact they are likely to be strongly influenced by the teacher's authority. But because they lack confidence, they find it difficult to think and act for themselves. A quick sketch of children's behaviors at the adjustment level is shown in this excerpt from *A Guidance Approach for the Encouraging Classroom:*

> Daily, teachers must respond to children who, fearing criticism, show anxiety over the completion of activities. Some children put off starting tasks, or don't start at all. Others ask the teachers or a friend to do it for them— or copy. Even when they have finished, many young children [at the adjustment level] show taxing persistence in pursuing the blessings of authority (38).

Harlow explained that children with few fears and a healthy sense of self are open to experiencing life fully. They are at an *encountering level* of social relations, where they are responsive to classroom interactions and are able to learn relatively easily. Kids at the encountering level are sometimes too independent for some teachers—if they know more about *Tyrannosaurus rex* than you do, they may let you know. It is useful to remember that these kids are young and need to exercise their developing minds. Even as they depend upon our guidance, we need to appreciate and support their mental health.

OBSERVATION: *On this day the sensory table was filled with shaving cream and toy people and animals. Vince watched closely as two other children got their aprons on and dipped their hands into the cream. I approached Vince and asked him if he wanted an apron, and he nodded his head. He quickly put one on and started playing with the figures. He made animal noises while he played with them. After about fifteen minutes, he went into the bathroom and washed his hands. When he came out, I asked him if he wanted some help taking his apron off. He hesitated for a moment and then said, "I'm not done in there yet," with a bashful grin. Vince joined the others at the table and played for quite some time.*

REFLECTION: *I was very pleased to see how involved Vince was in the sensory table. He is a very shy and quiet child, and I rarely see him really becoming engaged in an activity. I was happy to see that he did not shy away from the other children, as he often does. I feel like he is really making some progress. By watching Vince interact with this particular activity, I became even more convinced that* *it is extremely important to have a variety of different activities, because you never know when you will spark something in any child.*

Kali made a significant observation here, seeing Vince progress in this activity from the adjustment level of social relations to the encountering level. As children become more comfortable in learning activities, they take the initiative to engage fully in them. Children do so when they decide it is safe to venture forth. The sometimes challenging but ultimately non-threatening nature of sensory-table materials helps many children move from safety to growth—toward the encountering level of social relations. In other situations, Vince may be at the adjustment, or even the survival, level. But through successful involvement in one activity, the child gains the motivation to take initiative in other activities. In the process, the child, like Vince in the anecdote, gains experience, confidence, and beginning social skills—progress toward meeting growth needs and educational expectations.

Brain Research, Safety, and Growth

After 20 years of neuro-pyschological research, we have learned much about how children develop their brains—and yet we have so much more to learn. We know that children continually interpret their experiences during waking—and probably sleeping—hours. In the process of interpretation, their brains grow more cells and cell connections: the better to make more meaning (Julee Newberger, "New Brain Development Research—A Wonderful Window of Opportunity to Build Public Support for Early Childhood Education," *Young Children* 52 [4] May 1997, 4–9). Throughout the early years, every so often there is a spurt in this brain development, so that children's interpretive capacity increases dramatically. Tell a just-four-year-old child that it is raining "cats and dogs" outside, and with a puzzled expression he will go check by looking out the window. Tell him the same thing a year later, and he might look at you with a grin and say, "Yeah, and elephants even!" Children's ability to construct knowledge (understand things) progresses slowly and steadily, and then every once in a while leaps ahead.

In describing children's ability to learn, I used to use a record player analogy: most adults' brains work at about 33 rpm and most children's brains work at

78 rpm. Early childhood teachers are effective because they can usually get up to 45 rpm. I use this comparison less now because fewer people understand it, and because in addition to spinning at 78 rpm, children's brains are also building themselves while they spin.

The observation that follows shows children comfortable enough in the classroom to use materials in intelligent (creative) ways. Follow closely and watch these children's thinking—if not their brains—develop before your eyes.

OBSERVATION: *During choice time today in kindergarten, Dylan and Caleb were sitting at the art table making pictures. Caleb drew a box with a dot in the middle. He said to Dylan, "Look, this is a fly trap and I caught a fly."*

Dylan then said to Caleb, "I am going to draw a spider trap and catch a spider; then my spider is going to eat your fly."

Caleb: "It can't eat my fly because it can fly away and spiders can't fly."

Dylan: "If I draw wings on my spider, it will be able to fly and then it can catch your fly and eat it up!"

Their conversation continued for about six more turns. After they had finished, they put away their drawings and went to find something else to play with.

REFLECTION: *Dylan and Caleb were able to use their imagination and be creative in the pictures they were drawing. If they were given a coloring book, this freedom to be creative and imaginative would not have happened. Caleb and Dylan were also problem-solving. They figured out that if they drew wings on the spider, it could catch the fly. They were also working on the development of their social and verbal skills by the way they communicated with each other. Although their game had some rivalry to it, they left the table friends.*

Kalli, the student teacher who wrote the anecdote, showed understanding of the learning going on here for the two boys. We cannot force brain development, just as we cannot force learning that will be significant. What teachers can do, however, is provide the materials and the encouragement for children to engage fully in learning activities. With such opportunities on a daily basis, the growing body of brain research tells us that good physiological things happen inside the head of the child.

Teachers have often noted that when children come from functioning families and feel secure in the classroom and the home, they walk right into learning situations and try on the merchandise. When children feel threatened and insecure, they have difficulty opening themselves to classroom experiences. Learning becomes difficult, even painful. This pattern of behavior, of course, is what Maslow and Harlow were writing about nearly a half century ago. The recent brain research provides a physiological foundation for Harlow's and Maslow's ideas.

In prolonged stressful circumstances, the brain secretes hormones that heighten the child's "fight or flight" tendencies and restrict normal brain development. As Newberger points out in the article "New Brain Development Research," any prolonged stress impedes the healthy development of their brains, their ability to learn, and their ability to develop social skills. Because of brain chemistry, these children fear life and attempt to protect themselves from new experiences, including learning experiences, as a way to cope. This knowledge is important because it affects how we work with kids in the classroom, especially kids who are anxious and angry. Let's put the discussion in Maslow's terms. In the encouraging classroom, the teacher's task is to respect the child's need for safety, but not to give in to it. For the children's sake and our own, we don't want to build up their sense of helplessness and dependency on us. We need to nudge them toward growth so they can see that the world is not such a threatening place and they can do things for themselves, such as learn and develop their brains.

OBSERVATION: *Tim was sitting at the art table during free choice and asked me to help him cut out a "big head." I asked him what kind of head he was thinking about making. When he couldn't tell me, I asked him if he could draw it for me. He said he couldn't. I asked him if he could at least try. He drew it and then said, "See, it's not a head."*

I said, "Yes it is, why don't you cut it out and see if it fits on the body you made?"

After a little persuasion, he cut it out and glued it on the body. He ran over to Lois, the teacher, and said, "See the head that Gayle made for me?"

REFLECTION: *Tim needed reassurance that he could make the head himself. He lacked self-confidence and then didn't even realize that he had done all the work. I talked to him about how hard he worked to make the head and that it was his work. He does enjoy success, he just lacks confidence.*

Gayle's responses both in the observation and the reflection show the balance we are talking about. She respected Tim's frustration and lack of confidence at making his head. (Tim seemed to be at Harlow's adjustment level here.) She encouraged him to try, even if he was not yet ready to see his own developing ability. She did not impose adult standards about how a head should look or how it should correspond to the body. In fact, an important task of the teacher in nudging children from safety to growth, is to encourage them to put aside their sense of traditional realism—which they may not have the skills to duplicate—and encourage them to "do it" their own way.

Teachers are able to help children move toward growth by being "unrelentingly positive." Outside of the classroom, this means working with parents to the extent possible—as discussed in chapter two—to make life reliable for children. In the classroom, the teacher who believes in children's resiliency (the ability to overcome hurt and to thrive) does not give up on them. The teacher uses quiet but ongoing encouragement to let children who are hurting know that the classroom is a caring community and that they have a place in it. Some would call this "plain good old-fashioned education," but I call it *liberation teaching,* because it has such a lasting impact on children's lives—and children's brains.

PRAISE OR ENCOURAGEMENT?

The feedback that teachers give to children has everything to do with children feeling comfortable enough to try to learn. In this connection you may have heard that "Praise is good. Use lots of praise." Noted authorities such as Dreikurs and Ginott, as long as thirty years ago, have challenged this idea; their challenges are discussed in *A Guidance Approach for the Encouraging Classroom.* Praise is frequently used during groups and transition times (when a group is moving from one activity to the next) to "reward good behavior." Teachers select "only those children" who are listening "the most quietly" or waiting "the most patiently" for recognition and privileges. When I discuss with teachers this common use of praise, I often call out the names of a few people in the group to "praise" their listening and note taking. Then I ask how the rest feel. Typical responses are, "Upset that you didn't pick me," "Hurt, because I was listening too. Look at these notes," "You like them better than us," and "Angry, I'm going to get those two later." And these comments are from adults! When teachers single out children for praise, they may think they are being positive, but they really are setting up a conditional acceptance situation that unfairly compares group members and works against the encouraging classroom. Children often feel threatened if they are singled out—and if they feel they are being excluded. Praise does not help children feel safe in the classroom. Praise does not motivate children to learn. (A. Kohn, *Punished by Rewards,* New York: Houghton Mifflin, 1993).

OBSERVATION: *After most children are finished with their lunch, the teacher begins to call on them to bring their plates to her. Each child is called, one at a time, and hands the teacher the plate. The children are expected to wait patiently until their names are called. On this day the children were not very patient and kept leaving their seats before it was their turn. The teacher asked them to please sit down and wait for their turn, but it didn't work. She pointed out how one child correctly waited patiently and called on this child to bring up his plate. I was noticing that some children were more restless than others. I would say, "John looks like he's ready to give you his plate." My hope was to get the teacher to call them so they would not be singled out, or asked to sit down again. At one point the teacher turned her head to talk to the other teacher in the room, and I began to call the children. I chose a different way to select them. I called the children who were just about to stand up, but hadn't quite done it yet. As the children were called and handed me their plates, I thanked each one personally for being patient.*

While this worked for most of the children, I had to make a special deal with one child. He kept yelling, "Pick me, I'm ready!" Not wanting the other children to start yelling, I went over and told him that if he was quiet for a few seconds, I would call him next. I went back to the cleaning cart, and as soon as the boy was quiet, I called on him. When he got there, I thanked him for being quiet and waiting his turn.

REFLECTION: *I learned from this experience that using praise and criticism do not always stop a behavior. The teacher was hoping that if a student had his ability/inability to be patient mentioned to the whole class, the child would then want to behave in the way she wanted. I watched the children who were singled out for standing up sit with their heads down for a few seconds after they had the group's attention drawn to them. The one boy who did it right also seemed to look uncomfortable being singled out.*

Rather than focus on individual children, I tried to keep it from happening. Rather than asking a student about to get up to sit down, I chose to catch them right before they did and then thank them individually for exhibiting the behavior I wanted. The sad faces I had seen sitting at their tables waiting to be called on because they were impatient, were now smiling because they had been told they were being patient.

By avoiding stigmatizing by singling out, I was able to leave the children's self-esteem intact. I was also able to get the behavior the teacher was looking for. (She let me finish calling on the children after her conversation.) All it took was a little extra observation.

The problem with the traditional use of praise is that its real purpose is not to honor an individual so much as to manipulate the group. Traditional praise is a form of conditional acceptance because it singles out individual members of the community for comparison (Kohn). Some children have an easier time than others with the tasks of waiting, listening, and resting. It may be that kids who didn't wait so patiently, listen so quietly, or nap so easily are working a lot harder at these tasks than the kids who typically get rewarded. Joel recognized this and worked with the group's natural dynamics to make an efficient and harmonious transition. Joel also understood another principal of guidance: He did not single out individuals for either praise or criticism, but rather offered unconditional acceptance to everyone. (Whether this is the best way to end a mealtime is another matter.)

Using Encouragement

Instead of praise, teachers use encouragement. Traditional praise differs from encouragement in that praise is usually public and rewards children for results that teachers want to see. Encouragement appreciates efforts and progress without singling children out. Encouragement gives specific feedback that explains the teacher's thoughts; it is not the blanket shortcut, "good job." Most importantly, encouragement lets the child know that she can do it in her own way, and that however she does it is fine. Encouragement supports children in their decision to learn.

Encouragement can focus on an individual, or on a group. Group-focused encouragement does not single out individuals, but recognizes the effort and progress of the group as a whole: "You all are really working hard at waiting. Stay patient, and I will get everyone over here to clean those plates." When done effectively, group-focused encouragement builds group spirit, developing children's sense of community. In the next anecdote, Julia illustrates the effectiveness of group-focused encouragement.

> **OBSERVATION:** *Students in our kindergarten class were doing story pictures to send to some survivors of the Oklahoma City bombing disaster. I made a point of going around to look at each child's creation, not making any specific comments; then I stood in front of the class and said, "You are all working very hard on your story pictures. I'll bet that you are proud of your work." Some children smiled, and they all seemed pleased with the comment. They worked very hard. I noticed a few children even made comments to other children on how nice their story pictures were. By saying something positive to the group, they all wanted to share in that feeling; it was like the domino effect. (Anecdote first appeared in* A Guidance Approach for the Encouraging Classroom.*)*

Individual encouragement also focuses on efforts and progress more than results and is less evaluative of the child than praise. Individual-focused encouragement is usually private; then the child knows it is really meant for him. And, like group-focused encouragement, it is descriptive and specific rather than clichéd and judgmental: "Thank you, Becki, for waiting until your name was called," instead of "Good job, Becki, good waiting." Individual encouragement is the primary communication technique for inviting learning to occur and for building the encouraging classroom. As Joel mentioned, encouraging takes "a little extra observation," but the results make it worthwhile.

> **OBSERVATION:** *The children started arriving at kindergarten at about 8:30, and I was greeting them as they came in. They seemed very receptive to my greeting and I watched them disperse to the different centers in the room. There was*

one boy that was interested in striking up a conversation with me about a picture he had colored and this is how the conversation went:

Lamar reached out and handed me a picture of a frog that he had drawn.

Me: Wow! looks like you used a lot of green.

Lamar: Well yeah, frogs are green.

Me: Yeah, they are green aren't they.

Lamar: Yeah.

Me: You made an outline of your frog and then you stayed inside the lines so carefully.

Lamar: (smiling) I have a picture on the back too.

Me: What colors did you use?

Lamar: I used different colors!

Me: You made your own lines and stayed in the lines on this picture too.

He looked at me with a smile gleaming with pride.

Lamar: I would like you to have the picture that I colored.

Me: Thank you! I will put it on my fridge.

Lamar looked up from his picture and smiled in amazement. He looked so pleased that I would put his picture up in my home.

REFLECTION: *I used encouragement instead of praise. I tried to enlighten Lamar on the things he did very well and stayed away from bringing in any negative aspects that might "stunt" his creativity. Lamar didn't seem embarrassed or affected in any negative way by my comments.*

I was really nervous that I might give Lamar praise instead of encouraging him to keep on with his good work. I like to praise people and sometimes I have to be careful not to embarrass them and make them feel uncomfortable. I tried to stay away from, "Oh, you are so good at coloring." I tried to look at his picture in a different way and tried to pick out things that were unique and done well. I didn't get much of a response from Lamar when I told him he stayed in the lines so well, but he did show gratitude by giving a nice smile.

The final gesture that let me know that Lamar felt comfortable with the way the conversation went was when he made sure that I could have his picture to take home. He seemed to feel that I enjoyed his work on the picture and would enjoy having it for myself. He was really impressed when I said I would hang it on my refrigerator so that everyone could see it. I knew then that he was proud of his work and he seemed excited to show me other pictures he had colored.

Randolph picked up on a key point about using encouragement. It is not a shortcut phrase like "Good job" or "Nice picture." Children don't have much to say when teachers give these traditional, clichéd expressions of praise. Encouragement is supportive conversation about a child's efforts that helps him continue to make progress. Often just a brief descriptive comment will open the door. Listening and appreciating the child's response is as important as your initial comment. The interaction often is not long—Randolph's analysis was longer than his conversation—but it is enough to tell the child that you care enough to pay attention, enough to help the child make a connection with the classroom community.

OBSERVATION: *I have been working at an evening child care program while the parents are in group therapy for chemical dependency. On this evening I brought a bag of art supplies with me and decided to try some creative activities with the children. I wanted everyone to feel important and self-expressive, no matter what art activity they chose to do. Although I tried some group encouragement, I mainly wanted to practice making statements of encouragement directed towards individuals, because I thought that might be more difficult to do.*

To a child who exhibited level three (strong-needs) mistaken behavior during our previous meeting, I said, "You're drawing a truck." That's all I had to say, and he came back with "I saw a monster truck show." I had been having a difficult time communicating with this child, and when we discussed monster trucks for a few minutes, I was grateful that we were conversing.

When the same child then decided to trace some clown faces, I said, "You are tracing those faces very carefully."

"Yup," he responded to me with a smile, and he continued to concentrate on his project of tracing. This was the longest I had seen him do any activity since the program began.

REFLECTION: *Surprisingly enough, encouragement is a fairly easy habit to practice. For me, the key was to pay attention to what I was saying. For example, it is quite natural for me to say, "Wow! That's a really good picture," indicating a value judgment and praise. But if I am self-aware, it is just about as easy to come up with, "You're drawing a truck," and "You are tracing those faces very carefully."*

I also discovered that paying close attention to what they are doing leads to greater understanding about the children. It was necessary for me to try to figure out what the children were making, and then talk with them about it specifically. In this way, I learned more about their interests, backgrounds, and life experiences. This helped to make me a more productive child care provider.

Through encouraging conversations about their work, children gain and sustain the will to try, to persevere, and to accomplish. The secret to unlocking children's potential to learn is a simple one: Use encouragement.

Significant Learning

Some time ago an informal survey of architects about their favorite activities as children showed that a high percentage were always playing with Lego plastic building blocks. In fact, many said that they pretended to be sick in order to stay home to build with these venerable plastic blocks. The survey results are another indication of what we already know, that in sustained, non-pressured, playlike activity with materials that children value—Lego blocks, books, journals, musical instruments, ice skates (it's different for each child)—*significant learning occurs* (C. R. Rogers, *On Becoming a Person,* Boston: Houghton Mifflin, 1961). This is just what textbooks like the NAEYC publication, *Developmentally Appropriate Practice in Early Childhood Programs,* say happens (S. Bredekamp and C. Copple, eds., Washington, DC: NAEYC, 1997). Significant learning brings together new thinking, and personal gratification about the new thinking.

Over the years, writers have described this special kind of learning in different ways. One current description is the child's act of *constructing knowledge.* I especially like Maria Montessori's thoughts on the subject. Montessori considered peak learning episodes for a child to be spiritual in nature, experiences that should never be interrupted. In more terse modern terms, significant learning has both immediate and lasting meaning for the child. Significant learning almost always involves a challenge, but responding to the challenge is generally more pleasant than unpleasant. Significant learning can be encouraged, but cannot be forced.

OBSERVATION: *In the toddler room of our center, I was reading a book about a train called Thomas to a 20-month-old boy named Thomas. We enjoyed the book together, and I was ready to go on to another. Thomas said "Choo!" I asked him if he wanted me to read the book again. He nodded emphatically. We read the book three more times. Later that morning, I noticed Thomas doing puzzles. I went over and had to smile when I saw him putting together the Thomas the Train puzzle. I asked him what he was doing. He smiled and replied "Thomas." He spent over 15 minutes with that puzzle, putting it together quite a few times.*

REFLECTION: *That afternoon when his dad came to pick Thomas up, I told him about Thomas' interest in the book and puzzle. He laughed and said, "We have the book and puzzle at home, and I get tired of them way before he does!" The book and puzzle must have meant a lot to Thomas. He had a longer attention span for them than either his father or his teacher!*

If we watch for it, we will know significant learning when we see it. There is no question that significant learning is more likely to happen if teachers support it. I once heard a second-grade teacher comment that the work climate of her classroom changed completely when she stopped correcting children's writing in red ink and started encouraging their work with green ink. I heard another teacher comment that for her a child who has spelled the word "helucopter" this way, has gotten the word 90 percent correct. How teachers teach has everything to do, of course, with whether children have the oportunity to engage in significant learning. The whole point of the encouraging classroom is to make significant learning *inviting*.

RECOLLECTION: *In a primary-grade classroom, the teacher used a multi-dimensional math program that included small group problem-solving activities and many manipulatives. Periodically, though, he gave pencil-and-paper homework assignments. The following day during math time the children received the answers and corrected their own work. In pairs the children shared with each other a few mistakes they made in the problems. The teacher then asked for volunteers to share the mistake they made with the rest of the class on the board. Hands went up. A child was selected and analyzed his or her mistake for the group. When the child was done, everyone, including the teacher, applauded.*

On occasion, this teacher has had to tell the children to stop doing math during other times during the day. Each year the children in this gifted teacher's class do just fine on the district-required standardized tests.

DEVELOPMENTALLY APPROPRIATE PRACTICE

This section takes a "conversational approach" to developmentally appropriate practice (DAP). This means that we will look at DAP informally, using anecdotes to illustrate ideas. DAP by now is familiar to most early childhood professionals. Defined simply, DAP accommodates the developmental level and the personal circumstances of each child in the teaching–learning process. Several ideas already introduced in the book resonate with DAP. Emergent curriculum derives directly from the background and interests of the children and so is developmentally appropriate. Significant learning—learning that has meaning for the child—can only occur when activities are developmentally appropriate. Developmentally appropriate activity is inherently interesting to children, and so reduces their anxiety about engaging in learning acts. And, DAP is supported fully by the research on brain development. In "New Brain Development Research," Newberger says it this way:

> [Brain] research does not suggest drilling children in alphabet songs from different languages or using flash cards to promote rote memorization of letters and numbers. Rather, it reinforces the principles of developmentally appropriate practice (7).

Distilled to its essence, DAP guides adults to provide a successful learning environment for every child in the group. A successful learning environment is exactly what the neuropsychologists tell us each child needs for healthy brain development. This coming together of research trends is evident in the encouraging classroom.

While DAP has a common quality of being responsive to the developmental level and individual circumstances of each child, DAP has a particular look in different activities of the early childhood classroom. Through the anecdotes, we shall look in on block, art, writing, and library activities to see teachers using DAP in order to nudge children into active engagement in learning.

Blocks

In the following anecdote, Rachel describes her conversation with country preschoolers, playing with blocks, who had only visited Minneapolis and St. Paul and never lived there.

> **OBSERVATION:** *It was choice time, and the children were engaged in various activities (dramatic play, computers, reading corner, writing corner, and block area.) Three children were playing with blocks. They were stacking the blocks one on top of the other. I went over and asked them what they were building. "A skyscraper," said one child. I then asked them where they would usually find a skyscraper. "In the [Twin] Cities," said a child.*
>
> *I wondered how they would make a city with all the blocks. "By making a bunch of skyscrapers," said a child. I could see they were really involved in building their city so I acknowledged the comment, smiled, and walked to another group. The children proceeded to stack the blocks, but this time they had about six to eight separate stacks. Later on, I went over to the group and asked them if they could tell me what they made with the blocks.*
>
> *"Minneapolis," said one child.*
>
> *"See, here's 3M, the post office, and the grocery store," said another.*

When children are engaged in developmentally appropriate activity—as these children were—they integrate what they know and creatively hypothesize about the rest. They work to accommodate viewpoints different from their own and engage in high-level problem solving. We know that in order to promote brain development, activities must involve ongoing, hands-on engagement, so that children directly experience intellectual processes such as integration of information, concept formation, concentration, cooperation, creativity, language use, and problem solving.

It used to be that teachers thought children needed to complete defined activities to exact standards in order to learn. We now know that children are born with a built-in learning dynamic. Teachers don't have to mold this dynamic so much as encourage it. Yet, all around children are models for reality, models that they notice, but cannot yet replicate. As perceptive as they are, children frequently put themselves in the predicament of knowing how materials are supposed to go together, but not being able to put them together as the model suggests. To reduce children's anxiety about not doing it "right," teachers work to persuade children that their way is just fine; it doesn't have to be perfect. The teacher takes a developmentally appropriate position in this matter when she chooses not to introduce models to be copied, encouraging children instead to take the initiative to find and reach their own individual standards.

OBSERVATION: *It was play time and Shelda and Mindy, both age five, were playing with Lego blocks. Shelda called me over and said, "Ricole, we're having trouble building a helicopter like this one." She pointed to the picture of a big, perfect Lego helicopter on the side of the box. She said, "Will you help us?"*

I said, "Yes, but why don't we make our helicopter a little different. For one thing, we don't have all the Lego pieces to make one like the picture."

The girls agreed, but I could tell Shelda still was going to stick by the picture as much as possible. We started to build the body of the 'copter and she said, "We don't have propellers."

I asked Shelda if she could think of a way to make our own propellers. She thought we could take two long pieces and hook them together. She kept thinking of ways to build our own parts: the windows, doors, etc. Eventually we completed our own helicopter. I could tell she was comparing it to the picture, so I said, "I like it, and we did it on our own." She agreed.

Then Shelda wanted to build something else. She said, "Let's build an easier one." The two girls went back to the pictures on the box and started making the tow truck.

REFLECTION: *I guess I felt frustrated because I watched a child's creativity being inhibited. The child looked at the picture and wanted her helicopter to be perfect. I tried to encourage Shelda to come help make our own unique helicopter. Even though she agreed, I know she kept looking at the picture. If the picture wouldn't have been there, she would have felt free to make it how she wanted it, and would have been more satisfied with her creation. I don't feel that it's developmentally appropriate to have the pictures. There's no way the children could build objects like the perfect ones in the pictures. I couldn't do it, and I'm 22 years old.*

It was also frustrating to hear Shelda say, "Let's do an easier one." I felt like she didn't think she could do it. I know this child could do it, but because of the perfect picture, she felt theirs wasn't good enough.

When I have my own class I am not going to keep the pictures of what you can build with Legos where the children can see them. I feel that by taking away the pictures and letting them come up with their own ideas, we are setting them up for success. They won't have a picture to compare their work with, and therefore will be happier with their work in the end.

Ricole makes a strong case against a common practice in early childhood classrooms. It's simple. Remove the models and the patterns. The experience that the child gains with materials should be from their minds to their senses and back to their minds. We don't want older learners to copy someone else's work. We should not encourage copying in early childhood, whether or not the children are able to do it. A teacher who can put away predetermined expectations about products, and instead ask relevant, open-ended questions to prompt discovery, has mastered an important teaching skill in early childhood—one that will unlock children's initiative to learn.

Art

When teachers impose standards that young children are expected to meet in an activity, they are imposing roadblocks to learning. When this happens, the few children who can meet the standard may feel success at it (or just relief), but the children who do not meet the standard (often the majority) experience frustration. As described in Bredekamp and Copple's *Developmentally Appropriate Practice,* a common inappropriate use of standards happens when teachers substitute craft activities that have standardized products for open-ended art. Even when art activities truly are art, because they are open-ended, young children are aware of implied standards, based on realism, and feel anxiety as a result. Nonetheless, teachers encourage developmentally appropriate art when they use art centers with a variety of materials that the child can use in her own ways and when they motivate theme-related art with words rather than models.

A stereotype about young children is that before they can make pictures "that look like things," they can't really do art. The children in the next anecdote felt safe to express their ideas in many ways, including open-ended pictures. Because they felt safe, they explored ideas about their families, uniquely completing pictures in line with their stages of art development and their abilities. An adult who knows not to use premade models, or do parallel pictures that distract children from their own creative processes, is in an excellent position to encourage aesthetic development. It is not in the finished product but in the creative process that young minds grow. This anecdote is from a Head Start class of three to six year olds.

OBSERVATION: *In our Head Start class in an Ojibwe Indian community, we had been doing a theme on families. We had read a book about families the world over and some family members had visited the classroom. On this day I told my group of 22 children that at the art center today they could make "story–pictures" (pictures that tell stories) about their families.*

One of the six year olds came right over, but disdained the crayons and markers. She used a pencil "to get them all in." She drew over 40 figures on her paper, labeling each by name. She included "aunties" and "uncles" whom we teachers knew to be neighbors, but to her they were family, and that was fine.

One three year old drew her Mom as a collection of individual shapes. This kid told us the name of each body part, including some in Ojibwe that made the other teacher laugh quite loudly.

Then there was Joey. At age three and a half, Joey made seven distinct up-and-down crayon scribbles, each in a different color. On the right side of the paper, he made a circular scribble different than the rest. Joey used "personal script" (scribble writing) to write the name of each relative below each scribble. When we came to the circular figure on the right, I said, "I know who that is, Joey, that's your baby sister."

Joey shook his head in mild disgust, "Uh-uh, Dan, that's my dog."

REFLECTION: *This activity shows that young children, whatever their stages of development, are not just artists, but also communicators of ideas, capable of giving symbolic representation to their families. As to my own "symbolic" gain from this project, I learned to be careful about interpreting children's art work for them!*

A traditional notion about children's art is that children should not have to put their pictures into words. True, adults should not force a child to discuss a picture (or interpret a picture for a child). But children tell stories about their pictures naturally. Probably 90 percent of the art that they are familiar with is in picture books, helping to tell the story. They learn quickly that art can tell stories. It is the experience of the teachers I know that children love to interpret their pictures—a term for this kind of art is "story pictures." In my Head Start class, the children regularly did theme-related pictures of their families. In fact, for a child a story–picture is a form of authorship, and story–pictures strung together are journals. The blending of art into writing makes art not only art but also an important emergent-literacy activity.

Writing

Writing, like artistic expression, begins long before elementary school. Even more than with art, however, young children often learn that since they cannot form words on paper, they therefore cannot convey meaning on paper—be an author. If they try, others (often brothers and sisters—hopefully not adults) tell them that they "write like a baby." Without teacher support, they stop trying.

Later, as they progress though elementary school, these children learn the conventions of penmanship, spelling, sentence formation, and punctuation. But by then, for many, the years of skill-drill, red marks, and lack of encouragement have taken their toll. Even though they now can form words on paper, these children still believe they can't convey meaning on paper. The original, creative processes that they were ready to use in early childhood as young authors has been left undeveloped. Because of a lack of support for early writing, many older learners find that writing has become a major chore. They may suffer permanent writer's block as a result—a disadvantage in a society that depends on person-to-person communication in many forms.

Such is not the fate of all early writers, however. If, on a continuing basis, adults encourage the child to freely mark on blank paper and freely interpret those marks, he begins to see himself as an author. The teacher must take care to support the child if discouraging words are heard, of course, but with consistent support and ongoing opportunities to write, even preschoolers find wonderful meaning in the writing process.

> **OBSERVATION:** *James, the youngest child in my preschool center, is returning for his second year. He walks in the door and over to the writing center, smiling. He says, "Connie, we have journals! We have journals! Do you know who makes journals?"*

Wanting to hear his response, I say smiling, "No, who?"
James: "God did because he knows I love them so much."

Hipple and others have documented that writing in early childhood progresses through stages (M. Hipple, "Journal Writing in the Kindergarten," *Language Arts* 62 [3], 1985, 23–30). With encouragement, children's writing evolves from scribbles to squiggles to letters—random and significant—to invented spelling, to conventional spelling. In order to encourage development through the stages of writing, my experience has taught me the following: Refrain from writing down children's oral dictations for them—at least until after the children have written for themselves. Ask them to write their stories as well as draw them. They may tell you they can't write. Assure them that they write just fine for a four year old, and they'll write like an older kid later—or use other words that feel right to you. Be friendly but persistent. (Note: Some teachers offer to do a written translation of a child's writing after she has interpreted it for the teacher, "because not all adults can read children's writing.") Provide writing opportunities—journals, story–pictures— every day. Their writing, like their art, will develop over time.

In the following anecdote, notice that Jenner gives encouragement during the writing process when the child really needs it. After a picture is done or the story written, the child has the personal reward of the completed project. During the struggle with the task—when he may not be sure he can complete it—a child appreciates the boost that encouragement can provide.

OBSERVATION: *It was journal time in the kindergarten class. A girl was telling me about what she was working on. It was an Easter basket with eggs in it. On the lines below she had the letter E written. She said, "Will you tell me how to spell Easter?"*

I said, "You already have the first letter. I wonder if you could sound it out and spell it on your own."

So she said the word "Easter," then kept repeating the "Es" sound. She wrote the letter S next. Then she said, "Is this right?"

I sounded it out loud. After I made the "Es" sound, I said, "That sounds right. I think you're getting it, keep trying." I walked away for a few minutes to give her a chance to work. When I circled by her desk, I noticed she had EST written. I just walked by and let her continue thinking.

When she was done, she asked me to come over. "Look, is this the way you write Easter?"

So I asked her to show me how she did it. She sounded out the word and pointed to the letters as she went: "ESTR."

I said, "I knew you could do it by sounding it out."

She said, "Yes, I did, and I already know how to spell egg, it's E-G-G." She wrote it in her journal, finishing her work.

REFLECTION: *I found this experience to be very interesting because it's the first time I've ever worked first hand with invented spelling. I've always learned about it in classes and seen examples of it, but this time I got to see a student actually use it. I feel that writing journals is developmentally appropriate for these kindergarten children. Invented spelling was an appropriate level for this student to be at.*

When I was talking with her at first she wanted me to just tell her how to spell it. When I encouraged her to try it, and told her she had made a good start, she seemed very interested in trying it on her own. Once in a while she'd ask if she was right. I would sound it out and say, "Yes, that sounds right." When she received a little encouragement once in a while, she was excited to do it on her own. I learned that encouragement really works. By encouraging children, we are guiding them to achieve independence and increasing their self-esteem.

Educators have different names for invented spelling, such as *phonetic spelling* and *pretend spelling.* Whatever you call it, invented spelling is an important stage in learning to be as one child put it, an "arthur." Teachers need to let parents know that invented spelling is the right way for young children to write for now. Invented spelling teaches children phonetic skills so that later they will be ready for conventional spelling with all its irregularities, like the spellings of "chair" and "share." Because invented spelling looks "wrong" to many adults, children are vulnerable to criticism during the invented-spelling stage. They are often hesitant to try. Jenner's approach of giving encouragement and then actually walking away was just right in this situation. In the encouraging classroom you do as much as you need to—but only as much—to get the child to do the rest. Then he can truly feel that his decision to learn has been successful. Significant learning has occurred; no praise is necessary.

Reading

In early childhood education adults hear all the time that it is important to read to children daily. It is, but not just in a large group, waving that little book around too fast for some and too slowly for others. There is a place for large-group reading—especially with Big Books. But children naturally have things to say about books, and as we know, their comments do not necessarily follow the "official" lines of the story. The teacher's remark, "Not now, Jasper, let's see what happens to the Dirty Dog next," does not help Jasper engage intellectually with the story. In fact, the comment probably discourages him. For children to engage in significant learning through reading, the experience needs to be interactive. At the least children need the opportunity to follow up on the story—through "extender" ideas, such as making story–pictures and reading the book on their own. More important, though, children need to read individually and in small groups with adults.

When children get up-close and personal with books, they engage in the reading more fully. Seated on adults' laps, draped over adults' shoulders, or lying on their bellies in a circle, children respond to stories more personally, and they let their ideas flow. In the conversations that result, the child builds attachments with adults, with books, with reading, and with ideas. Reading with children individually and in small groups helps make books come alive. And learning to love books is the first stage in learning to read. In their vintage text, *Reading Is Only the Tiger's Tail* (Winnipeg, MB: Perquis Publishers, 1987), Robert and Mary McCracken argue that for many young children the "lap technique" (reading in informal, small groups) is the most developmentally appropriate form of reading.

In the following anecdote, notice how Lavonne uses encouraging responses in her contact talk over a book with Jake. Notice, too, that Lavonne and Jake don't actually start the book until after the discussion.

OBSERVATION: *In our kindergarten classroom, the children had been studying dinosaurs. They had just finished doing volcano science projects and had just started choice time. One little boy asked me if I would read him a dinosaur book in the book corner.*

Jake: Will you read me this book? (Tapping my hand while holding the book up in my face.)

Lavonne: Sure, let's sit on the carpet. (He held my hand as we walked to the carpet area.)

Jake: Look at the front, there are volcanoes like the one I made.

Lavonne: Yes, I see that.

Jake: Them ones got red smoke coming out of the tops.

Lavonne: I wonder why it's red?

Jake: It's red like mine because in volcanoes there is fire, so that's why it's red smoke.

Lavonne: What else do you see?

Jake: There's a big dinosaur in front of the volcanoes, but he's a nice dinosaur because he eats plants, not people.

Lavonne: How do you know he eats plants?

Jake: Cause he's a long-neck, our teacher told us that, and long-necks don't eat people, they eat plants, that's why I know.

Lavonne: Oh, I see.

Jake: The kind that eat people have sharp teeth, and see this one's teeth are not sharp so that's why he eats trees and branches.

Lavonne: I wonder how he reaches way up high to the trees?

Jake: He can reach the trees because his neck is like a giraffe's, it goes way up in the sky. That's why my teacher called him a long-neck.

Lavonne: Oh, that makes sense.

Jake: I really like dinosaurs, I have lots of books about dinosaurs at home. When we went to see my Grandma, I got to see a dinosaur.

Lavonne: Oh...?

Jake: It wasn't real, though, because all the dinosaurs died a long time ago, and there are no real ones anymore, just the bones.

Lavonne: I wonder what we can do with the bones?

Jake: The guy that worked at the place where the bones were told me a story about digging in the sand and finding different pieces from the dead dinosaurs. Then he said it's like a puzzle and he gets to put the bones together to make a skeletor and we can see what the dinosaurs looked like back then.

Lavonne: Wow, I bet that is a lot of fun making dinosaur skeletons. (I tried to ignore his way of saying "skeletor" and just repeated the correct word. It seemed obvious that he knew what he was talking about, so I didn't feel the need to correct him.)

Jake: Can we read now?

Lavonne: Yes we can, are you ready?

Jake: (He sat cross-legged and rested his head in his hands.) Yep, I'm ready.

Lavonne: All right. "Long, long ago..." (We began reading.)

Notice in the anecdote that Lavonne did not correct Jake's view that meat-eating dinosaurs ate people. The balance between correction and encouragement in early childhood education is a dynamic one, maintained by each teacher for each child. When there is a question about the balance, we weigh in on the side of encouragement. Kids have their whole lifetimes to sort out the accurate from the inaccurate. In the encouraging classroom, we give only correction that we believe the child can accept and is ready for. We save technical accuracy for the fourth-grade teachers, when kids have more living under their belts.

In the encouraging classroom, it is okay to read in large groups—when the sense of togetherness and interest in the story outweigh the restlessness. But to personalize the reading experience, so that children can safely try out their own ideas, reading needs to be done individually and in small groups. You will know that a story has been developmentally appropriate when a child's attention span for reading and re-reading a book is longer than yours. You will know that significant learning is occurring when your discussion of ideas generated by the book makes you and the child forget to turn the pages. In reading, as in all other activity in the encouraging classroom, DAP is simply empowering the child to decide it is safe to learn.

Learning about Human Differences: Social Studies

Let's define *social studies* as the study of culture and life. Both the NAEYC classic, *Anti-Bias Curriculum: Tools for Empowering Young Children* (Louise Derman-Sparks, Washington, DC: NAEYC 1989), and Stacey York's essential *Roots and Wings: Affirming Culture in Early Childhood Programs* (St. Paul: Redleaf Press, 1991), say that the beginning of learning about difference is for each child to be grounded in a positive sense of self, so that the human differences all around him will not be threatening, but rather will be sources of interest, learning, and the valuing of life. In this connection the NAEYC text and *Roots and Wings* both caution against studying cultures through "the tourist approach." The tourist approach happens when teachers introduce children to snippets of a people's culture—like "Eskimos live in igloos"—that often are inaccurate and trivialize a culture by suggesting it lives only in history, or is otherwise "exotic," as explained in *Roots and Wings*. Teachers need to be on guard against even "balanced" materials reinforcing stereotypes that children already have learned. They need to show leadership in going beyond the tourist curriculum, especially when children assume that tourist stereotypes about their own cultural groups are true:

OBSERVATION: *I was reading a book that two Ojibwe girls in the class picked out, called* Pueblo Boy. *It was about a little Native American boy's daily life and the traditions his family followed. The book showed pictures of the boy doing household chores and pictures of him in his headdress for a traditional dance.*

We got to the page where the little boy was all dressed up and Sondra (who is Indian) said, "Look! An Indian!" I said yes, he is Native American.

At this point I turned back to a picture of the little boy without the headdress on and asked her if he was an "Indian" in this picture, and she said no. Kari, the other little girl said, "Yes, he is." I went on to tell Sondra that he was a Native American even though he wasn't dressed up.

REFLECTION: *I think that Sondra has this image built up (unknowingly) in her mind that a person can only be an "Indian" if they are dressed up in the manner that the little boy was dressed in some of the pictures. Kari was aware that this was not true. When Sondra answered "No" to my question about the little boy being Indian in the other pictures, Kari piped up and said that he was an Indian in those pictures as well. Kari understood that he was Native American, not only when he dressed up. The manner in which Kari said this, it sounded like she was teaching Sondra something...She was sort of giving information to her. I liked how Kari was so respectful of Sondra not knowing this information.*

Even with materials designed to get past tourist curriculum, teachers like Julie are the ones—sometimes with the help of other children—who help children go beyond stereotypes. In this situation, Julie would do well to speak with the other teachers, and probably Sondra's parents, about helping the child to learn more about her cultural identity.

It is now well established that children as young as two recognize human differences such as skin color. Whatever the classroom setting—urban, suburban, or rural—children need permission to discover, discuss, and accept this basic point of human difference.

> **OBSERVATION:** *In order to infuse Minnesota's new graduation-standards content into our kindergarten curriculum, I was beginning a unit on "Peoples and Cultures" in our urban classroom. To assess and activate the children's prior knowledge, I asked, "What do you know about people?" The first comment was "Some people are black, some people are white."*

> **REFLECTION:** *When I thought about this response, I knew that it reflected the composition of this group of 18 students: three Asian, three African American, one European American, and 11 children of African immigrants. Their later comments were typical of kindergarten, "Some people have black shoes."*

In the classroom that promotes significant learning in developmentally appropriate ways, teachers watch how children regard such differences as skin color. Sometimes, as in the anecdote, children handle the matter comfortably, without undue emotion. But even when this happens, it is a result of a curriculum and a classroom environment that have taken careful building, as in Gretchen's case. On occasion, even in classrooms that celebrate diversity, teachers must take extra steps when a child shows signs of prejudice toward classmates. Whether we term it *anti-bias teaching* or *liberation teaching*, this leadership is essential so that all children feel safe.

> **RECOLLECTION:** *Becca was a student teacher in the group of older preschoolers at our child care center, and I was her cooperating teacher. One day at lunch, Charlie, who was Caucasian, came to the table reluctantly, I think because he saw he would be sitting next to Brandon, who is African American. Becca, who was eating at that table, greeted Charlie warmly. Charlie said quietly but distinctly, "I'm not sitting next to Brandon. He's dirty."*
>
> *Becca gave Brandon a hug and whispered something in his ear. Then she went over to Charlie, knelt down and told him, "Brandon's not dirty, Charlie. He just has more color in his skin than you do. Lots of people have different skin colors and that's fine. What's important in our class is that everyone is friendly." As she said this, she guided Charlie to his chair and continued, "Brandon, could*

you pass the milk to our friend Charlie?" Brandon did, and Charlie kind of thanked him.

Later that day, I noticed that Charlie and Brandon were playing together. I complimented Becca for how she handled the situation and mentioned that Charlie's dad had showed a bit of prejudice when I had met with him and his wife during parent conferences.

When Charlie's dad picked him up that evening, I noticed that Becca was talking to him. I asked her what she had said. She smiled and said, "Only that Charlie had commented that another child who was African American had dirty skin. I thought he would want to know, so he could reinforce what we tell the children in our class, that many people have different skin colors, but what's important is that we are all friends." This student teacher did something that I am not sure I could have done. The dad left with skin color a bit redder than when he came in! I was quite relieved to see Charlie in school the next day. Becca, to her credit, acted like nothing unusual had happened.

A central lesson of books about cultural diversity and anti-bias curriculum is this: When teachers explain human differences—rather than remain silent about them—and when they affirm each child's rights as a learner and class member—children begin to accept human differences. When a teacher fails to advocate for mutual acceptance, however, then the power of that silence may cause some children to think they have permission to see human differences as sources of ridicule. Whatever the differences between children—ethnic, religious, racial, gender, ability, appearance, or behavioral—the adult teaches mutual acceptance and appreciation. In doing so, the teacher makes the classroom an encouraging place for all children. As the next anecdote, by Verna, shows, this life lesson is often taught and learned in the dramatic play area.

OBSERVATION: *Janel, a preschooler with multiple disabilities, had been in our classroom for about a week. Janel was in a wheelchair and had trouble speaking, but she seemed really attentive and ready to join in.*

On this day Preston went over to the dramatic play area where Janel was. Preston looked at Janel, turned to me, and complained, "I'm not playing with her; she's a girl!"

I told Preston that Janel was a new girl in our class who got around in a wheelchair really well. I asked Janel what she was doing and she told us playing house. I said Preston could play house too and offered him the small carpet sweeper. Preston swept the carpet and told Janel, "The rug's clean now. I'm going fishing," and left.

REFLECTION: *At first I thought this was funny—with all that Janel had to contend with, the one quality Preston had a problem with was that she was a girl! Then I thought: Maybe the gender issue was the one difference that Preston could put into words. (He played with Sophie and Mercedes at other times.) I talked with Janel, and over the next few days I brought in some special education equipment like crutches and a wheelchair for the children to try. As a class, we read a book about a little girl in a wheelchair, and Janel's mom came in and talked about Janel's disability and the progress she was making. After that, I didn't hear Preston make remarks about Janel's being a girl, and the children played more with Janel—even Preston, once in a while.*

Verna did not give in to the "power of silence," but showed the leadership necessary to advocate for Janel. Verna's reflection about why Preston used gender as the reason for not playing with Janel was perceptive. Bias against a class member for any reason, including gender or disability, needs to be addressed by the teacher. Anti-bias curriculum means the teacher gently but firmly helps the child gain understanding to prevent early prejudice from becoming full blown. Depending on the situation, the teacher may conduct private "guidance talks" with the child as Becca did; use "class meetings" and themes, as Verna did; or even hold conferences with the child's parents. Verna did well to monitor Preston for "other remarks," including ones about gender, and to teach the group about disabilities and the importance of including children with disabilities as members of the class.

In the encouraging classroom, it's critical that teachers help all children, including those with early prejudice, feel welcome and safe. Children need to feel safe in overcoming mistaken impressions about others, just as they need to feel safe in other decisions to learn. When a sense of community exists in a classroom, we all learn from one another.

In this chapter on learning in early childhood, there has been little discussion of traditional academic instruction, that is to say, instruction designed to get the children ready for the next level, kindergarten or first grade. In the words of one kindergarten teacher, Pat Sanford, "My job is not to prepare children for first grade, it is to give them the best possible kindergarten experience they can have." The same, of course, is true for preschool. In the encouraging classroom, in which adults model and teach that it is safe to learn, children will learn, and the learning will be significant.

Suggested Readings

Achilles, Elayne. "Creating Music Environments in Early Childhood Programs." *Young Children* 54, no. 1 (January 1999): 21–26.

Crosser, Sandra. "Making the Most of Water Play." *Young Children* 49, no. 5 (July 1994): 28–32.

Dahl, Keith. "Why Cooking in the Classroom?" *Young Children* 53, no. 1 (January 1998): 81–83.

Dighe, Judith, Zoy Colomiris, and Carmen Van Zutphen. "Nurturing the Language of Art in Children." *Young Children* 53, no. 1 (January 1998): 4–9.

Engel, Brenda. "Learning to Look: Appreciating Child Art." *Young Children* 51, no. 3 (March 1996): 74–79.

Goldhaber, Jeanne, Marjorie Lipson, Susan Sortino, and Patricia Daniels. "Books in the Sand Box? Markers in the Blocks? Expanding the Child's World of Literacy." *Childhood Education* 73, no. 2 (Winter 1996): 88–91.

Gottschall, Susan. "Hug-a-Book: A Program to Nurture a Young Child's Love of Books and Reading." *Young Children* 50, no. 4 (May 1995): 29–35.

Leithead, Marion. "Happy Hammering: A Hammering Activity Center with Built-In Success." *Young Children* 51, no. 3 (March 1996): 12.

Low, Janie. "Letting Go: Allowing First-Graders to Become Autonomous Learners." *Young Children* 51, no. 1 (November 1995): 21–25.

Newberger, Julee. "New Brain Development Research: A Wonderful Window of Opportunity to Build Public Support for Early Childhood Education." *Young Children* 52, no. 4 (May 1997): 4–9.

Pica, Rae. "Beyond Physical Development: Why Young Children Need to Move." *Young Children* 52, no. 6 (September 1997): 4–11.

Puckett, Margaret, Carol Sue Marshall, and Ruth Davis. "Examining the Emergence of Brain Development Research: The Promises and the Perils." *Childhood Education* 76, no. 1 (1999) 8–12.

Russell, Ilene. "Of Course Kindergartners Can Write." *Young Children* 52, no. 7 (November 1997): 27–28.

Szyba, Chris. "Why Do Some Teachers Resist Offering Appropriate, Open-Ended Art Activities for Young Children?" *Young Children* 54, no. 1 (January 1999): 16–20.

Discussion Activities

For reasons of professionalism, as you respond to these discussion activities, please respect the privacy of all children, adults, programs, and schools.

1. Think back to your earliest memory of overcoming an anxiety and accomplishing a task in school. How did a teacher make your accomplishment easier or more difficult? What have you learned from this experience that will help you in working with young children in the classroom?

2. Think back to an experience that you, as a student, thought of as a failure. How did a teacher contribute to, or try to prevent, this "failure" experience? What have you learned from this experience that will help you in working with young children in the classroom?

3. An idea associated with DAP is that teachers should not put a child in a situation in which they think the child will fail. What are your thoughts about this idea? What about when a child puts himself in a position where he might fail? What should the teacher's approach be then?

4. How much priority should a teacher give to preparing young children for next year's educational program? How much should a teacher's priorities be on giving children an educational program that meets their present needs?

What are some sources of pressure on a teacher to follow one direction or the other? How can a teacher cope with these pressures in order to provide the best program possible for the children and their families?

Guidance and Mistaken Behavior

The encouraging classroom includes all members, right across the range of human differences. In this way, the classroom community differs from society at large. Unfortunately, society has its outcasts and its castoffs—people who don't fit in for reasons of culture, religion, physical appearance, or behavior. The teacher in the encouraging classroom includes all members, so that children don't begin to see themselves as stigmatized (negatively separated from the group) but as class members in good standing.

Back in 1900, a giant of American education, John Dewey, said that school needs to be "a microcosm of democracy" (*The School and Society,* Chicago: University of Chicago Press, reprinted 1969). Dewey meant that schools should model and teach the values and principles of democracy, the better to guarantee a democratic life for all. The way that educators can carry Dewey's legacy into the twenty-first century is to create an encouraging community in the classroom. A classroom in which the ideas, values, and character of all are respected is indeed a microcosm of the democratic society. When teachers help each child find a place as a contributing member of the classroom community, they are instilling the values and principles that the child will need as an adult to find a place in society.

So far in the book we have looked at how teachers help children cope with separation and attachment, retain healthy family identities, and move from safety to growth in the learning process. When a teacher has done these things, he has made a start in building the encouraging classroom. But now we get to where the playdough hits the fan, so to speak. As anecdotes in previous chapters suggested, children can be colorful characters, even in their preschool years. The challenge to any community, and especially the encouraging classroom, is this: How do we assist every member of the class to feel accepted when individual children see and react to issues so differently? For example, when one child takes a trike away from another, how do we help both children solve the problem and get along better?

Beyond Traditional Discipline

Monique, a Head Start teacher, wrote this recollection of coping with a second-grade teacher. The teacher shows what traditional classroom discipline too easily can become.

RECOLLECTION: *When I was in second grade, we had a teacher who was mean. I was very soft-hearted, so it didn't take much to make me cry. I don't remember exactly what happened, but it was just before we were to watch a filmstrip. I was never considered a problem child. She yelled at me, it seemed for no reason, and she made me cry. I felt awful that she yelled at me and even worse that she embarrassed me in front of the class. I just wanted to leave because I didn't want to be there. Because I was mad at her, I wanted to make her suffer. So I wrote my assignments extra small. I didn't want to do anything that would make her mad, but I just wanted to let her know in a subtle way. For most of the year I didn't want to participate because of how she made me feel.*

Like Monique in the anecdote, most of us encountered traditional discipline at one point or another while we were in school. The problem with traditional discipline is that it slides easily into punishment. Teachers think that they are disciplining a child when really they are punishing. Punishing is inflicting physical or emotional pain, or both, on someone for something she has done. Common punishments are blame and shame. The teacher blamed Monique for doing something—Monique did not know what—and she shamed Monique in front of the class about the presumed transgression.

Teachers who use blame and shame apparently think that these punishments will "teach the child a lesson" about how to behave. In reality, punishment has a different effect by making the child feel "bad, sad, and mad." The child feels bad and no longer wants to be a member of the class. Monique said, "I just wanted to leave because I didn't want to be there." The child feels sad because of the loss of connection with the class. Monique said, "For most of the year I didn't want to participate because of how she made me feel." Punishment also makes the child feel "mad," wanting to get back at the source of the punishment—the teacher, or possibly other children. In Monique's words, "I wanted to make her suffer." Shame and blame cause children to feel bad about themselves, sad about what has happened to them, and angry toward the teacher and the school.

You may have noticed that the tone of Monique's recollection suggests that the teacher's behavior is still affecting her. Contrary to what the teacher who uses punishment may think, the impact of punishment does not end after the lesson or by the next day; the impact stays with children, sometimes for years. You probably have pretty clear memories of being punished when you were in school, years or even decades ago.

Punishment works against the teacher's efforts to make the classroom an inclusive community. Punishment stigmatizes a child: It pressures the child to feel negative about herself, and it pressures classmates to see her as disqualified from full membership in the group. Not all children figure out such an ingenious way as Monique to get back at the source of the pain. What is in the future for children who already see themselves as outcasts or outlaws by the time they are in the primary grades? We do not want to do to children what this teacher did to Monique. Instead, we hope to be liberating teachers.

OBSERVATION: *We have a sensory table in the science area where during the winter months we put snow. The children have fun coloring and shaping and digging and getting cold. Since the snow is no longer available, we have put colored rice in the table. The size of the table allows two children to play with equal space. Nathan and Cody had the opportunity to be at the rice table at the same time. Cody is a tall, very active child who has just turned four. Nathan, a five year* *old, works very hard in his learning activities and likes to join in with other children and do what they do.*

The two boys tested me and the other adults to the limit in their rice play. Cody looked like he was intentionally spilling rice all over the floor, and Nathan was copying what he saw Cody do. Before I could get involved, the assistant teacher started saying, "Don't put the rice on the floor. You won't get to play at the rice table. Stop that!" They didn't, and I got to the area about when she said, "Both of you go and find some other place to play."

I suggested that they first help clean up the rice on the floor, and then choose a new place to play. The boys did help me clean up the rice. As we did the cleaning, I said, "The rice makes the floor slippery, and I would feel bad if someone got hurt. If we keep the rice in the table, there will be more rice to pour and move. I need your help to keep the rice in the table the next time you play at the table."

Nathan's comment was, "Cody made the rice wheel go fast."

Cody said, "The rice just flew."

I said, "Do you think you will remember how to play with the rice next time?" First Cody, then Nathan, nodded yes.

In the anecdote, we have a pretty clear contrast between traditional discipline and a more positive approach that many of us call guidance. The assistant teacher used typical practices of traditional discipline: "Don't" messages, threats, orders, and removal of privileges without explanation. If Clarisse had not intervened, the boys might have left the table with the message, "You aren't worthy of using the rice table." (You are not fully worthy of being a member of the community.)

Instead, Clarisse used guidance: She involved the children in cleaning up the rice. She gave them clear reasons why the rice needed to stay in the table. She described how she would feel if someone had gotten hurt. She explained how to use the rice next time in an acceptable way. In another situation, Clarisse might not have made the boys leave the rice table as part of the consequence, but the assistant teacher had already made this decision. (Part of the challenge in using guidance is to balance the views of all parties involved in a conflict situation. Because adults continue to learn just as children do, a discussion later with the assistant teacher might be a good idea.) Although there are no magic intervention techniques when a teacher uses guidance, there is a basic difference between traditional discipline and guidance: Traditional discipline punishes children for having problems they cannot solve; guidance teaches children to solve their problems. Traditional discipline punishes children for making mistakes; guidance helps them learn from their mistakes. Guidance is good teaching because it promotes healthy social and emotional development.

Although they can't always eliminate removal of the child from the scene, the traditional early-childhood consequence, teachers in the encouraging classroom try to use guidance rather than punishment to help the child learn acceptable behaviors. In the following anecdote, notice how the teachers work together to teach a new child how to fit into a large-group activity.

OBSERVATION: *Wyatt, a new child in our classroom, was just four years old and was showing a lot of nervous energy during our more quiet activities. Most of the rest of the class were "veterans" and enjoyed our daily large group story time. During story time Wyatt pushed another child who had accidentally leaned on him. He then stood up and began to wander around the room. Bernie, the assistant teacher, got up and asked Wyatt if he would like to help her wipe the tables for lunch, but he just stood by her and watched. One of the other children asked why Wyatt had left, and I explained he was still getting used to being with us. He would sit with us another day. The next day, before story time began, Bernie suggested to Wyatt that he sit by her during the first part of the story. Then if he wanted to, he could leave with her to wipe the tables. Wyatt did this for two or three days. After that, with a little strategic placement—seated next to either me or Bernie—he got so he enjoyed the stories enough to sit the whole time.*

Meredith, the teacher in the anecdote, worked with Bernie to help Wyatt learn how to solve his problem. In contrast to Clarisse's anecdote, the teachers guided Wyatt without withholding a privilege. Redirection to another activity, removal from a group, and isolation on a time out chair are interventions that withhold privileges. Because these interventions tend to be punitive, teachers in encouraging classrooms use withholding interventions only as methods of last resort. First, they use guidance techniques, such as building attachments with children, resolving conflicts, and holding guidance talks like the one Clarisse held with Cody and Nathan.

When problems occur, the choice of an intervention method depends a lot on how the teacher sees the child and the behavior. Guidance is not punitive, but neither is it wimpy. Clarisse, in her anecdote, decided that removal from the situation was warranted, but her additional efforts at presenting alternatives added an element of friendly guidance. On the other hand, Meredith and Bernie did not need to use removal. With guidance, the test of the teacher is the leadership he shows in a problem situation. Teachers who use guidance believe that children do want to get along, but just need to learn the life skills to do so. The teacher is there not to shame the child into being "good"—this method too often backfires—but to teach the child the skills he needs to be a successful member of the classroom community.

For an up-to-date discussion of guidance ideas, readers might want to look at the article in the appendix, "Beyond Discipline to Guidance," or my previous book, *A Guidance Approach for the Encouraging Classroom* (Albany, NY: Delmar/ITP Publishers, 1998). The next chapter will discuss conflict management and resolution specifically.

Mistaken Behavior

Guidance ideas fill the pages of this book because guidance is not just a way to deal with problems in the classroom; it is a way of teaching that builds the classroom community. Mistaken behavior is a related idea that helps us to understand more about guidance. We want children in the encouraging classroom to learn democratic life skills: the ability to express strong emotions in acceptable ways, to try to understand how others are seeing things, to solve problems together, to accept human differences, to get along with others, and to consider themselves worthy persons. In reality, we learn these skills into adulthood, and as we all know, some adults never learn them.

Young children, with only months of life experience, are just beginning to learn these vital yet difficult personal skills. In the process of learning new skills, children, like all of us, make mistakes. So the behavior that teachers have traditionally considered *misbehavior* is better seen as *mistaken behavior*.

The idea of mistaken behavior is central to the practice of guidance. Just to get you to think about this idea a bit more, I have two trick questions:

First, what kinds of kids misbehave?

Did you say children who are spoiled? rowdy? hyper? have ADHD or come from poor home situations? You didn't? Good. Because children who have gotten labels like these (usually from adults) are already in a process of being stigmatized.

Second question: What kinds of kids make mistakes in their behavior?

Did you say all kids? You are correct. If we recognize that all children make mistakes, then we are less likely to judge the child and inflict blame and shame. We are more likely to look at the situation and figure out how we can help the child learn life lessons from the mistake.

There was another correct answer to the second trick question: All children make mistakes except those who are afraid to make mistakes because adults have set such high standards for them. We almost *want* these children to show a little mistaken behavior now and then, instead of having a total breakdown later. Consider the following anecdote.

OBSERVATION: *I was talking quietly with a teacher and student teacher during rest time. It was dark in the classroom, and Lauren looked our way to see if we were watching. She must have thought we weren't looking, because she rolled over, pulled the hair of the three year old next to her, rolled back, and made believe she was asleep. The three year old, who had been asleep, sat up, rubbed his hair, complained to no one in particular, and lay back down again.*

I was curious how the teachers were going to respond. They looked at each other and grinned. The teacher whispered that the girl had almost been "too good" all year. Her parents were really strict. She was pleased that Lauren now felt comfortable enough in the class to loosen up.

Consider the alternative. The teacher tiptoes through a bunch of children trying to sleep, looks down, and wags a finger at the little girl. The teacher would have been a bigger disruption to nap time than Lauren was, and probably would have affected the girl quite negatively. When using guidance, sometimes a teacher reacts in firm but friendly ways, as Clarisse and Cheryl did, and sometimes a teacher lets something go. The teacher is a professional who evaluates each situation differently, not a technician giving a quick, standard reaction to whatever has happened.

We are now going to look at three levels of mistaken behavior. The levels are an extension of Steven Harlow's levels of social relations, introduced in the last chapter (Dan Gartrell, "Misbehavior or Mistaken Behavior?" *Young Children* 50 [5], July 1995, 27–34). Level one, experimentation mistaken behavior, corresponds to Harlow's highest level of social relations, the encountering level. Level two, socially influenced mistaken behavior, corresponds to Harlow's middle level, the adjustment level. Level three, strong-needs mistaken behavior, corresponds to the lowest level of social adjustment, which Harlow called the survival level. An explanation, with anecdotes to illustrate each level, follows.

LEVEL ONE: EXPERIMENTATION MISTAKEN BEHAVIOR

In Harlow's highest level of social relations, children are fully open to and involved in the experiments of life. Level-one mistaken behavior happens when children are fully involved, but because they lack development and experience, they run into problems. Sometimes situations get out of hand—an argument starts, for instance, or a request is made that a child does not understand—and the experiment becomes uncontrolled. Sometimes, a child does something intentionally (to see what will happen)—says a naughty word in front of a teacher, perhaps—and this is a "controlled" experiment. If there is not lasting, deep emotion behind the act, we say that each problem, controlled and uncontrolled, is *level-one, experimentation mistaken behavior.*

Several of the anecdotes in this book illustrate level-one mistaken behavior. By pulling the child's hair to see what would happen, Lauren (above) provided an example of "controlled" level-one mistaken behavior. In the next anecdote, David does not understand what the teacher is saying and shows an example of "uncontrolled" level-one mistaken behavior.

OBSERVATION: *We were making "puppy chow" for snack, and David was helping. After getting all of the ingredients into the bowl, one of the other teachers took it to the microwave and brought it back melted to pour over the cereal.*

David started to cry and said, "No, I don't want you to put that chocolate on the dog food." He pointed to the cereal and started to scream.

I explained to him that it was cereal, not dog food, and that we were going to put chocolate on it to make it look like dog food, but it would really be people food. He said, "No, I don't want to make it anymore."

Then he left the table.

REFLECTION: *David was upset because he didn't understand what the outcome would be. He must have thought we were making real dog food and knew chocolate didn't belong. We completed the activity without him and he later ate it for snack. He was not upset at that point and talked about it being "cool" to eat puppy chow.*

With practice, teachers learn to tell whether level-one mistaken behavior is controlled or uncontrolled. Andy, in the next anecdote, shows controlled level-one mistaken behavior. Sondra, in the one after that, first loses control and then gives a reaction that appears intentional—so she shows some of both. Note that the teachers in both situations take a problem-solving approach to the mistaken behavior, rather than a punitive approach. Even if there is not always a magic answer, "How do I help the child solve this problem?" is a productive mind-set for a teacher addressing level-one mistaken behavior.

OBSERVATION: *Andy was sitting at a table eating his snack and drinking his milk. I looked away for a minute and when I looked back at him, his cup was tipped just enough for the milk to spill out onto the floor. There was a puddle on the floor so he had spilled more than I first thought he did. He looked right at it, then at me, and turned away. When I asked him to help me wipe up the milk, he refused and walked away. Another teacher finally got him to help clean up the spill, but not willingly.*

REFLECTION: *It almost seemed to me that Andy spilled the milk on purpose. He knew it was spilling, yet he didn't try to stop it. It's not like him to not cooperate, but today he sure didn't. He didn't want to clean up after lunch either. I think he was having a bad day or just wanted some attention. I was surprised* *that he refused to help me wipe up the spill. He's usually friendly to me. I guess I haven't spent enough time with the kids to really know them all yet or how they typically behave.*

In adjusting to the early childhood classroom, many children have less trouble with informal play situations and more trouble with formal groups, such as meals, circle times, and rest. (Think of the trust required for a young child to let herself go to sleep in strange surroundings.) On this day for Andy, the difficult time was lunch. Sometimes student teachers try "guidance ideas" and may believe that "guidance doesn't work" when they don't get instant results. A Head Start teacher in northern Minnesota once told me that it took five years before she was confident that her efforts at guiding children would work most of the time. Guidance, like other advanced teaching skills, takes practice, but one thing is certain: The teacher and the child need to know each other well enough to build trust before they can expect to work together in crises. A teacher cannot build a trusting relationship with a child based solely on acts of discipline. Suzy, the student teacher in the previous anecdote, made a sensible decision: Concede the intervention to another teacher this day, watch how he handles it, and try again next time. In the meantime, get to know the child better.

OBSERVATION: *I was watching three girls in the block area, and they were busy building their room. Staci wanted Sondra to put blocks in a certain area, and Sondra did not want to do that. Staci got upset at Sondra and took the block out of her hand and put it where she wanted it. Sondra walked away, but stayed in the block area, and sat by herself, not talking to anyone. Another child, Zoey, walked over to Sondra and asked what was wrong. Sondra totally ignored her. Zoey kept asking her what was wrong. She said, "Don't be sad, Sondra." Sondra kept ignoring Zoey and the other girls. Dotty, the assistant teacher, saw the whole thing and asked Sondra to come over and talk to her. Sondra ignored Dotty as well. Dotty requested firmly that she come over and talk to her. Eventually Sondra did, and Dotty just told her that when people are talking to her, she needs to respond. After that, they discussed the block incident with the other girls. Sondra did not spring back from this incident quickly; it took her a while to warm back up.*

REFLECTION: *I have seen Sondra act this way on occasion, and I feel that it is her way of responding when she doesn't get what she wants. She also acts this way when she is reprimanded for something. I understand that the incident bothered her, and that Staci did not have a right to take the block from her, but I feel that Sondra needs to work on her communication skills a little more. She needs to know that she can tell someone when she doesn't like something. She can be vocal when it comes to playing, but when it comes to expressing her feelings, she's a little quiet. We may need to work on that.*

Learning to get along with others is a daunting task for a young child. Children have only limited experiences from home to bring with them into the classroom. They must shift roles, actions, and reactions in ways that are sometimes bewildering for all and frequently bewildering for some. This is why level-one mistaken behavior is a natural and frequent occurrence in early childhood classrooms. Though this idea may perhaps seem strange at first, teachers should not try to prevent all level-one mistaken behavior. Such a classroom would be sterile. Through the quarrels, the acts of empathy, and the guidance from teachers, children gradually learn to value themselves and others in social situations. For children and adults alike, the encouraging classroom is a human-relations laboratory.

In level-one (experimentation) mistaken behavior, the child is using personal resources to find out about the world, and though the experiment may go awry, the effort is still an attempt to learn on the child's own terms. In contrast, children showing level-two mistaken behavior are influenced by others and cannot yet muster their own personal resources to judge their behavior independently.

LEVEL TWO: SOCIALLY INFLUENCED MISTAKEN BEHAVIOR

Children at Harlow's second level of social relations, adjustment, are influenced in their behavior by significant others. If a teacher says, "Sheila and Henrico are sitting straight and tall," she is actually trying to influence the rest of the children toward adjustment behavior. Level-two mistaken behavior happens when children are influenced by significant others to take actions that teachers deem inappropriate. In other words, children exhibit level-two (socially influenced) mistaken behavior because others have influenced them, intentionally or unintentionally, to "do it too." A child shows level-one mistaken behavior when she gets others to say "poopy butt." She is the leader. But everyone she influenced to do it too is showing level-two mistaken behavior—they are the followers.

As with name-calling, and the classic with older children, spit balls, level-two mistaken behavior can be contagious. But level-two mistaken behavior can also result from influence on an individual. Children are adept at hearing a word that stands out to them in one situation, and recalling it when they think it's appropriate in another. When my son, Jesse, was just three, he didn't like the prospect of putting on his coat before going outside. "That's widiculus," was his comment. I later remembered that he had seen a Daffy Duck cartoon earlier in the week. A similar event that happened when he was almost four was remembered by Nellie, Jesse's child care teacher.

> **RECOLLECTION:** *Jesse was having trouble with a glue bottle. When too much glue spilled on his paper, Jesse said, "Oh shick" using a tone that sounded familiar to me. When Dan arrived later to pick up Jesse, I told him what I had heard and said the word wasn't quite right, but the tone sounded just like someone I know might say it. As I remember, Dan commented, "Must have been his mom."*

You are familiar with super-hero play? Over time the super-heroes change—Lone Ranger, Incredible Hulk, Ninja Turtles, Mighty Morphin Power Rangers, WWF Wrestlers, Pokémon characters—but the mistaken behavior that results is always socially influenced. These media "heroes"—they are not even real people—influence children to play more aggressively than they might otherwise, as in this observation from James's student teaching days.

> **OBSERVATION:** *The older preschoolers were outside on a summer day. I was with some children in the sandbox when I heard Vernon yelling. I went around the corner to where he was. Darnel was sitting on Vernon, Rydell was trying to pull Vernon up, and Voshon was trying to pull Rydell down! Vernon was still yelling and Darnel was rather large, so I didn't blame him.*
>
> *I got the four separated and had them sit down, take deep breaths, and we talked.*
>
> *Me: What was happening over here? I heard somebody yelling.*
>
> *Darnel: We was playing wrestlers and Voshon and me was Earthquake and Hurricane. Rydell was Hulk Hogan and Vernon was Jesse the Body!*

Vernon: But I was not 'cause I didn't want to be no wrestler.

Rydell: But you gotta be 'cause Hulk needs a partner!

Me: Okay, I've got it. You three were doing team wrestling and you wanted Vernon to be Rydell's partner, right?

Darnel: Yeah, but Vernon wouldn't wrestle.

Me: Well, we have a problem, because of the "No wrestling with other people" rule. (They knew the rule, this was why they were around the corner.) Okay, how's this? You either find something else to do that isn't wrestling, or you be one tag team and fight the invisible Phantom Wrestlers, but I don't know because they're kind of tough.

Darnel: (speaking as usual for the rest) Yeah, and you could too Vernon. (I left with all four wrestling the invisible tag team. It was hard to say who was winning!)

REFLECTION: *It seems like mainly boys have to get physical in their play. You can tell them no guns, but then they'll use blocks. They're going to do it anyway, so I guess you have to figure out how they can so nobody gets dragged in or hurt. My supervising teacher liked how I handled this. Before long they became firefighters fighting the fire in the skyscraper (climbing gym).*

The teachers at the child care center had previously held a class meeting to talk with the older preschoolers about the wrestling problem. The class and teachers decided on the "No wrestling with other people" rule as a way to solve the problem. Teachers hold meetings with children to identify and solve many kinds of problems, including level-two mistaken behavior. Group meetings are an important tool for building the classroom community. When you were a student, do you remember a teacher punishing a whole class for something that only a few did? Do you still have feelings about this experience? Class meetings—in which the teacher leads and makes sure each person's views are heard—are a more positive way to handle level-two mistaken behavior, even with wrestling preschoolers.

Level-two mistaken behavior often happens in the home when older and younger siblings play together and take on roles they have learned over time from family members. Usually teachers can give only indirect advice to parents about sibling issues, but in a program like Head Start, there is sometimes an opportunity for direct teaching.

OBSERVATION: *It was open house and parents had brought other children along with their Head Start kids. Two brothers were playing with the trucks and cars. Jim, age six, left; Tim, age four, remained playing by himself. He set up a road and used a gas station building in his play. He turned his back for a minute and Jim came and took the gas station over to where he was playing. Tim realized his gas station was gone and went over to Jim.*

Tim said, "That's mine," as he put his hands on the gas station.

Jim said, "I have it." They started pulling the toy and pushing each other.

Jim easily pulled it away and resumed play. Tim sat down and looked like he was going to cry, as though this had happened before.

Myla observed and then stepped in and said, "Wait a minute here, what's going on?"

Jim said, "He took my gas station."

In a frustrated tone, Tim said, "It's mine."

Myla said, "Let's work this out. What can we do?"

Jim said, "I will use it, then he can."

Myla said, "No, no. Can you both play with it?"

Tim said, "No."

Myla said, "What if we put it here in the middle and you can share it?"

The kids didn't say anything, but started playing. After about three minutes, Tim left and Jim stayed to play.

REFLECTION: *The children were getting pushy so I stepped in before someone (probably Tim) got hurt. It was pretty clear that since Jim was older, he was going to do what he wanted. As I guided the children to try and solve the argument, their mother observed. This was good for her to see. I know the boys are pretty active with her. The boys, I think, showed they were beginning to work* *together and problem-solve. Hopefully, their mom can pick up on this from her visits at Head Start.*

Adults help children solve many instances of level-two mistaken behavior by using *social problem-solving,* which is also called *conflict management.* In research for the second edition of *A Guidance Approach for the Encouraging Classroom,* I came across seven widely used models of conflict management that utilized between four and 21 separate steps. This important guidance process is discussed more in the next chapter, but for now, I will mention that many of the models seem to have these five steps, which you can probably pick out in adults' responses in previous anecdotes:

1. Cool down, if needed (all of you).
2. Agree what the problem is.
3. Brainstorm solutions all can live with.
4. Select a solution.
5. Try it out, with the adult's guidance if needed.

The student teachers in both preceding anecdotes, James and Myla, used problem solving. In Myla's case, even if she didn't use the technique perfectly, she headed off a likely fight and modeled for the mother a clear alternative to doing nothing or using punishment—not small challenges for a student teacher. Myla probably could have involved the children more actively in step three, coming up with solutions for using the garage. Nonetheless, one need not use social problem-solving perfectly in order for the parties involved—and even onlookers such as the boys' mom—to gain from it. Social problem solving is a high-level teaching skill that for most of us takes practice, but which even beginners can use with success.

When children show level-two, socially influenced mistaken behavior, they have not yet developed the personal resources to make independent choices about their actions. They are acting under the influence of others important to them and have learned the mistaken behavior as a result. A child showing mistaken behavior at level two is motivated more by the social influence of others than by deep unmet needs that he is acting out. In contrast, children who show strong-needs mistaken behavior, level three, are governed in their actions by their own strong emotions. Due to unmet psychological and/or health needs—abuse, neglect, untreated physical conditions—these kids hurt. They are on the edge. And it does not take much for them to jump, fall, or get pushed over.

LEVEL THREE: STRONG-NEEDS MISTAKEN BEHAVIOR

Behaviors such as getting upset frequently, biting and hitting, throwing blocks, using extreme language, and withdrawing from the group are serious. Everyone is entitled to a level-three day once in a while (even teachers). We can understand why a child is grouchy when her sleep was disrupted at home, she got up too late for breakfast, she missed the bus, and her older brother, who drove her to school, refused to tie her shoes. The teacher helps a child through such a day, but monitors to see whether this is just one bad day or a pattern. Consider Kirby's anecdote.

> **OBSERVATION:** *During a "limited choice" center time (only some play centers were open), one of the teachers brought out Candy Land so a group of children could play. Only four could play at a time, and Andy was not one of the four selected. He instantly became upset and ran (crying and screaming) to the other side of the room. He continued to cry and pout in the corner for quite a length of time. After a while he stopped making noise because no one was paying attention to him. I then helped him get into another activity until it was his turn to play the game.*

> **REFLECTION:** *Andy has a history of getting upset when things don't go his way. His actions today were very similar to previous ones. He has a really hard time accepting things. His crying and screaming are not unusual, and although he usually settles down, sometimes his unpredictable behavior is unsafe. He sometimes gets violent when he's upset. After talking with the teachers, I think his home life is really affecting his behavior at school. Andy's behavior is a result of what happens in his home, and it is very evident that there are problems in that environment. The teachers have been working with the mom for a while now and are trying to get the family into counseling.*

The concept of mistaken behavior, especially at this level, asserts that there is no such thing as a bad child. There are only children with bad problems that they cannot cope with on their own. Children with strong unmet needs show mistaken behavior in the classroom, often because it is the safest place in their lives. They are acting out, sometimes in extreme ways, but they are doing so because it is the only way they can ask for help. Children who show level-three mistaken behaviors are difficult for teachers to work with. They may be the most difficult children to like, but they are probably the ones who most need a guiding relationship with us. The last line of Kirby's observation is significant: "I then helped him get into another activity until it was his turn to play the game." Kirby showed the active leadership needed to teach Andy that he has a place in the classroom community.

> **OBSERVATION:** *We were watching a video of Dr. Seuss, and all of the other children were lying quietly on their cots. Jason was not. One of the teachers asked him to lie down so that the other children would be able to see. Jason started yelling very loudly, not words, just loud noises. Carla, the assistant teacher, walked over and reminded Jason of the rule that everyone must lie down during rest time. He continued to yell, and Carla gave him the choice of lying down or leaving the room with her. He immediately stopped yelling and said, "Let's go out into the hall!" Then Carla took him out, and he didn't return until after rest.*

> **REFLECTION:** *Jason clearly was looking to go out of the room. It was a mistaken behavior used as a way to not have to rest with the other children. Jason has used this type of behavior to get out of circle time, lunch, rest, or anything he does not want to do. He enjoys the time he spends in the hall because of the one-on-one attention he gets from the teacher. We staff have talked and believe he does not get much attention at home—large family, overworked single mom. I think it would have been more effective to give him the choice of lying quietly or moving his cot to a different location in the room. We need to talk more to help him deal with his problems.*

When there is a threat of serious harm or disruption, a teacher intervenes in a firm but friendly way that relates directly to the mistaken behavior. In this anecdote, another set of choices might have been, "Jason, you can choose to lie quietly here or over there where you won't be bothered by other children. Which will it be?"

By itself, a single action like removing a child from the group fails to address the underlying problem that is causing the level-three mistaken behavior. Even if done consistently, withholding a privilege adds to the child's negative feelings as well as reinforcing a less-than-ideal way to get teacher attention (a level-two mistaken behavior). Teachers need to do more. After the incident is over, in this case after rest time, a teacher might talk with the child about how a similar situation could go better next time (a guidance talk). He could involve the child in suggesting ideas and implementing them; he could actively guide the child through the situation the next time it occurs, offering acceptable alternative behaviors. To summarize these points, in holding a guidance talk, the teacher:

- Explains to the child why the mistaken behavior was not acceptable.
- Helps the child understand how the other child felt as a result of the mistaken behavior.
- Brainstorms with the child alternative acceptable behaviors she can choose the next time a similar situation comes up.
- Asks the child how she can help the other child feel better. (Note that this is different from forcing an apology, which puts all parties in a position of having conflicted emotions.) If the teacher can't help the child think of a way to make amends, the child can be asked to think about it and come up with an idea later. She usually will.

Gretel, the teacher in the anecdote to follow, had worked hard to develop a relationship with Nick and to help him, largely by guidance talks, to control his mistaken behavior through thought and words.

OBSERVATION: *We were making a video for the parents, and during one of the songs Nick chose to take himself out of the singing. He said, "I don't want to sing this song."*

I asked, "What are you going to do, Nick?"

His comment, "I'll sit on a chair."

I followed with, "That would be fine. The rest of us want to finish singing for the movie."

Nick sat out for two songs, and then when we started with the instruments he stated, "I want to play."

I remarked, "If you are ready to come back, that is fine."

REFLECTION: *Nick has had a lot of difficulty all year controlling his impulses and participating in activities planned for the group. We teachers have been working hard with him and his parents to help him increase his impulse control. Choosing to sit out for a few minutes has helped him, so that he doesn't get into trouble with other students, and to get his composure back. He was told at the beginning of the year that when he was ready to return to what the other students were doing, he could. He was given the opportunity to monitor himself. And now in April, he has made a giant step while we taped the video, by sitting down and not interrupting the other children. I hope he will be in Head Start again and that we can continue to help him with his social development.*

Because some teachers still consider time out the standard method of dealing with mistaken behavior, "the chair" is probably the most misused discipline method in early childhood education. But as Gretel's anecdote shows, when children show long-term serious problems in the classroom, there are ways of using brief, temporary removal—as a last resort, in a comprehensive plan. Perhaps a way to think about temporary removal is as a cooling-down time, when a child has lost control and needs help regaining it. If a child has engaged in serious mistaken behavior, but has not lost control, the teacher uses social problem-solving or guidance talks rather than isolation.

When a child is too upset to do social problem-solving or to have a guidance talk, the adult removes the child from the situation, but sits with her for a cooling-down time, until she is ready to talk. In short, the key difference between the traditional time-out chair and a cooling-down time is that in the cool-down, the teacher usually stays with the child. In addition, the teacher helps the child reunite with the group through social problem-solving with other children or through a guidance talk between teacher and child.

When a child's mistaken behavior becomes so destructive that it affects other children, a teacher may call a class meeting to give all children a chance to discuss and better understand the situation. A class meeting to discuss a child's behavior is serious, and the meeting must be handled with care. Children need to be reminded that class meetings are for speaking from the heart and that all class members are to be respected. The teacher may give the child in question a choice of attending; if the meeting is held without the child, the teacher may want to discuss the meeting with the child.

OBSERVATION: *One of the children in my primary-grade class exhibited mistaken behavior on a regular basis. He did things like tipping over his desk, lying on the floor, getting up from his desk on impulse, and other types of mistaken behavior. On this day, Darren started out on the wrong foot, and things grew progressively worse as the day wore on. Right before lunch, after a series of crises, I ended up having the special education teacher physically remove Darren from the classroom.*

I knew the children were bothered by what they had seen. When we returned to the classroom after lunch, I held an unscheduled class meeting. I started out by saying, "Sometimes when we come to school, we don't feel good about something that is going on at our home or with our friends. Many of us go to our parents or to someone we trust and talk about how we feel. Sometimes when we haven't been able to let our feelings come out, they start to sneak out in ways that maybe we don't want them to. I think that is how Darren is feeling today. I think he has some feelings that he needs to get out because they are starting to sneak out in ways he can't help. Before lunch today, Mrs. O. helped Darren down to her office so that she could maybe help him get rid of some of those scary feelings."

One child raised a hand and said, "Yeah, one time I was so mad at Joe I could have hit him, but I went home and talked to my Mom and that helped."

Another child said, "So you mean that Darren doesn't tip his desk over on purpose?"

I said, "Yes, that is what I mean."

Another student raised her hand and said, "But sometimes I get mad and I don't tip my desk."

Her neighbor said, "Maybe you aren't mad like Darren."

We had just finished an Ojibwe story about a boy and a butterfly. The story was an analogy about people and their feelings. The last comment made was by one of the girls, who said, "Darren is like the butterfly with the broken wings."

It was so sweet I could have cried. I said, "Yes, Darren has a broken wing." We ended the class meeting, and I felt like the children had a better understanding of their classmate.

REFLECTION: *I can honestly say I have learned a great deal each time I had to deal with a problem, not only about solving problems, but about kids as well. I think the biggest thing I learned here was how effective a class meeting can be at helping children understand their classmates. The class meeting allowed them to really think about how Darren felt. I saw this when Joe related his story of being so angry that he wanted to hit someone else. After discussing this, they had a better understanding of Darren. I also felt they needed to know that Darren was not out there tipping his desk over for the fun of it. Deep down inside, Darren is a hurt little boy trying to cope with a problem that is bigger than he is. I wanted the class to try to see that in him. When Sue made that reference to the butterfly, I knew I had succeeded in that area.*

Another thing that I learned was how effective a class meeting can be at solving a class problem that could have gotten worse. If we didn't have that talk, maybe some of the kids would have teased Darren when he came back into the room. Instead they treated him with respect. I was very pleased to see this response when he did return. Darren did continue with his mistaken behavior during the remainder of the day, but the kids ignored it. They seemed to understand that Darren was having a bad day and needed his space.

The encouraging classroom models compassion for its members. If a member is having a problem, that is no reason to stigmatize the child. Marchale's anecdote illustrates well how the teacher in an encouraging classroom may have to remove a child showing level-three mistaken behavior, but the removal is temporary, and the child still has a place in the class.

With level-three mistaken behavior, teachers sometimes overlook an important element: improving the teacher–child relationship. Rather than wait for a child to act out in order to get attention, teachers must schedule daily quality time with the child, perhaps at arrival, to build important attachments. The degree of success of a crisis intervention comes down to the relationship the teacher has built with the child over time. Teachers cannot help children deal with level-three mistaken behavior when their primary contacts take place during crises.

> **OBSERVATION:** *Kaylee and her mom were in a dilemma. Head Start requires a dental exam, and Kaylee had already bitten two dentists. In several conversations with mom, she expressed her fear that local dentists had been sharing their experiences with each other, since she hasn't been able to set up another appointment in the town.*
>
> *I suggested another option—a dentist 50 miles away who has a reputation for working with "difficult" child situations. Kaylee's mom, the other teachers, and I set up a plan where I would be drawing positive attention to children in the class that had gone to the dentist and try to pull Kaylee in. It worked. When the class discussed dentist visits, Kaylee expressed that she was going to the dentist. She later told me, "Carrie, when I go to the dentist, I'm not going to bite!"*
>
> *"Wow," I said, "This is the news we have been waiting for. Can we call your mom and you tell her?"*
>
> *On the phone to her mom, Kaylee said, "If I bite the dentist, I'll say I'm sorry."*
>
> *"Kaylee, that is not what you just told me," I said.*
>
> *Kaylee told her mom on the phone, "Okay, okay. I won't bite the dentist."*
>
> *After several reminders of her promise, a week later Kaylee's dental exam went fine.*

Not your everyday classroom problem, but Carrie clearly practiced guidance to help Kaylee address her mistaken behavior. Using the relationship she had built over the year with Kaylee, Carrie worked with the child to get a commitment about her behavior. Carrie involved the parent as well. Between the two of them, they taught Kaylee another way to behave at the dentist's office, and it worked.

Guidance is good teaching, because it helps with personal development as well as with academic areas. Good teaching in the encouraging classroom means working closely with the parents. With a partnership begun at the very beginning of the school year, the kind of informal contact that Carrie had with Kaylee's mom is often enough to solve the problem. If the situation does not improve, however, the teacher needs to meet more formally with the family to do some social problem-solving. Depending on the circumstances, the teacher may even request that relevant professionals be included, such as other staff, directors, principals, special education teachers, and mental health workers. During the meeting, the teacher may propose an individual guidance plan that has some or all of these parts:

- A strategy for helping the child cope with difficult times when the mistaken behavior is more likely to occur. Often a teacher who gets along well with the child will take the lead in these situations.
- A plan for staff to improve relations (build attachments) with the child. The plan may include regularly scheduled one-on-one time. Regular contact talks reassure the child she has a place in the class and help the staff get to know the child beyond the mistaken behavior that they often see.
- An agreement for how parents and teacher can work together to help the child at home as well as school. Referral for other services may be part of the agreement.
- A schedule for a second meeting to review problems and progress.

Just as with families, the teacher alone does not handle difficult situations involving mistaken behavior. The more serious the mistaken behavior a child shows, the more comprehensive the intervention needs to be—and often, the more adults need to be involved—if the problem is to be solved.

These days, children with level-three (strong-needs) mistaken behavior are members of virtually every early childhood classroom. As children at level three progress in dealing with the deep hurts in their lives—impossible without active adult support—their behavior begins to change. Their mistaken behavior shows signs of the guidance alternatives we have been working so hard to teach. These children improve in impulse control, begin to use words to express emotions, start to consider others' viewpoints, and play more cooperatively.

We teach all children to use their personal resources to make thoughtful decisions about their behavior—including children at level two, who don't require quite as much intervention. However, the greatest reward comes when a child who used to hit and kick says to a classmate, "Stop bugging me, you rodent," and comes to the teacher to complain. The teacher's job here clearly is not done! But the child's mistaken behavior has risen from level three. Progress has been made.

Strange as it may seem, children who demonstrate level-one mistaken behavior tend to be healthy kids. Engaged in the ongoing experiments of life, we all make mistakes, and kids will make their share. Our goal with young children is not to try to make them perfect kids, but to teach them to solve the conflicts they find themselves in as a natural part of living. As children learn this ability—and only children progressing toward level-one mistaken behavior can—they are developing an essential life skill. Who knows, with further guidance the kid who used the "r-word" may another time say, "I am busy at the moment, can you return at a more propitious time for this discussion?"

This chapter has looked at the guidance approach for addressing children's mistaken behavior and for building and sustaining an encouraging classroom. The test in working with mistaken behavior is how the teacher manages to help children cope with their problems, while at the same time helping the class learn to live together as a caring community. Conflict resolution, a real and important dilemma for teachers, is addressed in chapter five. In the encouraging classroom, where guidance is practiced, children want to attend, even if they are angry or ill, as opposed to not wanting to attend when they are well. Even young children know where they want to be, and the classroom of the teacher who is using guidance is one of those special places.

OBSERVATION: *In our kindergarten classroom we use a mistake jar. When you make a mistake, you need to think about two things:*
> *1. Why you have made it.*
> *2. How to avoid doing it again.*
> *Pluck the mistake out of your mind—no need to write it down. Put it in the jar, put on the lid, and it's history!*

In the encouraging classroom, it's all right to make mistakes—everybody does. We just need to learn from them.

Suggested Readings

Boyd, B. J., "Teacher Response to Superhero Play: To Ban or Not to Ban." *Childhood Education* 1 (1997): 23–28.

Curry, Nancy, and Sara Arnaud. "Personality Difficulties in Preschool Children As Revealed through Play Themes and Styles." *Young Children* 50, no. 4 (May 1995): 4–9.

Froschl, M., and B. Sprung, "On Purpose: Addressing Teasing and Bullying in Early Childhood." *Young Children* 2 (1999): 70–72.

Gartrell, Dan. "Misbehavior or Mistaken Behavior?" *Young Children* 50, no. 5 (July 1995): 27–34.

Gartrell, Dan. "Beyond Discipline to Guidance." *Young Children* 52, no. 6 (September 1997): 34–42.

Goldberg, E. "Including Children with Chronic Health Conditions: Nebulizers in the Classroom." *Young Children* 2 (January 1994): 35–37.

Levin, Diane, and Nancy Carlsson-Paige. "The Mighty Morphin Power Rangers: Teachers Voice Concern." *Young Children* 50, no. 6 (September 1995): 67–72.

Manning, Diane, and Patricia Schindler. "Communication with Parents When Their Children Have Difficulties." *Young Children* 52, no. 5 (July 1997): 27–33.

Discussion Activities

For reasons of professionalism, as you respond to these discussion questions, please respect the privacy of all children, adults, programs, and schools.

1. Think about a time in school when a teacher intervened in a situation you were involved in. Did the teacher handle the situation with guidance or with traditional discipline? What makes you think so? As a teacher, would you handle the situation similarly or differently?

2. A common misunderstanding about mistaken behavior is that if it's an accident, it's mistaken behavior, but if it's on purpose, it's misbehavior. What does the chapter say about this issue? In what ways do you agree or disagree with the author's position?

3. Recall a child who was involved in one or more problem situations, either when you were in school, or when you were observing as an adult. What level of mistaken behavior was the child showing? Why do you think so?

4. What, for you, are some differences between the traditional time-out and the cooling-down time? Referring to the chapter, how would you assess these differences if a teacher's goal is to build an encouraging classroom?

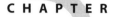
Conflict and Resolution

Social Problem-Solving

In everyday classroom life, teachers place a high value on children's ability to get along with others. There is validity in this position; research indicates that children who do not learn by first grade to get along have problems throughout their schooling and drop out in higher numbers than their peers. Still, early childhood teachers sometimes place developmentally inappropriate social expectations on children. In fact, some teachers value getting along so highly that they practice *conditional acceptance* based on this ability. The teacher accepts children as full members of the group as long as they get along with other people (especially the teacher) most of the time and do not openly disagree. The teacher considers as less acceptable, or even unacceptable, children who for reasons of development, background, or personality have trouble getting along.

Getting along with others is one of those life skills that, especially for some children, takes a while to learn. If a young child hasn't yet acquired the skill, and is shunned for this inability, he is going to have an even more difficult time learning it. Fredrich Froebel, the originator of the kindergarten, wrote that it is another person, often even the teacher, who causes children to be "bad." The teacher does so by attributing the natural exuberance of youth to a will towards evil, and by administering frequent punishments to "break the child's will." Children who experience repeated punishment become stigmatized, with long-term personal consequences that include feelings of unworthiness, alienation, and hostility.

Though it's perhaps less obvious, teachers who use conditional acceptance also affect children who "go along in order to get along." In conforming to the teacher's will, these children learn that they are only acceptable if they agree. Children who pick up this message feel that they have little authority over their lives. The authority of others instructs them how to behave. In early childhood, that authority tends to be significant adults. With development and experience, children gradually learn that adults make mistakes too. As this awareness grows, and if children have not developed a positive sense of self, they look elsewhere for people to identify with, such as older acquaintances and peers.

In the encouraging classroom, teaching young children to get along is an important goal, but we need to teach this skill with developmentally appropriate expectations. It is important to realize that getting along is not a passive skill, but an active one. Every day, children in our classrooms have conflicts. Conflicts are a natural part of living and learning. Rather than make moral judgments about children for not handling their disagreements "nicely," we need to appreciate their efforts and teach them the skills of social problem-solving—how to disagree and still be friends. Most people take years to learn how to disagree in ways all can live with.

Our challenge then is to guide young children to respond to conflicts so that social problems can be settled peaceably. In our day, as in Froebel's, teaching this life skill to young children is difficult. But this is exactly what is asked of the early childhood teacher. And the amazing thing is that when we do model and teach social problem-solving skills—imperfectly is okay—young children learn them.

OBSERVATION: *It was rest time and some of the children were extremely active and having a difficult time lying down. Irene was almost asleep on her cot when another child took her stuffed animal and ran off with it. Irene became extremely upset and was really crying. The teacher went to her cot and said, "Irene, I can see that you are very upset, but crying will not help. Can you tell me using your words what is wrong?"*

Irene responded, "Sam took my animal." The teacher then asked Irene if she could tell Sam how that made her feel. Irene marched over to Sam and said, "That's my animal and I don't like you to take it like that." Sam immediately handed her the stuffed animal. The teacher thanked Sam for returning the animal. Rest time quieted down.

REFLECTION: *Irene was obviously very upset at first and I think it was very effective that the teacher talked to her first before encouraging her to talk to Sam. I think it's also important to remind children from time to time that crying really does not help and using words is much better. The sooner children learn to talk things out and express their feelings, the better.*

A traditional discipline approach in Krissy's anecdote would be for the teacher to scold Sam and make him return the stuffed animal to Irene. Sam would have felt punished for "not getting along." And, if you think about it, Irene would too. By not giving Irene a chance to stand up for herself, the teacher would have been reinforcing Irene's status as victim and her dependence on others to make things right. By using guidance to problem-solve, the teacher did not focus on Sam's level-one mistaken behavior. She avoided conditional acceptance. Moreover, she gave Irene permission to solve the problem for herself. The teacher gave each child an opportunity to reaffirm their place in the classroom community. Irene responded, and so did Sam.

Teaching children to solve social problems is a long-term process that begins with infants and toddlers. Teachers of very young children model the skill as much as they teach it, so that children have connections between their living and their learning. From the beginning, teachers convey that children are capable of solving problems on their own and without harm. Even before the very young have word power, this understanding is important because it is the basis of all future social problem-solving.

OBSERVATION: *All year, the teachers in our campus preschool had been working with the three-year-old group, encouraging them to "use words to solve your problems." One day on the playground, a teacher noticed that Krista wanted to take Yolanda's trike. As the two grew more upset, the teacher was about to step in. Just then she saw Yolanda scowl and with determination say to Krista, "Words! Words! Words! Words!" Looking surprised, Krista immediately handed the trike back to Yolanda!*

In the encouraging classroom, teaching democratic life skills is sometimes exasperating and sometimes amazing. As the anecdote illustrates, young children willingly involve themselves in learning how to resolve conflicts. Even if they don't have the exact words yet, they are learning the process, and they want to use it successfully. Yolanda knows she should use words when she has a disagreement. She just isn't quite ready to identify, select, and use the particular words. Her commitment to solving the problem on her own without hurting is what is significant here, as was Krista's understanding of Yolanda's intent. By their actions, the two children showed they are learning they can solve their own problems.

In the anecdote, the teacher might watch the situation, after initial resolution, to see if the children need assistance to feel fuller satisfaction from the process. She might give the children some specific words to use:

"Yolanda, you really solved that problem with Krista. Next time you could tell her, 'I'm not done yet.' Those are some other good words to use."

"Krista, thank you for giving the trike back to Yolanda. Next time you could say, 'Are you done with the trike?' Then you will know if she is finished."

Of course, a teacher can never be sure what a child will do or say "next time," so monitoring children's progress in problem-solving skills is important—and in the encouraging classroom it is sometimes even fun!

HIGH EMOTIONAL STAKES

When a young child makes a mistake in learning self-help skills (buttoning a sweater wrong) or early academic skills (printing his name backward), teachers do not criticize. They realize that mistakes like these are normal in the learning process. But when children make mistakes in behavior—especially mistakes that cause disruption or harm—the teacher's emotions become involved. Conflicts over objects, territory, and privilege—three common conflicts in early childhood settings—cause some teachers to react with reduced understanding and a sense of lost control. Perhaps without meaning to, the teacher resorts to traditional discipline. She may "restore order," but in the process she punishes not just the children involved in the conflict but other class members as well.

OBSERVATION: *In our preschool classroom today, I noticed two boys arguing over a small truck. This is what happened:*

Antonio: I want to play with the truck! Don't you know you have to share?

José: I had it first, Antonio!

Antonio: But I want the truck now, you have been playing with it all day long. (José ran away with the truck.) JOSÉ!!!!

At that point Antonio found something else to play with, and seemed to forget about José, who left the area with the truck. About five minutes later, José reentered the scene, and Anthonio headed straight for him.

Antonio: José, can I play with the truck now?

José: (using a loud voice to capture the teacher's attention) No, Antonio, I'm not done with it yet!

Teacher: (arriving on the scene) You boys have to share the truck.

Antonio: He's played with the truck all day long. I want it!

At this point, Antonio was becoming demanding of José, and José was really getting angry.

Teacher: Antonio, you are going to have to wait until José is done playing with the truck.

Antonio: (reaching over to grab the truck) José, are you done yet?

José: Stop it, Antonio!

At this point, José began to cry. José's crying caught Antonio by surprise at first, so Antonio backed off a little bit, but when José stopped crying, Antonio continued to try and grab the truck. This is what happened then:

   Antonio: I want the truck, you have had it long enough!

   José: (raising his voice toward the end of the sentence) I'm not done with it yet!

   The two boys began a tug-of-war with the truck, and the teacher again stepped into the situation. She decided to take the truck away from the two boys, and put it on a shelf where no one could reach it. Needless to say, the boys were not happy about this. José sat on the floor with a sad expression, and Antonio glared at the teacher's back. Even the teacher walked away like she was angry. The other children in the class seemed puzzled. They didn't appear to understand what was going on or why nobody could play with the truck. The entire mood of the classroom had changed, and the noise level began to drop, as the children played quietly by themselves.

REFLECTION: *In this situation, I believe the teacher did not use professional judgment, and tended to be a boss rather than a leader. She was telling them what to do. Instead, she should have been helping the two boys to solve their conflict over the truck. I feel she hurt the boys' self-esteem by giving them the idea that what they were disagreeing over was not important, and that because they were arguing, they deserved to be punished.*

   The teacher also punished the entire class for the two children's mistaken behavior. The truck was put away so that no one could use it. They all became very quiet, and even I didn't want to make a wrong move. After about five minutes of quiet play, the teacher made a transition into another activity. The children seemed to accept it and move on, but I thought the atmosphere remained tense for the rest of my observation.

A practical definition of *conflict* is "words or actions taken by an individual to which another individual objects." José and Antonio provided a classic example of an early-childhood conflict over an object. Because of discomfort and possibly even danger, a conflict like this sets high emotional stakes for children and adults. In handling the conflict, the role of the teacher is central and difficult: The one task harder than using democratic life skills yourself is teaching them to others.

In the anecdote the teacher's act of taking away the truck might be considered a logical consequence of the boys' not using it peaceably. Her thinking probably was that José and Antonio would feel shame and so be motivated to behave better next time. The reality is that without specific, positive teaching, young children usually do not know how to behave better. The teacher blamed Antonio and José for having a conflict, but did not help them learn how to resolve it.

Brittany, the observer, suggested that some of José's reactions were intended to get teacher assistance. By her response, the teacher probably discouraged José from requesting help in the future. Likewise, José was not taught how to respond to Antonio's demands. Shaming children who are unable to resolve conflicts may well discourage them from trying to respond in future conflict situations.

Some children who are blamed for problems may feel not discouraged so much as angry, making hostile reactions more likely in future conflicts. Unless handled by a skilled adult, anger expressed by children tends to precipitate adult anger. At another time, the angry glare from Antonio might be seen and challenged by a teacher. The message a child receives from an adult in such a situation cannot be positive. The teacher in the anecdote relied on traditional discipline. There are better ways of handling conflicts, ways that preserve places for all children in the classroom community.

EMOTIONAL INTELLIGENCE

Emotional intelligence is the ability to empathize with others in order to solve social problems in mutually satisfactory ways. The term may be new, but back in the 1930s Jean Piaget, the important developmental psychologist, defined a similar concept, *autonomy.* Autonomy is the ability to make decisions intelligently and ethically—using thinking skills to solve problems in a manner responsive to the rights of all concerned. When social problems arise, an autonomous person is creative yet conscientious, taking all viewpoints into account to figure out how to reconcile them.

Piaget believed that young children progress toward autonomy by constructing meaning from experience. Early in the twentieth century, Lev Vygotsky observed that to do this, children rely in part on their interactions with peers. By contrast, early interpretations of Piaget's ideas held that because young children are developmentally egocentric, not yet able to understand viewpoints other than their own, they are not capable of being socially responsive. More recent interpretations follow Vygotsky in pointing to clear instances of generosity and kindness in young children and conclude that social relationships do affect intellectual development. While young children may not be able to comprehend and discuss multiple perspectives on social matters, they can understand broad matters of right and wrong and identify feelings of happiness and anger. Young children are "works in progress." They show beginning emotional intelligence, beginning autonomy. With successful social experiences—including conflict management experiences—and with ongoing support of their brain development, children make remarkable progress indeed.

OBSERVATION: *During free choice I helped a group of kids to make pumpkin cookies. While we were making the cookies, Joe came over to "help." He grabbed a bowl of flour, one which was extra. I explained to him that the flour was extra and only to be used "if needed." He wanted to know what "if needed" meant. I told him that it meant we would only use the flour if, when we were all done mixing, the dough was still too sticky. I also mentioned that I didn't think we would need to use it.*

He looked at me and said that it was "no fair" because he didn't get to do anything. I tried to explain to him that the other kids were there first, from the beginning, and that he was joining in after we started. Joe asked if it would be all right if he just watched them put all of the "stuff" in and maybe he could stir a little. I said sure.

When it came time for Katie to put in her can of pumpkin, she took her spoon and scooped out some of the filling. After a few scoops, she held the can up so that I could see the inside and asked me if I thought she had scooped out about half. I said that yes, I thought that she had scooped about half, and reminded her that we needed the whole can. She told me she remembered and that she wanted Joe to scoop out the other half, and she passed the can to Joe. Joe scooped out the filling and we continued stirring the cookies.

REFLECTION: *I was really happy to see that Joe accepted the fact that he would just be able to stir. I think that earlier in the year he probably would have* *hit or kicked me or the closest person to him. I thought it was great that he could think of that solution on his own.*

I was also happy to see Katie share her part with Joe. As I already said, Joe has had some problems in class and sometimes he picks on Katie. I thought it was really considerate of her to offer to share. I thanked them all for working together, and by working together we were able to enjoy some really good cookies!

In the anecdote, Joe showed beginning emotional intelligence in his way, and Katie in hers. These children were showing just the progress that a teacher who is building an encouraging classroom is gratified to see.

Three Levels of Conflict Management

A traditional priority of teachers in a conflict situation is to support the child who is the "victim" and punish the child who is the "perpetrator." For conflict management to be successful, the teacher needs to fight this temptation and put aside judgments about who is right and who is wrong. Instead, the teacher in an encouraging classroom needs to persuade herself, other adults in the classroom, and the children themselves to look for ways in which all parties can be "right," through the mutual satisfaction of a successful resolution. To give direction to the teaching of "win-win" social problem-solving, some teachers use a variation of Wichert's thee levels of conflict management (S. Wichert, *Keeping the Peace,* Philidelphia: New Society Publishers, 1989):

1. High-level mediation
2. Low-level mediation
3. Child negotiation

Don't confuse these three levels of managing conflict with the three levels of mistaken behavior discussed in the previous chapter. The three conflict management levels indicate children's progress toward being able to handle conflicts peaceably on their own, without adult assistance.

Most children begin at high-level mediation, with the teacher as a coach, leading the children through the mediation process step by step. Some children need high-level mediation longer than others do. While children are showing strong-needs mistaken behavior, they are likely also to show a need for high-level mediation.

With consistent modeling and teaching, most young children progress to the use of low-level mediation within a few months. In low-level mediation, the adult is in the background, allowing the children to take as much of the lead as they are ready for in resolving their problems. She is ready to step in, of course, if emotions are high or if one of the children is showing strong-needs mistaken behavior. At the low-mediation level, the teacher is more a helpful facilitator than an active coach.

Child negotiation happens when children manage the conflict on their own without a third-party mediator. When young children negotiate a conflict, they can make gnarly old professors weep tears of joy. Child negotiation is not for the faint-hearted. Sometimes it happens after one child does another child wrong, so to speak—clobbers him, for instance. Instead of hitting back, the second child protests, "Hey, you're supposed to use words," and takes the lead in using words to settle the problem. (It does happen. Remember Yolanda and Krista.) Child negotiation is the goal that teachers work toward with children. Due to factors beyond our control—such as strong-needs mistaken behavior—some children make only a little progress in the time they are with us, but many make lots, because children want to get along, just like we want them to.

Anecdotes that illustrate each of the three levels of conflict management follow. Remember that in this book we are going to "feature" a five-step conflict management process that is an informal composite of several conflict management models. So that you will keep in mind the five steps, whatever the level of mediation, here they are, fresh from the last chapter for your review:

1. **Cool down, if needed (all of you).** Try having everyone take deep breaths, count to ten, or otherwise calm down enough to discuss the problem. Sometimes a cooling-down time is necessary.
2. **Agree what the problem is.** Ask each child to talk in turn about what happened.
3. **Brainstorm solutions all can live with.** Remember in steps two and three that the teacher's job is to empower the children to come up with their

own solutions, to the extent possible. A solution you impose may work better for you than it works for the children.

4. **Select a solution.** Again, as much as possible encourage the children to select one that all can live with—even it is not the ideal solution you may be thinking of.

5. **Try it out, with the adult's guidance if needed.** Observe, encourage, review if necessary, and compliment.

To remember the five steps for social problem-solving, some adults post them on the wall. Some count them off on their fingers. I know one teacher who tattooed them on her wrist—she said she had to put something there to cover up her old "I love Bob" tattoo. Whatever method you use, remember that even in high-level mediation, the adult may not formally follow each step. Almost always, though, these five steps are evident when an adult mediates a conflict or when children negotiate it for themselves.

On occasion, children may be ready to progress to low-level mediation, or even child negotiation, before a teacher is. Most of us teachers find it difficult to let go of control in conflict situations, just when our emotions, as well as the children's, are running high. We may think, why should we give up control of the solution? Isn't the teacher paid to be in charge? Kirby's experience in the following anecdote illustrates some of these issues.

OBSERVATION: *We had just finished up with lunch and were ready for rest time. The kids got their blankets and pillows and found cots to lie on. The kids tend to take the same cot every day. I overheard Zoey and Stacie arguing over who would have the cot they were both sitting on. It was the place that Zoey usually lies. I walked over to them and asked what the problem was. Zoey replied, "This is my cot and Stacie is on it. It's mine!"*

I asked Stacie who was on it first and Stacie replied,

"She was." I said, "Okay, since Zoey was on it first, then I think Stacie should choose another cot to lie on for today." Stacie got up in a "pouty" way. I pointed out a few other cots that would be a good place to watch the video from. Stacie eagerly raced to another cot by the television.

REFLECTION: *I think that maybe Stacie wanted Zoey's cot because another of her good friends was on the cot next to it. It is understandable that she would want to lie by her friend, but this was not the way to get the cot. Looking back, I should have asked the two girls how they could work this situation out for themselves. I should have had them work out the problem or at least try. I was too quick to find a solution—lesson learned. I'm sure they would have come up with the same solution.*

By imposing a solution, even though it was masterfully done, Kirby relied on her own expertise rather than cooperative problem-solving, as she mentioned. The advantages of involving children in solving problems are many:

- Cognitively, the children have to integrate contradictory information into a hypothetical compromise.
- Linguistically, they have to put complex thoughts and feelings into acceptable words.
- Emotionally, they have to control angry impulses, accommodate a contradictory point of view, and take the risk that they may end up frustrated.
- Socially, they have to listen and reach a compromise with a person who they are angry at.

A whole lot of learning is going on! This is why many educators say that social problem-solving and conflict management need to be part of the core curriculum of all educational programs from infant/toddler programs on up. In learning to articulate and respond to diverse thoughts and feelings, children are really engaging in an advanced language arts and social studies curriculum. The resulting life lessons happen most fully when the teacher shares authority with children and guides them through the process.

HIGH-LEVEL MEDIATION

OBSERVATION: *At center time Dakota decided to play in the block area. Katrina decided she would play in the block area and the kitchen area. Dakota went over to the blocks and took out the Duplos. He started to build with them. Katrina began to play with the dishes in the kitchen area. After about ten minutes Katrina put away all the dishes and went over to the block area. Katrina approached Dakota.*

Katrina: Can I play with you?

Dakota: No.

Katrina immediately ran over to me. I was working on a puzzle with Roger Lee.

Katrina: Dakota won't let me play with the blocks.

Lorrie: Let's go over and talk to him.

I took Katrina's hand and we walked over to the block area where Dakota was playing.

Lorrie: (to Katrina) Please ask Dakota if you can play with him again.

Katrina: (shrugging her shoulders) Can I play here?

Dakota: No.

Lorrie: (bending down beside Dakota) Could Katrina take some of the blocks and play over there?

I pointed to a spot about five feet away from Dakota.

Dakota: Yes.

So Katrina picked up some of the blocks and took them to the spot I had pointed to. Both children played in the block area until cleanup time.

REFLECTION: *I knew that Dakota liked to protect his territory when he used the blocks. I wasn't sure Katrina could persuade him on her own to let her play in the area. With me taking the lead, I think Katrina got to use the blocks and Dakota began to learn he could share the space and the blocks.*

This conflict was over territory, Katrina wanting to play in the area where Dakota was. In deciding whether and at what level to mediate, teachers first consider the development of the children involved. These children were four year olds, a year or more older than Yolanda and Krista. A second consideration is experiential. With another child, Lorrie might have encouraged Katrina to use child-negotiation skills, standing by in case low-level mediation were needed. In this situation, the teacher had made home visits to Dakota's family and knew him well enough to not be sure how he would react if Katrina asked him again on her own. When Dakota said no to Katrina a second time, Lorrie did not argue, but redefined the problem and offered a solution in terms both children found satisfactory.

Did you notice that the two children played together after the conflict was resolved? A successful resolution of a conflict is often that the children involved come together in a later activity—sometimes even the activity that previously was the matter of dispute. Children's ability to forgive and forget is an important life lesson for adults.

OBSERVATION: *One day when I was observing, two children were fighting over a keyboard and earphones in the music center. Ennis was upset with Callie because he felt she was taking too long in the area. Ennis said that Callie had forgotten to set the time for ten minutes and had been there a lot longer.*

Callie: I set the timer. Look at it if you don't believe me.

Ennis: You just set it a few minutes ago when I asked you how much time!

Callie: I'm staying until the time is up.

Ennis hit Callie on the back. Callie kicked at Ennis from her chair, and the earphones fell around her neck. I had been observing during the entire argument and was staying close, but not too close, in hopes that maybe these children would be able to work out their own problem. I went over, got them both sitting on chairs, and calmed them down. I asked Ennis what had happened. He told me his version of the story, what I had seen. I said, "That is a problem, but I can't let you hit other students, and I won't let them hit you. Let's hear what Callie has to say." She told me her side.

I told her she should set the timer before she starts playing the keyboard, so that she doesn't forget, because other children do not want to be left out. I asked, "How can we fix this so you don't fight?" The two children seemed bummed out, so I said, "How about if Callie sets the time for five minutes to finish up, and then Ennis can set the timer for the full ten minutes?" They agreed, and I said that next time they should remember to set the timer right away during their turn. A few minutes later I observed Callie giving the earphones to Ennis when the timer rang.

REFLECTION: *I took the opportunity to teach the two children how to solve the problem next time a situation similar to this comes up. I tried to stay out of it and let the children solve their own problem, but I had to intervene when it got serious. I could have just told Ennis that he can't hit and Callie she shouldn't kick and ended the discussion there. But I took the time to tell the two why their behavior was unacceptable and to offer some alternative, acceptable behaviors. I took discipline that extra step to teach the children the important life skill of solving problems involving other people. I discussed it with them and took their differing opinions into consideration and thus modeled a skill so that they could do the same thing in a similar situation.*

The dispute was over privilege—who had the privilege of using the keyboard for how long. Earlier, I mentioned that when teachers try to mediate conflicts, they don't need to do things perfectly. Considering that Siew Lee was a practicum student trying conflict mediation for the first time, she deserves many compliments. Let us explore how Siew Lee followed the five steps of conflict management, at the high-mediation level:

1. **Cool down, if needed (all of you).** She didn't go into detail (like having each child take deep breaths), but she did calm them down enough so they could discuss the problem.
2. **Agree what the problem is.** Siew Lee heard both children's versions of what happened. She explained to each child why the hitting and kicking were mistaken behaviors. She did this in a way that did not punish, and she guided the children about what they could do differently next time. The children didn't dispute what she said, because they knew it

was true. They all pretty much agreed to what the problem was; the agreement was apparent later when they agreed to a solution.

3. **Brainstorm solutions all can live with.** She invited the children to give ideas for "how to fix this so you don't fight." One of the reasons for this high-level mediation is that the children were not ready to suggest solutions, so she suggested one.

4. **Select a solution.** A key difference between conflict mediation and traditional discipline is that the teacher does not force a solution. Siew Lee suggested a solution that the children accepted. If the children don't accept a solution, the teacher goes back to step three, brainstorming more possibilities. Step four offers an opportunity for a guidance talk, and she might have reminded them here about hitting and kicking being unacceptable and to use words instead. She did get them set up with a solution to try, however, and this key in step four.

5. **Try it out, with the adult's guidance if needed.** Siew Lee observed the children putting the solution into practice. Step five is the other place for a guidance talk, usually with one or both children separately. Reinforcement for how the children are solving the problem peaceably is a useful way to start the talk.

If one or more children lose emotional control in a situation, then high-level mediation usually becomes necessary. But no one, even adults, can talk through a problem when they are upset. This is why step one is so necessary. The teacher takes a momentary break—two deep breaths, or counting to ten by twos—to calm down. She then separates the children, helps them cool down, and mediates. The teacher guides, encourages, and coaches the children, giving them usable information so that they can solve the problem and perhaps be more successful in handling the problem next time. All in all, with Siew Lee's first try at high-level conflict mediation, she has taught the children quite a bit, and informed us with her observations, as well.

LOW-LEVEL MEDIATION

By modeling and teaching the steps of conflict management, we encourage children to take more responsibility for resolving conflicts by themselves. In low-level mediation, the adult is more a helping facilitator and less an active coach, looking on and offering suggestions if needed, but allowing the children to see if they can do most of the managing on their own.

OBSERVATION: *I was just finishing a center activity that involved a race-car game. The game used rubber race cars for the pieces. The children were given time for play after they finished the activity. One boy, Chad, was holding his car and playing with it. Another boy, Sam, came up to Chad and grabbed the car away from him. Chad's reaction was to reach out and grab for his car. Sam pulled back a little so that Chad couldn't grab the car. Sam didn't want to give it back, and Chad looked at me, really upset. I told Chad that he needed to use his words to tell Sam that he wanted the car back.*

    Chad: (looking at Sam and pleading) Please give it back. I want my car.

    Sam: Please can I keep it? Look at what's on the end of this car! It's really neat!

    Sam went on to say a little more about the car and why he wanted it. He was talking so fast and so much that Chad didn't get a chance to say anything. Then Sam ran around the table with the car, and eventually threw the car on the table next to Chad.

    I thanked Chad for using words and Sam for giving the car back. Sam found something else to do until Chad was done and gave the car back to Sam.

REFLECTION: *I was surprised at the way things turned out, because for a minute it looked like the boys were going to get into a fight. It didn't surprise me that Chad first grabbed for the car when Sam took it away. I don't know if Chad would have gotten up to hit Sam, because they were across the table from each other, and it wasn't really easy to reach him. I guess I was surprised at Sam's answer when Chad told him what he wanted. Sam tried to plead with Chad the same way that Chad pleaded with Sam. When Sam realized that wasn't working, he distracted Chad by talking about the car's features. Chad didn't have a chance to say anything else before Sam ran around a little and gave him back the car.*

    I didn't think that Sam would give the car back, but he did! By not getting upset with Sam, and by encouraging them to use words to solve the problem, I helped the boys end their disagreement without physically hurting each other. Usually children hit the other child who took their toy, because they don't know how else to express their anger. I think encouraging them to use words is very effective, although I wasn't sure it was going to work in this case. I was pleas-antly surprised, though!

The conflicts that most young children get into are first over property (the rac-ing car); second, territory (Katrina and Dakota in the block area); and third, privilege (Ennis and Callie's argument over how long to use the keyboard). Teachers can never be sure how children will respond in conflict situations. Scott, the observer in the race-car anecdote, mentioned this when he said that for a minute he thought Chad and Sam might fight. A common and often effective approach, used by Scott, is to encourage children to use words to work the prob-lem out on their own. The adult stands by and monitors the situation, to see if child negotiation will work, or if high- or low-level mediation proves necessary. The adult gives only as much help as the children need in order to do the rest on their own.

In this case, Scott used low-level mediation. All he had to do was ask Chad to tell Sam what he wanted. At his request, Chad managed his own steps two, three, and four of the mediation process, with Sam cooperating at step four. Scott fol-lowed up (step five) only by thanking each boy and monitoring the results.

CHILD NEGOTIATION

A goal for teachers—and not just early childhood teachers—is to empower chil-dren to resolve their problems by themselves, peaceably. If you think about it, you can probably recall a couple of kids in any class, including young preschoolers, who were able to negotiate. The truth is that some young children are better at conflict management than some adults. Teachers usually find that young chil-dren are more able to engage in negotiation towards the end of the year than at the beginning. But with a few children, teachers may see child negotiation sur-prisingly early, especially when then they have modeled and actively taught the process from day one. Two keys to enabling child negotiation are to watch for signs of it, and to stand back and allow it to happen.

OBSERVATION: *During play time I observed two boys playing with the blocks and trucks. They were cooperating with each other in building a mall parking lot so that their trucks could fit. I have never seen two kids so involved* *in what they were doing. Reese picked up a block that Delray was about to take. Delray got really upset at Reese and started to argue with him about who had their hand on the block first.*

Delray said, "I was the first one over to the block station and then you came over."

Reese said, "My foot got here before your foot did." They were arguing with each other, but they were doing it quietly enough so the teacher wouldn't hear.

Delray said, "Come on Reese; you know I was here first."

Reese said, "No you weren't, I was here first!" He paused, then went on, "I'm not going to invite you to my birthday party if you don't let me play with you."

Delray said, "I don't care. That way I can keep your present." Then Delray hit Reese on the back. I just heard a big thump. Reese looked really shocked by what had happened. Mrs. A., the teacher, looked up and noticed that Reese was almost crying. I watched her sit there and wait to see what was going to happen next. I think I would have been over there scolding Delray for what he had done.

Reese said, "That really hurt, Delray; I don't care if you have the block, but I'm not going to play with you any more."

Looking really sad, Delray said, "I didn't mean to hit so hard. Why don't we just throw this block out, because it made us fight."

At first Reese just walked away and got involved in a painting activity while Delray just sat there all alone. After Reese finished his painting, he came back over to Delray and said, "If it is not too late, could we forget what happened and just finish our building?"

So together they threw the block in the box and used a different one instead. Mrs. A. came over and quietly took Delray aside and told him that hitting is not a good idea when we get frustrated. She also told him that he could have hurt Reese by hitting him so hard on his back. She let them continue playing. A while later when they had finished building, Delray looked at Reese and said, "Thanks for helping with the blocks. We really worked hard."

REFLECTION: *For the rest of the day, everything they did, they worked together on. These children were learning through their play how to balance blocks so their mall parking lot could be made. They also learned conflict resolution, by themselves.*

Even young children can show consideration in conflict situations. They can summon personal resources, grasp the other's point of view, solve problems, and forgive. The magnificent gains that are possible in managing conflict peaceably—even at ages three, four, and five—can only happen if children see adults who are able to show their own emotional intelligence by modeling and teaching conflict resolution. We're lucky to have those adults, whether with a doctoral degree or with an eighth-grade education, who practice and teach the active process of getting along, the ability to integrate contradictory viewpoints in ways that respect the perceptions and needs of all concerned.

Putting It All Together

In the encouraging classroom, the adult helps children resolve conflicts at whatever level of assistance the children need—high-level mediation, low-level mediation, or child negotiation. Unless the negotiation is between them and a child, (it happens every day), teachers observe but don't help during child-negotiations. They just stand by, chew their fingernails, hope that the management lessons they've taught have taken hold, and celebrate when the children solve the problem for themselves. When teachers believe children have a good chance of solving the problem themselves, they do well to let them try. Because if the kids work it out, it means they are progressing toward democratic life skills, emotional intelligence, and autonomy. A case in point is Jeremiah.

RECOLLECTION: *Jeremiah was almost three when I started teaching at the center. He was one of those very physical kids, whose feelings and thoughts always moved through his body first. He'd had a turbulent life, and when I came to the center, he was living mostly with his mom, and some with his dad. They were separated, and neither made very much money. Jeremiah was a shiningly bright kid, curious about and interested in everything, who loved stories and connected with others with his whole heart. He knew a lot about the natural world and was observant and gentle with animals, insects, and plants.*

When I first started working with Jeremiah, he had a lot of angry outbursts. The center used time out at that point (the dreaded "green chair") and Jeremiah spent considerable time there. While I was at the center, we moved away from using time outs. Instead we introduced a structured system of problem solving called "peer problem solving" developed by a Montessori teacher in New Hampshire. By the time Jeremiah graduated to kindergarten, we had been using the system for three years, and he was one of the experts.

One day, I overheard a fracas in the block corner. I stood up to see what was going on, ready to intervene. The youngest child in the room, who was just two and only talking a little bit, was in a dispute over a truck with one of the four year olds. I took a step forward, ready to go to their aid, and then I saw Jeremiah approach them.

"What's going on, guys?" he asked (my standard opening line). He proceeded to facilitate a discussion between the two children that lasted for five minutes. He made sure both kids got a chance to speak; he interpreted for the little one. "Jordan, what do you think of that idea?" he asked. Jordan shook his head and clutched the truck tighter. "I don't think Jordan's ready to give up the truck yet," he told the four year old.

It was amazing. Jeremiah helped the kids negotiate an agreement, and then he walked away with a cocky tilt to his head that I'd never seen before. His competence was without question; his pride was evident.

In the process of mediating a conflict between two other children, Jeremiah was helping all of the children in the group affirm the promise of the encouraging classroom community.

Suggested Readings

Dinwiddie, S. A. "The Saga of Sally, Sammy, and the Red Pen: Facilitating Children's Social Problem Solving." *Young Children* 5 (1994): 13–19.

Gartrell, Dan. *A Guidance Approach for the Encouraging Classroom.* Albany, NY: Delmar/ITP Publishers (1998).

Gruenberg, Ann. "Creative Stress Management: Put Your Own Oxygen Mask on First." *Young Children* 53, no. 1 (January 1998): 38–42.

Honig, Alice, and Donna Wittmer. "Helping Children Become More Prosocial: Ideas for Classrooms, Families, Schools, and Communities (Part 2)." *Young Children* 51, no. 2 (January 1996): 62–70.

Jackson, Beverly. "Creating a Climate for Healing in a Violent Society." *Young Children* 52, no. 7 (November 1997): 68–70.

Manning, Diane, Samuel Rubin, H. G. Perdigao, Remigio Gonzalez, and P. Schindler. "A 'Worry Doctor' for Preschool Directors and Teachers: A Collaborative Model." *Young Children* 51, no. 5 (July 1996): 68–73.

NCTA. "The National Television Violence Study: Key Findings and Recommendations." *Young Children* 51, no. 3 (March 1996): 54–55.

Discussion Activities

For reasons of professionalism, as you respond to these discussion activities, please respect the privacy of all children, adults, programs, and schools.

1. Describe an example of social problem-solving that you or another adult used with one or a small group of children. Was the example of conflict management most like high-level mediation, low-level mediation, or negotiation? Why do you say so?

2. Describe an example of social problem-solving that you or another adult used with one child or with a small group of children. In what ways did the use of social problem-solving contribute to an encouraging atmosphere in the classroom?

3. One characteristic of social problem-solving is that teachers do not respond to children in terms of victims and perpetrators. Instead, they focus on helping children solve the problem at hand and learn from the experience. What effect do you think it might have on the children in a dispute not to be cast in victim/perpetrator terms, but to be helped instead to solve the problem?

6

Loss, Liberation, and Resiliency

A sense of connection with family members in the home and with peers and adults in the classroom is the healthy state of mind for young children. By knowing they belong both at home and in school, children gain the initiative to learn, cooperate, and solve social problems. The mistakes that such children make are the natural ones of everyday living, "level one" mistakes to learn from but not be consumed by.

The state of grace in a child with healthy attachments at home and in school is often attributed to all children, in the form of the stereotype of childhood as "that happiest time of life." It's a stereotype, not a truth, because most children, at one time or another, experience the profound emotions of loss. We associate serious loss with disruption in the home—the death or absence of a family member, or the breakup of the family. However, young children also experience loss at child care or school—for instance, when a valued teacher leaves for another job, or when a child transitions to another level of the program. Separation from a friend or peer group at school can also provoke feelings of deep loss.

The emotions of loss range from sorrow, to anxiety, to depression, to anger. Whatever the cause of loss, the child always feels less connected to home or class, or both. The feeling of "detachment" that comes with loss is natural: the child's reliance on others for nurturance has been shaken. Children are just learning the high-level skills of putting feelings into words. As a result, strong unexpressed emotions may show up in the classroom in the form of strong-needs mistaken behavior. Teachers can often head off mistaken behaviors if they are receptive to the child and encourage her to talk through the grief. Unless teachers do this, and recognize that the reason for the mistaken behavior is the child's grief, they may react with traditional classroom discipline. Punitive reactions toward a child in a state of loss do not help, of course. Such reactions stigmatize the child and further complicate the child's fall from grace.

Few teachers would intentionally discipline a child if they recognized that the cause for the mistaken behavior is grief. But often the problem is that teachers cannot take the time, or do not know the child and family well enough, to perceive that loss is the motivating factor. The challenge to early childhood teachers is to be continually sensitive to the signs of loss among children in the class. Guidance generally is easier when the reasons for behavior are understood. With guidance, teachers can support the child and her sense of belonging in the classroom community. Regained connectedness at school cannot cure the child of a loss, of course, but it can strengthen the child's resiliency (the ability to work through the grieving process and to bounce back) (Maxine Weinreb, "Be a Resiliency Mentor: You May Be a Lifesaver for a High-Risk Child," *Young Children* 53 [2], January 1997, 14–20).

This chapter is about the child's experience of loss and the teacher's responses to it. The anecdotes tell of several loss experiences and show how the teachers in these situations assisted children to recover a sense of connectedness. The types of loss we look at include:

- Loss due to death of a family member
- Loss due to family discord
- Loss due to dislocation from familiar circumstances
- Loss due to lack of personal control

Anecdotes appear under each heading, and the implications of each type of loss for the child are discussed. The path from loss to resiliency is different for each child, but all grieving children share a common need for the active support of a teacher who cares.

In my work with teachers over the years, I have seen two main difficulties in reaching children who grieve. First, teachers miss the signs of loss in children's behavior. Second, at times even veteran teachers have difficulty finding the words to comfort a child. They give reasons such as, "The child can't really understand," and, "It is better not to get involved with the family's beliefs." The anecdotes show that "just the right words" are not necessary, but a sincere effort to listen and to help the child give voice to difficult feelings is. Through the anecdotes, we discuss each type of loss and its effects. We also look at teacher responses that lead children back to a sense of community in the classroom.

Helping Children Cope with the Death of a Family Member

The death of a loved one is a profound loss for a young child. To help children cope, teachers may listen attentively, ask questions, make room for conversations about grief in ordinary classroom activities, follow up on conversations from home, and share their personal experiences.

Perhaps the most frequent loss (other than that of a pet) in the lives of young children is the death of a grandparent. This is sometimes a young child's first significant experience of loss. Children need to talk about this experience, both at home—to reestablish connectedness there—and in the classroom.

OBSERVATION: *Today a little girl named Brook came up to me as soon as her mother dropped her off. She took my hand and when she said my name and I knelt down, she told me very matter-of-factly that her grandpa had died.*

I touched her shoulder and asked her how she felt. She responded by saying, "Sad." I told her that it was all right to feel sad. I also told her that any time she wanted to talk to me or just sit by me, she just had to come and get me. That day, I made it a point to pay special attention to Brook. We read some books in the rocking chair, and played in the housekeeping area. During our play she did mention that her grandpa was "old" and she talked more about his death.

REFLECTION: *I felt very glad that Brook was able to talk about her feelings, and about her grandpa's death. I felt I needed to be quietly supportive and let her say the things she needed to talk about.*

I feel that talking about something that is worrying them can help kids a lot. But I don't believe we should bombard kids with dozens of questions, which could just add to their confusion and grief. Brook came to me and told me her feelings in her own time.

In the encouraging classroom teachers like Carin find different ways to talk with a child about the death of a grandparent. The choice of words can be difficult, and children's books such as *Nana Upstairs & Nana Downstairs* (a classic by Tomie dePaola) can sometimes help. In the next anecdote, notice Tina's approach with Ashley, a bit different than Carin's conversation above. When helping a child deal with grief, there is no given set of words to use. The teacher listens and says what she thinks might help and listens some more. She is there for the child and conveys this; that is what's important.

OBSERVATION: *Rest time was over and I was standing in the dramatic play area. Ashley came and stood by me and said, "My grandpa died."*

I said, "I'm sorry to hear that." She was quiet. I said, "I'll bet you miss him." She continued to stand next to me. I put my hand on her shoulder and said, "What did you and your Grandpa do together?"

Ashley said, "He tickled me."

I asked, "What else did you and your grandpa do together?"

She said, "We played with my puppy and he took me to McDonald's."

I said, "It sounds like you had lots of fun together."

Ashley said, "Um-hmm. He bought me stuff. Sometimes he bought me candy."

I said, "Sometimes it helps to remember the fun times when you're missing somebody. Do you think it would help to think about the fun things you did next time you are really missing your Grandpa?"

She laughed and said, "Um-hmm." She walked over to the doll cradle and picked up a doll and started playing.

REFLECTION: *This was a "teachable moment." It was also a time when I was grateful for my background. I was glad I was able to "actively listen" and was* *able to respond. There were no other children around when Ashley told me about her grandpa. I could tell she really missed him and she needed some comforting. I chose not to explore her sadness, but instead to try to get her to focus on her good thoughts about her grandpa. I feel I did validate her feeling of sadness and missing him and tried to let her know it's okay to miss him. But—I wanted to give her something. I hope in some small way, I helped her to think about the good times and to keep those memories in her heart.*

Grief felt with loss of a grandparent may be tempered somewhat by the child's understanding of the association of old age with death, although of course it's still difficult. Given the special relationships many children have with their grandparents, and the slow passing that sometimes is involved, family members sometimes talk with children about a grandparent's dying. Such conversations in the home are important, and like Tina in the following anecdote, teachers can often tell when they have occurred.

OBSERVATION: *I was reading a story dealing with Easter to a small group of kindergartners. I was just reading along when Dean interrupted me, saying, "My grandma died, will she be up in heaven?"*

I replied, "Of course she will, Dean."

Dean went on, "I wasn't in school one day because I was at her funeral."

I asked, "Was it sad?"

Dean said, "Yes, it was very sad, but you know what? They said that now my Grandma can rest and be comfortable. When she was alive, she just laid in bed always in pain. She cried a lot, and she didn't even know who I was. But she looked so young and happy at the funeral. She didn't even look the way she did when she died. She looked all old and wrinkled when she was alive."

When Dean was through, I went on to finish the story. After the story, more of the children had experiences to tell the rest of us about relatives, cats, and dogs that have died. These children wanted to say something because Dean's sharing got them thinking about similar experiences.

REFLECTION: *Even though I was reading a book, I chose to let Dean talk, not only to make himself feel better, but also so that the other kids would understand how he was feeling. After the story was over, they all had a chance to talk, so Dean wasn't being singled out. Also, I noticed that after Dean got his chance to talk, he seemed more relaxed. I think that if I had not let Dean talk, he might have thought that I didn't think it was important that his grandpa had died. I know sometimes it is hard to read a book without being interrupted by the children, but I think sometimes, like this time, it is okay. I think that it helped Dean to talk about his feelings since it had just happened a couple of days earlier.*

Especially in non-sectarian early childhood classrooms, teachers may need to monitor their words so as not to teach their personal views about death and the hereafter. But Tina's approach illustrates that whatever the setting, the teacher is there essentially to listen. The teacher shapes prepared activities to give the children permission to talk about a topic that is important to them if that seems necessary. By doing so, she affirms a child's place of worth in the classroom community during a time of grief.

It is at least as hard for children to cope with the death of a younger family member due to accident, illness, or violence. As those who have experienced it know, the loss of a parent can be devastating. Children try so gamely to go on, but their behavior tells us that they need to grieve. When we let them, and at the same time teach them about grieving, we are supporting resiliency.

OBSERVATION: *I heard the words, "Shut up," and walked around the corner to the bathroom to find out what was happening.*

Shayna was sitting in the corner crying. I said, "Shayna, why are you crying?"

Shayna said, "Amanda and Christina said they aren't my friends anymore."

I asked her if she had told them to shut up. Shayna said yes. I told her I was sorry that what they had said made her feel sad and angry, but we don't use those words in our center. Amanda and Christina were watching and listening to us talk. I explained to Shayna that maybe next time she could tell the girls that it made her sad to hear they didn't want to be her friends. I told Amanda and Christina that Shayna was feeling sad. They came over to Shayna and gave her a hug and said they were sorry.

A little later, Shayna walked over to the breakfast table. She started crying again. I asked, "Is something making you feel sad, Shayna?"

She said, "I miss my daddy." Her father had been killed in a car accident a few months before.

I sat down on a chair, hugging and holding her. I said, "Shayna, my daddy died when I was a little girl and it made me very sad, too. I am so glad you told me why you were crying." We sat by each other and ate breakfast.

Shayna went to the housekeeping area for choice time. Later in the day she came up to me and said, "I'm over my daddy now."

I said, "Shayna, it's okay to feel sad about missing your daddy. I still miss my dad. If you need a hug or want to talk, you come and tell me."

REFLECTION: *This incident gave me the chills. I felt sad for Shayna, but I also felt good that she was able to verbally express her feelings about her father's death. This experience reinforced the importance of listening to young children.*

As a teacher I need to take the time to listen and open the door for these opportunities to be a listener. Shayna had a need to talk about her father's death. Hopefully Shayna can talk more about her feelings, and she knows that I care about her.

Later I talked with Shayna's mother about the incident and Shayna's behavior at home. With Shayna's mother's approval, we asked our mental health counselor to observe and talk with Shayna the next time he came to our center. I also gave Shayna more personal attention and made other staff aware of the incident. The next day Shayna sat on my lap at the playdough table. We made cookies together.

By sharing her own personal experience, Kay was able to help Shayna understand that grieving doesn't just end. It goes on for a while, sometimes years or even a lifetime. Personal disclosure can assist children to understand and cope with their grieving. The connection they are able to make with the teacher helps children feel that they have a place within the classroom community.

Helping Children Cope with Loss Due to Family Discord

Communities still exist where virtually all families are in first-time marriages and both fathers and mothers live in the home. This is not to say that some of these families aren't "broken," just that the breaks may not show. By the same token, large numbers of single-parent families are intact, just functioning with fewer adult members. Nonetheless, the classic loss around family disruption is the separation of parents with one leaving the home. Studies indicate that when separated or divorced parents stay on civil terms after separation, children suffer fewer long-term problems. Obviously, teachers are not marriage counselors and cannot control parents' feelings, attitudes, and actions. They can, however, be responsive to children, who will share their concerns with teachers they trust.

OBSERVATION: *Karly and I were sitting at the lunch table eating. Some of the children at the table were talking about what they had done at spring break, where they had gone, etc. Karly quietly said, "I didn't see my daddy at Easter."*

I said, "Oh?"

She said, "He isn't good with kids. He doesn't like them. My grandma and grandpa don't like kids either."

Knowing about the situation, I said, "I'm sorry Karly. I bet you have other grown-ups who like kids."

She smiled and said, "Yes I do! My other grandma and grandpa love me. And Uncle Tim and Aunt Judy like to play with me. And my Mom really loves me!"

I said, "Then you are a very lucky girl to have so many people who love and care for you." She nodded seriously, and that ended the conversation.

REFLECTION: *My immediate response was sadness. Being a parent myself, I can't imagine having a child but not being involved with the child, not loving it, etc. I know that it happens, like in Karly's case, but it's hard.*

What also struck me was the matter-of-fact way she was dealing with it. The statement, "He isn't good with kids," sounds like what her mom may have said to her explaining her dad's absence. I thought it was a good explanation, rather than saying he doesn't love or like Karly. Karly isn't left feeling bad about herself, at least, that's the feeling I have. The feeling I was left with is that Dad has the problem, not Karly.

I was left with a more optimistic feeling when she spoke of her other relatives. She does have people around her that care about her, and I think it was reassuring to Karly that we could talk about them.

When parents separate, friends and relations often feel pressure to take sides and support one member at the expense of the other. The teacher's job is to remember that the child loves both parents, even if one "isn't good with kids." Whatever thoughts the child—or for that matter a parent—shares, the teacher's job is to listen and help the child make the best of the situation. The child is an extension of the family, whatever circumstances the family faces. To the extent feasible, the teacher works with both parents, separately when he must, to help the child cope with the loss of a family structure that she has come to rely on.

In two-parent families, children experience loss, as well, when discord and violence erupt. In this situation, the child loses trust in family members as sources of nurturing and support. She must summon all of the resources in her young life to cope with fear and anxiousness when parents fight.

OBSERVATION: *While we were eating breakfast, Vincent started talking about his mother and father fighting.... "Mom was fighting with Dad last night. She hit the phone and it fell on the floor."*

Dottie (the assistant teacher) heard this and said, "Your mom and dad were fighting last night and she hit the phone and it fell on the floor?"

Vincent said, "Uh-huh (nodding). She was real mad."

Dottie asked, "Were you scared?"

Vincent said yes. Dottie asked him what he did while they were fighting, and he said he tried to stop them. Dottie told him it might be a good idea to just go sit on his bed and read a book or play with a toy if it happens again.

We later found out from Vincent's mom that they fought for six hours straight...no wonder he was scared.

REFLECTION: *I felt horrible when I heard this. I'm lucky to not have gone through that. I would have a hard time with that at my age now. I can only imagine what Vincent has to be feeling to have heard and witnessed all of this. What* *some of these kids have seen in their five years of life, I haven't seen an ounce of in my 24 years. My heart goes out to them.*

I feel it really made a big impact on Vincent's life because he rarely comes to school and talks about home. It was obvious that he was shaken up over the situation. I'm glad he brought it up because we all need to know what he is going through at home. If we know what is going on at home, it is easier to understand his behavior at school, which is usually perfect. The teachers talked for quite a while with the mother about what happened. Needless to say we are all looking out for Vincent.

With the stress Vincent experienced, strong-needs mistaken behavior would certainly be understandable. Instead, even after the events he experienced, Vincent's behavior remained "usually perfect." In home situations where violence is a guest, some children cope by trying to put themselves beyond criticism. Children sometimes believe that by being "bad" they provoke violence in parents. By being "extra good" they hope they can prevent further loss of the family system that they need so much. The danger here is that they will internalize feelings of fear and self-doubt—and possibly develop post-traumatic stress syndrome: anxiety intruding on the child's everyday life sometimes long after the trauma has been experienced.

Kellie's reflection describes the feelings of many teachers when children share traumatic experiences. In the anecdote, Dottie used reflective (active) listening appropriately and professionally. By repeating back exactly what Vincent reported in Kellie's presence, she was verifying Vincent's story. Talking with the mother was important, and encouraging referral to relevant agencies also is important. When a child is suffering from family circumstances, staff members need to work together. Together they may be able to accomplish what they cannot alone.

Helping Children Cope with Loss Due to Dislocation

In this book dislocation means being separated from familiar life circumstances that have special meaning for the child. Dislocation is seldom a happy experience. Dislocations that children experience can be dramatic or subtle. Major dislocations often involve leaving the home, even for a few days, such as for hospital stays, joint custody situations, foster home placements, and living with non-custodial relatives. When families move and change early-childhood placements, children also feel dislocated. In all dislocation situations, the teacher communicates with parents as much as possible and provides support and encouragement to minimize the child's feeling of loss.

OBSERVATION: *We were on a tour of our hospital. Chris had been involved in a car accident about three months before, which resulted in his being hospitalized for four days. He was with us and was very anxious! He wouldn't let go of my hand. He was breathing rapidly and perspiring. I told our tour leader how Chris knew a lot about the hospital since he had recently been there. She sensed his distress and was very good at encouraging him to help with the tour. He slowly relaxed and eventually took some leadership. After the tour he stated, "The hospital really isn't so bad!"*

REFLECTION: *Chris was traumatized by his hospitalization. His cousin was born about a month and a half ago, and he wouldn't consider a visit to see the new baby. We talked about the trip with his parents, and we were all quite concerned about his reactions. We even gave him the choice of going or not going on the tour. He decided to go with us, and I was really glad he did. The tour was a real time of healing for him.*

The teaching staff talked long and hard about whether to take the trip to the hospital, because they knew of Chris's experience. They talked with his parents and decided the trip might benefit all concerned, including Chris. They didn't know what the outcome would be, of course, and Carrie monitored Chris's reactions closely. Because of Carrie's responsive teaching, and Chris's readiness to confront a major dislocation, "the tour was a real time of healing for him."

Helping Children Rebound from a Loss of Personal Control

Teachers don't typically think of children as suffering traumas in the classroom that they need to grieve. I didn't either until I interviewed retired adults about experiences they could remember in school (Dan Gartrell, *A Guidance Approach for the Encouraging Classroom*, Albany, NY: Delmar/ITP Publishers, 1998). The majority of the experiences these senior citizens recalled were of being embarrassed in the public situation of the classroom, often by teachers. The teachers probably thought they were just reacting to a problem of the moment, but the hurting words and actions stayed with the folks over a lifetime. These seniors needed to work through the events and rebound from their grief, but they did not have the opportunity. They were still feeling pain from their losses after half a century or more. What have children actually lost when they are seriously embarrassed in the classroom? Not a loved one, perhaps, but something still quite tangible: They have lost self-esteem, control over their own lives, respect by significant others, connection with the class.

Children feel such loss when they are "made" to do things against their will. They feel such loss when they feel they have failed at important activities. They feel such loss when they are shamed for their behavior. Obviously, life has its share of frustrating events. Occasional frustrations in day-to-day classroom life can actually strengthen children's resources for dealing with reality. But little failures only help to build character when the child feels basic acceptance and security in the group situation, and when the experiences are not overwhelming. When the hurt is too much, lost personal control results in those same emotions that the more recognized loss experiences generate. Teachers monitor children's reactions to everyday frustrations. They provide support and guidance when children need to be reassured that their place in the encouraging classroom is secure. They do not set children up for failure.

OBSERVATION: *After our hospital tour, I was driving some of the children back to the center in my car. I looked in the mirror, and Stephanie got big eyes. "I have to go—I went." Stephanie had wet herself and my back seat! The rest of the children were so quiet, almost like they were waiting for my reaction. I just*

145

said, "That's okay—we all have accidents of some kind now and then." The children agreed with me, a couple sharing about accidents they have had!

We arrived at the center. We were out of our usual stash of extra clothes, so I called her mom to bring some in. She came in immediately—totally embarrassed. I assured her she did not have to be. No one seemed to need to talk any more about the accident.

REFLECTION: *This could have been a very embarrassing and humiliating incident for Stephanie. Instead it showed the children that perfection isn't always possible and that it's okay to make mistakes. It also shows that we, the adults, still care about them no matter what happens. Stephanie stayed with us for the rest of the day, participating as if the accident had not happened.*

In new situations, especially if challenged by them, people feel pressure to be "perfect." The implication is that unless we do things completely right, we will make mistakes and be stigmatized, negatively separated from the group. Until they feel accepted for who they are, children are likely to feel these same pressures. When children make mistakes, as when they make accomplishments, we need to communicate that their status as members of the encouraging classroom is not in doubt. The encouraging classroom is there for them, to help them rebound from the loss of personal control. In Stephanie's case, being resilient was no big deal, because both her teacher and her mother were on her side.

The following anecdote shows a side that we see in many older preschoolers. They know how things are supposed to work in the class, but they can't always make them work. When things go wrong that are not supposed to, total frustration results—frustration that can stay with a child and build, or can be dissipated, depending on the response of the teacher.

OBSERVATION: *It was play time and all the children were busy in the areas they had chosen. Robby had picked the art area. He decided to paint a picture at the easel. When he had completed his picture, he reached up on the easel to remove the clasps holding it up. As he removed them, all the paper clasped up to the easel came down with his picture and landed on the floor. When this happened Robby began to cry and stomp his feet. Dana, the assistant teacher, was working with Jamie at the art table. When she saw what had happened she* *immediately got up and walked over to Robby. She said, "Can I help you?" Robby said nothing and kept crying. Dana said, "Robby, is there anything I can do to help you feel better?"*

Robby said to her, "Fix my picture."

Dana responded, "I wish I could." She added, "Let's pick up all the papers together." Dana bent down and started to pick up the papers. Robby waited about 30 seconds and then silently started to help her. As they finished picking up the papers, Robby began to talk excitedly about a picture he wanted to paint especially for Dana. When they finished talking, Robby returned to the painting easel with a big smile on his face.

REFLECTION: *Dana was a very effective helping professional. The first way she demonstrated this was by immediately recognizing that Robby needed her help. Second, Dana consoled Robby. I believe the most significant thing she did was ask Robby how she could help him. This gave Robby the opportunity to verbalize his feelings. Robby in return showed Dana his gratitude by painting a picture for her.*

Responsiveness by the teacher empowers a child to realize that loss of personal control, which we all face at times in our lives, is not the end of the world. We can learn and grow from the experience. In early childhood education, teachers are there to help. When we do, children show resiliency—and make us pictures!

In two important studies, Ladd found that children who were unable to make friends in kindergarten became quietly stigmatized and experienced difficulties all through school. In fact, these kids dropped out in much higher numbers than their peers. By kindergarten, most young children have a beginning awareness of the importance of acceptance by the group. Mistaken behavior that results in rejection by classmates must be a serious loss indeed. Ladd's work suggests that the loss of self-esteem by the stigmatized child may cause grieving from which he does not recover. So what does a teacher do when a child shows strong-needs mistaken behavior, behavior that hurts others and comes back to hurt herself? In the following anecdote, by assisting both Ray and Brandon in a difficult situation, Carin illustrates how *liberation teaching* helps children recover from a loss of trust and self-esteem.

OBSERVATION: *I heard Ray crying at the table. I walked over and said, "Why are you crying, Ray?" Ray said, "Brandon cut my shirt," and pointed to the sleeve of his new Star Wars shirt, which had a hole cut in it. Brandon was sitting next to Ray with his scissors. I said, "Brandon, did you cut Ray's shirt?" Brandon said, "Yes, he tried to take my paper."*

I said, "Brandon, what would have been a better way to let Ray know that you didn't want him to take your paper?" Brandon replied, "Tell him." I said, "I think that would be a much better idea." The class left the room for a walk to the playground. When we arrived at the playground, I quietly asked Brandon to come over by me. I sat down and he sat on my lap. I asked, "Brandon, how would you feel if someone cut a hole in a shirt that you liked a lot?" He said, "Sad." I said, "How do you think Ray feels about his Star Wars shirt?"

Brandon said, "Mad and sad. I will tell him I'm sorry." I said, "Okay, let's find Ray." Brandon said, "No, you stay here. I want to go by myself." He ran over to Ray, put his arm around him and said, "Sorry about your shirt." Ray smiled and ran off to play. Brandon came back over and I said, "Brandon, I think Ray is feeling better!" Then I added, "Brandon, what can we do if we damage something of someone's or wreck it?" Brandon said, "Pay for it." I asked, "Do you have any money at home?" He said he did, in his piggy bank. I said, "I need to talk to your mom about what happened today and if she thinks it's a good idea, maybe you could give Ray some money to help buy a new shirt." Brandon said, "Okay, I'll ask my Mom." I called Brandon's mother and explained what happened. I made a home visit the next day, and Brandon gave me two quarters from his piggy bank. Brandon's mom was very supportive. The next day at the center, Brandon, Ray, and I got together. I had written a note to Ray's mother with the 50 cents taped on it, with an explanation. I asked Brandon to tell Ray what the money was for. He said, "To help pay for a new shirt." Ray smiled and said, "Thank you." He gave Brandon a big hug.

REFLECTION: *In this situation, guidelines for behavior were set: We respect other people's property. I tried to guide the children by using words to settle their problems. I addressed the problem, but I respected Brandon by involving him in the decision making and not embarrassing or humiliating him individually or in front of others. I continued to build on the established partnership with Brandon's mother.*

The reason I suggested Brandon give some of his own money to help pay for the shirt is after several episodes of level-three mistaken behavior, he has been very apologetic, but repeats the behavior. I am hoping that the money will give him a stronger message about being responsible for his behavior. He accepted the idea and gave the money willingly. Rather than shaming him in front of the class, I wanted him to take pride in the restitution.

Liberation teaching was at work. After the episode, Brandon appeared to value himself as a person. He made a mistake but in the guidance process his self-esteem was a priority. Each day I give Brandon a hug as a greeting. As it says in A Guidance Approach to the Encouraging Classroom, *"Children most at risk for stigma are those who show chronic mistaken behavior. These are the children who need a positive relationship the most, but often are the most difficult for the teacher to like and accept" (300). I used liberation teaching by "showing a clear acceptance of Brandon as a worthwhile individual and member of the group."*

Most difficulties children experience in classrooms are the result of loss, due to death of a family member, discord within the family, dislocation, or lost personal control. Ray experienced lost control of his personal space when Brandon cut his shirt. Brandon experienced lost control of his emotions, resulting in his level-three mistaken behavior. In response, Carin used liberation teaching with both children.

Liberation occurs when teachers help a child to overcome a vulnerability and reinforce the child's individual worth and membership in the group. Loss frequently puts children at risk for stigma as a result of the mistaken behavior, done to or by them. Carin helped Ray overcome feeling victimized, which is common when a child's personal control is diminished by another person. His hugs and smiles for his friend, Brandon, attest to his resiliency.

Carin helped Brandon overcome the negative self-messages associated with doing violence and being confronted about it. With Carin's guidance, Brandon both took the initiative to apologize, and engaged in restitution—that most logical of consequences. Both children were encouraged to keep their place as worthy members of the classroom community, and both responded. Taking leadership to reaffirm children's participation in the encouraging classroom, despite the effects of loss, is liberation teaching.

Suggested Readings

Fassler, D. G., and I. S. Dumas. *Help Me I'm Sad.* New York: Penguin Putnam (1997).

La Cerva, V. "Adverse Effects of Witnessing Violence." *Child Care Information Exchange* (November 1999): 44–47.

Read, Laurie. "Amos Bear Gets Hurt." *Young Children* 50, no. 4 (May 1995): 19–23.

Sang, D. "The Worry Teacher Comes on Thursdays: Clinical Consultation in a Kindergarten Class." *Young Children* 50, no. 2 (January 1994): 24–31.

Weinreb, Maxine. "Be a Resiliency Mentor: You May Be a Lifesaver for a High-Risk Child." *Young Children* 52, no. 2 (January 1997): 14–20.

Discussion Activities

For reasons of professionalism, as you respond to these discussion activities, please respect the privacy of all children, adults, programs, and schools.

1. Think about a time when, as a child, you experienced loss. Can you recall another person who helped you through your time of loss? What did the person say and do to help? What life lessons were (are) there for you in the person's responsiveness?

2. Recall from your experience in classrooms (as either child or adult) a child who was suffering from a loss. If you were to work with this child now, what actions could you take that would constitute liberation teaching?

3. Recall from your experience in classrooms (as either child or adult) a child who showed resiliency after a loss. As you think back, who or what helped the child to recover from the loss? What changes in behavior do you recall as the child recovered? How long did significant recovery take?

Wonder and Delight

In previous chapters we have looked at broad dimensions of teaching that together build the encouraging classroom. "Teaching" is the right term to use, although for some the word has a set schoolhouse meaning that is pretty restrictive—"instruction" in the narrow sense. In this book we are referring to a kind of teaching that includes guiding children's social and emotional development, as well as their developmentally appropriate cognitive education. This broad definition is in keeping with the National Association for the Education of Young Children's publication on developmentally appropriate practice—geared to the entire developing child and not just his mind (S. Bredekamp and C. Copple, eds., *Developmentally Appropriate Practice in Early Childhood Programs.* Washington, DC: NAEYC 1998). The definition is also in line with the concept of emotional intelligence (D. Goleman, *Emotional Intelligence,* New York: Bantam Books, 1995).

Back in the 1980s, an "assertive" model of discipline maintained that the role of the teacher is to teach and the role of the student is to learn. If one is teaching for healthy social and emotional development, "whole child" education, then this sentiment is only partially correct. The teacher also learns, and the child also teaches. Teaching is interactive; it includes listening, learning, and sharing, as well as leading and guiding. Certainly teaching is not just "instruction."

Building the encouraging classroom is a significant goal for teachers. In the encouraging classroom, children decide it is safe for them to be, to grow, and to learn. They willingly engage in activities. They initiate contacts and relationships with others. They allow themselves to be comforted. They grow in empathy. They begin to make choices intelligently and ethically—with consideration for those around them. A large reason for productive learning and living in the encouraging classroom is that children feel they have a part and can contribute. The teacher is there not just to tell them what they should know and do—and by extension what they do not know and cannot do. The teacher is there leading, but also learning and living with them. This is why the encouraging classroom is a caring community. All are helping all others in a process of healthy life development.

This chapter is different from the others. It is about what children in the encouraging classroom contribute to us, even more than the other way around. With only months of development and experience instead of years, they come without the benefits (and the baggage) of centuries of historical tradition. Lacking the entrapments of cultural sophistication, children really do see that the emperor has no clothes, or sometimes too many clothes—or maybe even both! Not always sure where reality ends and imagination begins, young children see the world so literally, yet so freshly. Not yet equipped with the brain development and personal experience to fully comprehend other people's perspectives, young children view events with "developmental egocentrism"—the innocent kind. In making sense of situations, children don't yet understand adult sophistication, symbolism, and not-so-naive egocentrism.

After more than 30 years in classrooms with young children, the wonder and humor in their actions and words still totally beguile me. "Been there, done that" is such an adult—or rather adolescent—expression that some of us wince the first time we hear a child say it. Maybe this is the key: If we don't begrudge our own lost innocence in how children interpret situations, we are free to celebrate life with them. The wonder of children helps us to stay fresh—despite the poor wages, benefits, and working conditions that many early childhood teachers endure. In early childhood education, we have a gift that is missing in most other professions: the promise of our own renewal.

So it is no mystery that teachers delight in the things that young children say and do. In fact, the humor we find in the classroom is vital. Our enjoyment celebrates the community we are creating with children. If we grin discreetly and convey appreciation to the child, then we are not laughing at, but with, our fellow community members. We are not putting down the younger members of our community, but appreciating one another's unique worth. One concern I have about the book, and especially this chapter, is its "voyeuristic" nature (viewing for selfish gratification). After some thought, my response is that by looking fully at what young children say and do—and by understanding how they touch us and our lives—we can better reach and teach them.

The anecdotes in this chapter show children openly sharing their personal thoughts with the adults in their lives. Note how the teachers support and encourage children's honest expressions. Note as well the many reminders of the innocent intelligence that is inherent in young children. In the encouraging classroom, one way to look at our job is helping children retain their intelligence even as their growing up erodes their innocence. As mentioned, good teaching is interactive. As the teachers encourage children in the open exploration of ideas, the children are enriching their teachers' lives.

The anecdotes that follow are divided into these topics of conversation between adults and children:

- Word meanings
- Colorful language
- Dealing with emotions
- Their bodies—themselves
- Holidays, holy places, and ceremonies
- Wonder
- Grandmas and other wondrous things

Readers may notice that teachers' reflections about the observations are generally missing in this chapter. Most of the teachers who submitted these particular anecdotes didn't offer commentary. Without further ado, here are the anecdotes—with just a bit of professorial definition.

Word Meanings

A famous quote on language development states that children use language not to learn about language, but to learn about life. The idea is that we shouldn't diminish children's efforts at communicating by correcting their choice of words. We listen to the content of what they say and model the conventional language in our response. With our listening and modeling, they will use "the correct terms" when they are developmentally and experientially ready. Nonetheless, language holds magic for children who have been encouraged to use it. When a young child uses words imaginatively—even if not quite conventionally—we can appreciate the miracle of a developing mind at work. The first two anecdotes in this section are from early childhood educators about their own children, a reminder that a child's love of language begins in the home.

OBSERVATION: *We had ordered pizza and were having a carpet picnic. I looked over at Alex and told her, "I think you are too cute and I love you to pieces!" She leaned towards me, smiled, and said, "I love you to pizza too!"*

Who would correct the language, when the sentiment is so clear?

When encouraged to use language, children find fascination in words. As they approach school age, young children even appreciate words that are "secret." Adults enjoy a child's secret as well, especially when it is kept as well as this one:

OBSERVATION: *Last night Tyler came running. "Mom, I have a secret!" I said, "Wow, can you tell me what it is?"*

"I can't tell you," Tyler said, "I don't even know it. It's so private, I can't even tell myself!"

Some of life's mysteries are better appreciated than probed.

Children sometimes have difficulty explaining their connections to relatives. Who can blame them, as complex as family structures can be? Perhaps we should just be content with giving them credit for trying, as Sherry, the mother in the preceding anecdote, discovered in her kindergarten class.

OBSERVATION: *Two of the little boys in my class came up to me today, and one said, "Teacher, did you know that Ron and me are regulated?"*

"Really," I said. "Tell me about that."

He explained with pride, "We're cousins!"

For children to share their ideas about the world, they have to know that the teacher is listening. Sherry's comment, "Tell me about that," made this situation interactive. When she shared this comment with the two parents later that day, Sherry mentioned that all three laughed and wondered who was doing the regulating—it wasn't any of them!

Conversations with young children do have their moments of hilarity, of course, which teachers invariably handle with the utmost respect and decorum. Well, at least they try:

OBSERVATION: *We were reading name cards today, when the names "Presley," "Peter," and "Petula" came up in a row. We discussed how each name started with a "P...P...P." Later Petula, quite taken with this spontaneous lesson about her name, came up to me and said, "Teacher, I have to go "p...p...potty."*

Smiling benignly, I said, "Go ahead, P...P...Petula."

When she came out of the restroom to wash her hands, she proudly announced, "Teacher, I went p...p...pee and p...p...poop too!"

Colorful Language

When children and the world of words get together, there is no guarantee that kids will always choose the words that teachers would prefer. As with all words, young children are learning the meaning of expletives. This learning process was once brought home to me in a nonverbal way when a child, angry at a student teacher for taking away his truck, flipped her off using the wrong finger! An example from my own experience with the "s-word" illustrates this learning process.

OBSERVATION: *I had heard Karen talking to herself in the corner of the room. She must have been practicing because when I approached her, she looked up at me with a grin and said, "Shit, teacher."*

Now, this was Karen's second year in my class, and she was a pretty strong-minded kid. I knew if I ragged on her that I never wanted to hear that word at school again...I would. So, I knelt down to look her in the eye and said quietly but firmly, "Karen, I like how you are always learning new words, but this is not a word we use at Head Start because it bothers people. You keep learning new words, okay, but maybe don't use that one?" Karen considered what I said and nodded, with just a touch of indignation. I didn't hear her use that word at Head Start again.

It is hard enough for a self-respecting kid to learn the actual "bad" words, but then there are those "sanitary" word substitutes. They can get complicated for a kid and sometimes take a while to get right:

OBSERVATION: *Paula on the bus, "Teacher, Sheila used the four-letter word."*

I was worried because I knew that Paula's father was "big in law" in our community, so I asked, "Oh, she used the four-letter word?"

"Yes, she said shut up!"

And another example:

OBSERVATION: *I was listening to some kids play today. One little girl was pretty vocal. When in one sentence she got out the words "piss," and "shit," and "ass" and "hell," I was on my way over there!*

All of a sudden, this same girl screamed, "Teacher, he said a bad word to me!"

I said, "Well, I've been hearing a lot of words we don't use in school."

She said, "Yeah and this was the 'b' word," and then she whispered to me, "Be quiet."

At least the child was beginning to show phonetic recognition skills! Many times when children use strong words, they are doing so in place of acting out physically. The angry language often is a request for teacher assistance, before they lose total control. For teachers who use guidance, using words instead of hitting is progress; this is step one. With our assistance over time, we will see children make further progress toward step two, using language we can all live with.

While we have a right to enforce standards of civility in our classroom communities—and should—we have to remember that swearing is pretty common among adults. We might as well not make a federal case about something that is happening on every street corner. Still, as the final anecdote about expletives shows, a teacher (me in this case) never stops trying:

> **RECOLLECTION:** *A few weeks into the year, I noticed that a young four year old, Rodney, had a habit of saying, "Damn it to hell," whenever anything went wrong—which seemed to happen a lot. The assistant teacher told me I had to do something about it, so I did. When Rodney and I had finished reading a book, and he was relatively relaxed, I told him, "Rodney, you know those words you say when you are bothered about something?" Rodney said them, so I knew he did. I explained how those words bother people at Head Start and I would give him some other words to say when he got upset. I noticed real interest in Rodney's expression, so I whispered significantly, "Ding-dong it."*
>
> *Rodney nodded knowingly. The next day when he got upset about something, he exclaimed, "Oh ding-dong it, damn it to hell!" Realizing that I had increased his vocabulary rather than changing it, I did the broken record routine and explained it all again, much to my assistant teacher's amusement.*

Dealing with Emotions

Because we are human and neither angelic nor robotic, emotions play a central role in our lives. A baby feels hungry, tired, lonely, or uncomfortable, and cries. As children grow, putting these feelings into words becomes a great challenge for them. Young children know what their task is, but experience shows that even some adults have not mastered emotional intelligence. We adults do well to remember that young children have months of life experience to draw from, not years. When an adult listens and gives children credit for their efforts, she is encouraging them to keep trying. Often, though, before giving the encouragement a teacher can't help but smile.

OBSERVATION: *Jaime, who had just turned three, wanted a toy that another child had. Jaime started whimpering. Sue, the teacher, said, "Jaime, use your words." After a lip-quivering moment, Jaime replied, "I can't find any!"*

The teacher might suggest some words that Jaime can try, and stay with Jaime to see him through the problem. Over time, she encourages the child to find the words on his own. At the moment, she smiles.

In some situations when children do find the words, however, not smiling can be a challenge. You have to admire how hard Clara, the kindergarten teacher in the next anecdote, must have worked to remain encouraging to Dean.

OBSERVATION: *In my kindergarten I had a little boy named Dean who was very shy. One day for "Show and Tell" he raised his hand and quietly mumbled, "I had to wear these shoes today because I got b'ture on my good ones." I asked him what he had said. He again mumbled it. I said, "You got what?" He looked at me in frustration and said loud and clear, "Cow shit!"*

Sometimes you have to accentuate the positive, especially when you've put your foot in it yourself. "Oh, Dean, now I know what you said! You got cow manure on your shoe. That's not much fun, is it?" One of the most widespread phobias in the United States is a fear of public speaking. When a child speaks up in a group situation, we need to be inclusive of his comments—even when they are embarrassing—so that he still feels part of the group and not separated from it. Anyway, who has not gotten manure of one kind or another on his shoe?

Some children (like some adults) enjoy playing but not picking up after themselves. When the time comes to put things away, early childhood teachers often put on music to induce a cleanup frame of mind. Still, the following musical expression of feelings was not what this teacher had in mind.

OBSERVATION: *As they played with the table toys this morning, Darla and Chelsea were singing the commercial, "What would you do for a Klondike Bar?" over and over. At the end of work time, I got after Darla because she was letting Chelsea do all the picking up. As Darla began to help, she was quietly singing to the tune of the commercial, "What would you do for a new teacher?"*

At least the kid was cleaning up! If we watch for it in their actions and words, we can see children putting effort into expressing their emotions acceptably. Sometimes their efforts make us shake our heads and grin. Sometimes, as the following anecdote suggests, they make us feel proud.

OBSERVATION: *Sean and Tevin are cousins in our center-based Head Start program. While in the active playroom, they both wanted the tricycle with the larger wheels. After a short pull-and-tug session, Sean overpowered Tevin and rode away. Tevin began to cry very loudly. Sean stopped, came back and gave him the tricycle. Sean spotted me watching their exchange and said, "He felt more bad than me and he was crying harder."*

Their Bodies, Themselves

Children have a natural interest in their bodies and body functions. They should; it's where they live all day long. Children bring an uninhibited thoughtfulness to their curiosity. Who else but a four year old could link up George Washington and going to the bathroom in the same sentence?

OBSERVATION: *One February we were talking about the presidents. Chelsea was really interested in George Washington. Her mom said she talked about George when they got home, so they looked him up in the encyclopedia. The next morning the farmer near our center was unloading manure from the barn—and the wind was just right. Chelsea asked what that awful smell was and we explained what the farmer was doing. Chelsea asked what manure was, so we told her. Later that day Chelsea was sitting in the bathroom and yelled out to me, "I'll bet George Washington hasn't gone manure for a really long time!"*

Using the bathroom is a matter-of-fact thing for young children. A child just naturally learns and brings to school her family's practices around the bathroom.

OBSERVATION: *Annie, age four, was in the bathroom one afternoon, and I was waiting for her in the hall. A maintenance worker was hanging a bulletin board right outside of the bathroom door. He was pounding nails. Annie heard this knocking and yelled, "It is all right, you can come in." Besides being hilarious, I thought it was great that she must have privacy at home and adults must respect it.*

Children are curious about your body too, which any early childhood teacher who has ever worn panty hose at work has discovered, so I'm told. Sometimes, their comments just make you smile.

OBSERVATION: *I habitually wore jeans or casual pants to work, but one day I had to go to a state meeting right from work. Near the end of the day I went into the bathroom to change into a suit and stockings. I came out in my new attire. One of the two year olds, Crystal, looked at me with absolute astonishment, caressed my nylon-clad legs in wonder, and stammered, "What, what... who are you?"*

Did you ever notice how easily children work human physiology—especially yours—into the early childhood curriculum?

OBSERVATION: *I was lying down with my eyes closed during rest. Tawny whispered, "Teacher, can I ask you something?" I said sure. "Where do your eyes go when you're sleeping?"*

"Owies" have significance for children, of course. They also are concerned about your owies, so be prepared.

OBSERVATION: *I had just had surgery. During story time, Scott, age three, said, "Can I sit on your lap?" I answered, "Not yet." He whispered, "Do you still have your owie?" I said yes. Then he asked, "Can I see it?" I whispered back, "No, I'd have to take my pants down." He didn't say anything for a while, then whispered, "Let's go in the bathroom."*

If I use the terms "storks" and "cabbage patches," younger readers may guess that I am talking about dolls or Saturday morning television, which is good. Because of discomfort with "the facts of life," adults used to make up stories to explain to children where babies came from. Two famous ones were, "The stork brought you," and "We found you in a cabbage patch." The other extreme, of course, is to be totally honest and give a detailed explanation. There is a famous story about a father who did this when his son asked him where he came from. After the dad finished some minutes later, the son responded, "That's funny. I thought we came from Chicago."

There are anatomically correct picture books out there, and I know of a Head Start teacher who uses this approach to sex education: She lets the parents know ahead of time, invites a nurse in, and the nurse reads the books and has very interesting discussions with the children. The teacher says the nurse lends a note of authority to the situation, and the children really pay attention. They probably would anyway if the teacher read the book—but whatever works.

In any case, even young children are a bit more knowledgeable than previous generations about the reproductive process.

OBSERVATION: *My daughter-in-law, who is a massage therapist, came to visit our family child care. While visiting, she talked about a client who was pregnant and couldn't lie in bed. A child in the program, Nadine overheard and asked, "How could she get pregnant if she can't lie down?"*

The teacher did not say how they answered Nadine's question. Sometimes, when adults do take time to explain things to children, the message may get lost when the context changes.

OBSERVATION: *A group of children were playing basketball. They were four and five year olds so the boundaries were the fence enclosing the playground. Many times one would run by with the ball, a group of children chasing behind. I was nine months pregnant at the time and had on a red jacket stretched tightly over my stomach. The basketball bounced past me and Jordan ran over to me and asked me for the ball. I told him, "I don't have the ball."*
He put his hands on his hips and said, "I want the ball!"
Once again, I told him, "But I don't have the ball."

He looked at me angrily, put his hand on my stomach, and said, "Then what is that?"

I loved his comment because it shows just how children think. It also showed me that what may be so obvious to adults, children may be oblivious to. We had discussed the fact that I was having a baby many times.

Holidays, Holy Places, and Ceremonies

Children are careful onlookers to the formalized events of families and schools. They often feel grown up if they are allowed to participate, and left out if they are not. Formal holiday events are important landmarks for them, even if their take on an event is a bit different.

OBSERVATION: *A few years ago at Christmas time, a little girl's granddad volunteered to play Santa Claus. We were all waiting for Santa to arrive, and the little girl was kneeling on the couch watching out of the window when her grand-dad drove up. He was in the Santa suit and driving his red Suburban. The little girl got very excited and stated, "I did not know that Santa drove a red Suburban!"*

In the following anecdote, two children show unauthorized creativity while making "Frosty the Snowman" and justify their efforts by telling stories about their artwork:

RECOLLECTION: *A kindergarten teacher had read the book* Frosty the Snowman *to her children, and together they had watched the video and sung the song. It was now art time, and the teacher showed the children a model of Frosty, and explained the traced parts and how to cut them out and glue them together. She put her Frosty model face down and told the children, "But you don't have to make Frosty if you don't want to. You can make your own snowman."*

As the teacher helped children on one side of the room, a group from the other side came up, grabbed the Frosty model, and took it back to their table so they could copy it. Some children, of course, started right up and made Frosties approximately like the teacher's. Some started, then stopped and said, "Teacher, help me." A few children didn't start at all.

Two children had Frosties different from the rest. One accidentally put the biggest circle in the middle. When the teacher stopped by his table and gave him a quizzical look, he grinned and said, "My Frosty's been doing body building."

Another took the white piece of paper that had the traced circles on it and turned it over. With a black marker he made a ground line with a mound in the middle. He then took his yellow marker and colored the mound. The teacher couldn't believe her eyes when she saw his picture, and made him explain. He did: "My Frosty melted and my dog came and peed on him." The teacher later called the parent to report what had happened. To the teacher's surprise, the parent laughed and explained that this series of events had actually happened to Preston's snowman over the weekend!

Even around holidays, a developmentally appropriate approach to art is to not use a model. Instead, the teacher discusses a broad seasonal theme, then asks the children to make their own creations, expressing what the season means to them. When one preschool teacher used the "spoken motivation" approach before winter break, she was delighted with the picture that Karen decided to make about Rudolph. Karen drew Rudolph with a yellow nose, "So Santa can see better." In her creative picture, Karen actually improved on the whole Rudolph concept. After all, where do you want your headlights and where do you want your taillights?

When children see their teachers outside of school, in stores, at movies, or on the street, they are excited to see them. With each such experience, including home visits, their definition of "teacher" expands, and they begin to view these important adults not just as role players, but as human beings. (Ask an early childhood class where they think you eat and sleep after school and see what they say.)

OBSERVATION: *One Sunday my husband and I were ushers at church. Following the service, the mother of one of my kindergarten students said that her son had been so excited to see me in that capacity that he said, "I can't believe it! Pat's a gusher today!"*

Pat, an experienced kindergarten teacher, takes ceremonial occasions in her classroom with a grain of salt. She does what she needs to, like allowing the American Legion to come in and hand out little flags, but understands clearly that young children are just starting to understand what ceremonies are about.

RECOLLECTION: *I usually wait until late in the year to introduce my kindergarten children to the Pledge of Allegiance. My decision to delay was more than reinforced when I once heard a child say, "I pledge Norwegians to the flag...." And, another comment "...And to the Republicans, for which I stand..." I get them used to reciting the Pledge, but I sure don't expect them to understand the words!*

Back in 1950, when I was in kindergarten, Miss Brannic had us say, "Red, white, and blue, we all love you." I guess times were simpler then.

Wonder

Wonder is a delightful word, in spite of the bread company that co-opted it. Wonder happens for both child and adult in much of what we find amusing in children's words. We wonder for a moment at the wondering that children do so naturally, so much of the time. For children, wondering is serious business, their way of learning about the world. We need to appreciate the sense of wonder in children. But at the same time, while we wonder at their wonder, sometimes it is hard not to chuckle, or at least smile.

OBSERVATION: *Before the home visit I was about to go on, I had a quick breakfast with the three-year-old group. That was something! They were talking about birthdays when I sat down at the table and one little boy said, "I have one more birthday left!"*

Debbie, the assistant teacher, replied, "You only have one more birthday left? Why is that?"

The little boy answered her, "'Cause then I'll be four!"

Debbie said, "I hope you have another birthday, you don't stay four years old all your life, you know."

The little boy looked at her and then joined a discussion about another topic. I think that maybe he had been hearing about other kids' fourth birthdays throughout the year. His birthday is coming up and this was a big accomplishment—so that's as far as he can see right now.

OBSERVATION: *I was sitting at the breakfast table when Karla said to Lois, the teacher, "We have a long, long way to go before we die." Lois asked her how she knew that. Karla said, "Just 'cause we're little, and we have a long way to go." She then picked up her plate and cleared away her utensils and napkin.*

Julie, the student teacher in these two anecdotes, indicated that neither she nor Lois knew of a loss in Karla's family. It is possible that Karla and her mom had simply had a contact talk, and this was what Karla took away from the conversation. The wondering by children about birthdays, the length of a lifetime, and even death, reminds us how much about life there is for them to learn. Sometimes there are no answers; our role is to listen, reassure, and perhaps wonder ourselves.

A source of wonderment for teachers is the variety of topics that children wonder about—not just life's big questions, but also more practical matters.

OBSERVATION: *Matt and I were doing an activity with paper when our conversation began.*

Matt: I know where paper comes from.

Kellie: You do? Where?

Matt: From trees!

Kellie: You are right. Do you know how they get paper from trees?

Matt: Yep! It's inside.

Kellie: So, if I go to a tree out there and peel off the bark there will be a piece of white paper inside?

Matt: (holding his hands about one foot apart) Yep. But you gotta go in about this far.

Kellie: Oh! So let me see if I got this right. If I go peel bark off a tree and go in about this far, there will be a bunch of white paper inside?

Matt: Yeah! But you gotta go way to the top! That's a very dangerous job, you know.

Kellie: I bet it is. Well, what about this purple paper? Where does purple paper come from?

Matt: Oh, that comes from apple trees!

Kellie: What about red paper?

Matt: Lava. That comes from lava.

Our conversation faded here and we went back to doing the activity.

A traditional concern of teachers is not to pass incorrect information on to students. When children have their facts mixed up, we often feel a need to correct. However, it's important to remember that children are not only expressing ideas in their conversations with adults, but also getting feedback about the worthiness of their conversing. What message do we give them if we consistently correct them?

As children grow, what seems true to them today will not seem true next year. The teacher's goal in talking with children is neither to impart truth, nor to correct children's thinking. Our goal is to encourage confidence and competence in children's communication skills as a lifelong means for acquiring, evaluating, and sharing information.

To state this another way, we are less concerned with the correctness of children's information than with their ability to improve their own sense of correctness as they grow and learn over time. When children's insight is appreciated even though their information base is limited, they gain the confidence to continue in the process of finding meaning for themselves.

OBSERVATION: *We were outdoors one afternoon during winter. At this time of the year, the Alaskan sky was very dark all day. A quarter moon was up. An older (age five) sister, Shayla, had slid down the hill with her younger (age three) sister. They were lying at the bottom of the hill. Shayla pointed to the moon and said, "Look, it's broken."*

At that time of the year, with the light being so dim, kind of like twilight, everything seems magical. I remember thinking that Shayla's conclusion seemed so natural. As I think back about it now, I wonder if there were stories about the moon in Shayla's Inuit community of Kotzebue.

Grandmas and Other Wondrous Things

Because they are so unpredictable to teachers, the many topics of children's wonder contribute to our own wonderment. Sometimes children's wonder is tied to the natural world—the source of paper, or the shape of the moon. Other times, children's wonder comes back to persons dear in their lives. Often that person is a grandparent. One reason may be that grandparents so obviously care about their grandkids.

> **OBSERVATION:** *When I was outdoors with the toddler group, I was admiring Frannie's boots. I told her that my feet were cold and that I sure wished I had a pair of boots like hers. She asked me why I didn't. I said that I just didn't and she said, "Didn't your Grandma buy you any?"*

Another reason may be that grandparents sometimes are distant from the child and are missed. Perhaps because they are not always there when needed, grandparents can have a mystique for children—can be a source of elaborate wonder. The following anecdote reminds us of the rich generation of ideas we see in children when we let them express their wonder to us.

> **OBSERVATION:** *I had the following contact talk in a child care center with a four year old named Linnea:*
>
> *Linnea: Where Nikki (a cousin) lives has a lot of snow.*
> *Sharon: Yes, there sure is a lot of snow where Nikki lives.*
> *Linnea: We have a lot of snow too.*
> *Sharon: Yes, we have a lot of snow. What do you think about all of this snow?*
> *Linnea: It's very assiting!*
> *Sharon: It is very exciting. What is your favorite thing to do in the snow?*
> *Linnea: We maked angels last night. Mom and Dad and Eric did too, but Dad said mine was best.*
> *Sharon: You made angels last night? I love to make angels!*
> *Linnea: But my hat fell off and my head got real freezy so I had to go in and put on a different hat instead.*

Sharon: I bet that was pretty cold. I like to catch snowflakes on my tongue when it snows.

Linnea: Me too, they feel funny on my tongue. Sometimes when I do that they get in my eyes, but it doesn't hurt, it's just that oochy feeling. Hey, do you know how it snows 'cause I do.

Sharon: Will you tell me how it snows?

Linnea: Well, I think that Santa brings the snow in his sleigh and drops it over us—the clouds tell him when to. He has a machine on the back that shoots it out.

Sharon: Wow! I didn't know that was how it snowed. Santa is sure busy.

Linnea: Yeah, but Rudolph and Clixen and all those guys help. (whisper) Do you who fixes the snower when it's broke? (No time to respond.) Mrs. Claus does and my mom says girls can do that.

Sharon: It's good that Santa has all that help, and I bet Mrs. Claus is good at fixing things.

Linnea: Yeah, but Santa doesn't bring it everywhere 'cause my grandma lives in Azizona and she said they don't ever get snow there.

Sharon: Why do you think they don't get snow in Arizona?

Linnea: It's too far for Santa to drive. My mom says it's too far for us to drive. I wanted to go last night. We went one time on a big airplane, it was scary, but only a little.

Sharon: It is a long way to Arizona. Your grandma must be a pretty important person to you and I bet you miss her.

Linnea: She's my favorite.

Sharon: What is your favorite thing about your grandma?

Linnea: But—I think there might be another way it snows.

Sharon: I'd like to hear about it. Could you tell me about the other way it snows?

Linnea: Maybe the clouds just melt cause they move in front of the sun and the sun is hot and then they melt.

Sharon: That's neat, maybe the sun does melt the clouds. It's pretty sunny in Arizona, do you think that if it got cloudy there that it might snow?

Linnea: (Laughing) No!! There's too much cactuses. Didn't you know there are cactus everywhere there? We saw big ones that were bigger than my dad and they had really sharp prickles on them.

Sharon: How do the cactus keep it from snowing?

Linnea: Because, silly, snow doesn't like the prickles on the cactuses! When the snow gets on a prickle, it hurts them and they don't like that, so that's why.

Wonder involves the use of imagination in a particularly open-ended way. Where there is wonder, there is thinking, brain development, and learning. In this final anecdote of the chapter, an underlying message in Linnea's conversation with Sharon is that Grandma is her favorite—perhaps because Grandma, like Sharon, is easy to talk to. Yet, Linnea talked about so much else as well. When we allow children to wonder, so much learning goes on. Of course, teachers learn, as well as the children.

When children fully engage their imaginations and share their wonder with us, we need to appreciate both the child and the experience. Through the expression of wonder, children begin to explore what is true and what is not—and risk adult criticism. When children share their wonder with us, they are hoping for a bond of trust. With this bond, the developmental process of making meaning about the world can continue. An additional benefit of supporting wonder, of course, is that it makes the classroom a pleasant place to be. Wonder and humor are central to building the encouraging classroom. By our responses to the things children say and do, we teachers both encourage the caring community to happen, and delight in the positive interaction that occurs as it builds.

Suggested Readings

Chenfeld, Mimi. "Do Spider Webs Ever Wake You Up? (Oh the Wonder of It All!)" *Young Children* 50, no. 5 (July 1995): 70–71.

Chenfeld, Mimi. "Welcome to Lala's Land." *Young Children* 51, no. 5 (July 1996): 4–5.

Fuhler, Carol J., Pamela J. Farris, and Maria P. Walther. "Promoting Reading and Writing through Humor and Hope." *Childhood Education* 76, no. 1 (Fall 1999).

Discussion Activities

For reasons of professionalism, as you respond to these discussion activities, please respect the privacy of all children, adults, programs, and schools.

1. Recall the funniest thing a child ever said—either to you or in your presence.

What might an adult reaction be if he or she chose to laugh at the child for the comment made? What might an adult reaction be if he or she chose to appreciate the child for the comment made? What impact might each adult response have on the child?

2. How do you decide whether an adult is appreciating the humor in a child's comment, or making fun of the child for the comment?

3. What might be the reasons that an adult chooses to make fun of a child's comment—in front of the child? Later with other adults? What might you do to help an adult who seems to be making fun of a child's comment realize that this reaction is not okay?

The Encouraging Classroom

The encouraging classroom is a place where children want to be even when they are sick, as opposed to not wanting to be there when they are well. It is a caring community within the physical boundaries of the class. It is a place where children feel at home when they are out of the home. In fact, if this were a textbook, the definition of an encouraging classroom would be:

The physical surroundings of a school, center, or family child care program, in which adults provide ongoing guidance in order to maintain an equilibrium between the needs of each developing member, and the right of the caring community to mutual appreciation among its members. It constitutes the creation and sustenance of a caring community among children and adults, within the physical boundaries of the group.

Good thing this isn't a textbook.

The encouraging classroom begins within the minds of its teachers. In the encouraging classroom, teachers work hard to sustain the dynamic balance (the equilibrium) between the changing needs of each individual (adults and children), and the right of the community to mutual appreciation. The equilibrium between the individual and the group is difficult to maintain because young children are just learning to express and meet their needs. Remember that expressing and meeting individual needs in socially acceptable ways are long-term democratic life skills. We work on these skills our entire lives. Young children are just starting this lifelong work.

In an encouraging classroom, a teacher guides children to a good start, even, and especially, when children make mistakes in the learning process—when they show mistaken behavior. Guidance, which is the approach teachers use to build the encouraging classroom, actively teaches children to express and meet needs acceptably. Unlike teachers who use traditional discipline, teachers using a guidance approach do not threaten the child's membership in the community in order to motivate better behavior. The child's place in the classroom community, except in rare situations, which must involve parents, is not up for discussion.

These days teachers work to build encouraging classrooms within the context of a broad trend called "educational accountability." We now are hearing discussions about educational accountability even in kindergarten and prekindergarten classrooms. Early childhood teachers increasingly hear words such as *portfolio, observational assessment, anecdotal observations,* and *outcome attainment.* Educational accountability, which means teachers need to be accountable for the education they are providing, is vital at all levels of education, including early childhood. One benefit that has come from this movement is general acceptance of *developmentally appropriate practice,* a priority of the National Association for the Education of Young Children.

A danger in the trend, however, is the confusion of educational accountability with political accountability. When officials put inappropriate pressures on schools and programs to achieve, for the sake of reputation and appearances, they put both teachers and children at risk. Teachers begin to expect too much of children and use forced teaching and discipline techniques—and inappropriate methods of assessment. With the imposition of developmentally *in*appropriate practice, children are unable to meet teacher expectations. They experience frustration, resentment, and a sense of failure. Creating an encouraging classroom becomes very difficult under these circumstances. To keep the difference clear, we need to remember the words of my friend Pat, who teaches kindergarten. She said, "My job is not to prepare children for first grade. My job is to give children the best possible kindergarten experience they can have." This statement—which pertains as well to preschool—is an eloquent reminder of what educational accountability really is and what political accountability is not. Educational accountability in the encouraging classroom consists of observing the progress children make in beginning to learn democratic life skills. The current chapter shares with the reader indicators of that progress, by observing the words and actions of children in relation to the issues raised in the book:

- In chapter one we noted children's progress in separating from the home and attaching to adults in the classroom.
- In chapter two we saw children able to affirm family identity through the classroom community.
- In chapter three we examined children's ability to move from safety to growth and take the initiative to engage in learning experiences.
- In chapter four we observed children showing minor mistaken behavior from full involvement in life.
- In chapter five we viewed children's progress in social problem-solving as they move from high-level meditation, to low-level mediation, to child negotiation—and ultimately to cooperation.
- In chapter six we examined the progress children make in moving from loss to resiliency.
- In chapter seven, we witnessed the gains in thinking and communication skills when children feel free to engage in wonder.

Separation and Attachment

In chapter one, we looked at children's transition process as they separate from the home and build an attachment with teachers in the classroom. Teachers build attachments by supporting children through the transition, and by modeling and teaching mutual appreciation. As we might expect, the attachment process takes longer for some children than for others. The following anecdote from Janeen, a Head Start teacher, charts one child who has found a secure enough place in the classroom to accept the teachers' guidelines for solving problems. The other child, feeling the weight of personal difficulties from outside of

WHAT THE KIDS SAID TODAY

school, is having problems adjusting. In a clear conflict situation, the teachers work as a team to support both children.

OBSERVATION: *I walked out onto the playground and immediately saw that a child from another room was hitting Kevin, who stood against the fence with his arms up over his head. I hurried over and arrived at the same time as the teacher of the other child. She pulled the child off of Kevin, and we both knelt down, holding each child, to talk to them. Before either of us said anything, Kevin looked at the other child and said, "It made me very mad when you hit me." He told the other boy, "You're supposed to use words, not hit." The boy from the other class did not respond in any way during the discussion. I thanked Kevin for using his words and not hitting back. The teacher stayed to talk with the other boy.*

REFLECTION: *Kevin knew that he should not hit the other child. However, he did not feel comfortable using his words until there was a teacher standing near him. Once he had a chance to express himself, he kept talking, even though he was getting no response. For some time Kevin has showed us that he is learning to solve problems maturely, and he sure showed us that today.*

When children who have serious problems act out in encouraging classrooms, they often do so because it is the safest place in their lives. They are asking for help with their problems—inappropriately, but in the only way they can. The other child's teacher indicated to Janeen that there would be a staff meeting concerning him that day, and that they would meet with the family soon. Some children need extra help to find a safe place, even in encouraging classrooms. In the caring classroom community, teachers assist all children to get the help they need to find a place.

Attachments in early childhood classrooms are never permanent. The security of a child's connection to a classroom is tried when staff leave. Turnover is a problem in early childhood programs, because of low salaries and challenging working conditions. In the following observation, a student teacher is leaving because the semester is over, and a child is working hard to understand and adjust.

OBSERVATION: *I was sitting on the carpet when Jared came up behind me and gave me a big hug. He said, "I'm gonna miss you."*

I said, "I'm gonna miss you too, but I'll come back and visit."
Brief pause, then he said, "Would you read me a book?"
I said, "Sure." He walked off to find a book.

REFLECTION: *My last day was hard for me, and I think it was hard on the children too. Jared is very sensitive, and we formed a bond, so I will have to go back and visit. I was glad we could read the book together.*

The difference between how children first leave their homes for school and how they part with a teacher they have become attached to says so much. Jared has extended his world to the classroom, and the community there has made it possible for him to say good-bye.

Identification with the Family

In chapter two, we noted that the child is an extension of the family, and children in the classroom need to be able to find meaning in this identification. Teachers cannot impose change on family situations. Neither should they criticize families in ways that force the child to choose between the culture of the family and the culture of the school. So what does a teacher do when a child shares something inappropriate, like "Teacher do you know how to wrap a joint? The striped paper works better." Teachers talk together and make hard decisions (no joke here; four year olds shouldn't have this information). If they decide there is immediate danger to the child, they follow the reporting policy used by the school or program. If not, they say something like, "Jed, talking about how to wrap a joint bothers a lot of people. It is something we don't do or talk about at school." Hopefully, teachers have developed relationships with parents, so that they can bring the matter up in a way that won't escalate the problem. They also monitor Jed's behavior for other signs of inappropriate influence by others.

Through partnerships with parents, as well as attachment with the child, teachers demonstrate acceptance both of the child and his family. One indication of a child's awareness of this acceptance is a growing ability to express pleasures and concerns about family life. The ability to talk about family life with a teacher marks a degree of trust in the relationship. The teacher handles such conversations sensitively with the child, and professionally when speaking to other adults about it.

> **OBSERVATION:** *I was talking with Brody while we were reading a book during play.*
>
> *Brody: Teacher, my mom is divorced, right?*
> *Me: That's right, Brody.*
> *Brody: (pausing to think) That means she can get married, right, teacher?*
> *Me: Yes, she can.*
> *Brody: Well, if she does, then I would have a dad that lives with us, or at least in Minnesota this time.*
> *Me: If your mom got married, probably he would live with you, Brody.*
> *Brody: Good.*

> **REFLECTION:** *Brody had been hurting all year about his parents' divorce. The dad was now someplace out of state. I'd talked with Brody's mom and we have been working together with Brody. This was the first time he had talked about the divorce with me. I was pleased he could put his thoughts in words. I'd better let his mom know, though, sounds like Brody may be making plans!*

Young children feel a real sense of connection when they know that parents and teachers are on friendly terms. Children do better in school when teachers and parents work together as a team. By doing so, they bring children's separate worlds together.

Initiative and Learning

In chapter three we examined children's ability to move from safety to growth and take the initiative to engage in learning experiences. Authorities who want to hold teachers politically accountable invariably prioritize assessment. Often their focus is too narrow, measuring academic or pre-academic skills. In early childhood, the most significant cognitive gain children make is the leap from safety to growth, taking the initiative to become consistently engaged in learning experiences. Through active engagement in the encouraging classroom, brain development happens and developmentally appropriate learning occurs (Julee Newberger, "New Brain Development Research—A Wonderful Window of Opportunity to Build Public Support for Early Childhood Education, *Young Children* 52 [4], May 1997, 4–9).

To document this all-important process of *engagement,* we can look at a beginning effort by a younger preschool child, and advanced efforts by three big kindergarten kids and three older preschoolers.

OBSERVATION: *Caleb, who had just turned three, was playing in the house area by himself. He had a bunch of food set out on the table and was making sandwiches and other dishes. I sat at the table with him and tried to get a conversation going, but he's extremely quiet and didn't say much. When he did talk I could barely hear what he said over the noise of the room.*

Eventually more kids came over and started playing with the food. Caleb shared the food he had and also played along with them. He helped them sort things and make more meals. He didn't say much of anything, but he did play.

REFLECTION: *Caleb is extremely quiet and not vocal at all. He always plays by himself and never says a word. He never even says anything if someone takes a toy he is playing with. I was surprised today because he actually played with some other children. It was nice to see him do that and not play alone. He didn't talk to the other children very much, but at least he was with them and didn't leave the house area. It's not that he can't talk, he just seems like he's not ready to.*

So how does this anecdote illustrate a child's progress toward taking initiative and learning when the kid isn't saying anything? The big difference between political accountability and educational accountability is this: To boost appearances, political accountability overlooks children's individual situations in favor of group results. When teachers are being educationally accountable, they work very hard for progress, but they appreciate each child enough to look at her circumstances and nudge her toward progress at a rate she can handle. With the encouragement Suzy and the other teachers are giving Caleb, he is already coming around and showing initiative. Keeping anecdotal records of this individual child over time would show his progress clearly. Would he be this quiet in his play interactions in another year? Probably not.

The differences in cognitive and social skill between a young three year old and big kindergarten kids are truly amazing. In the next anecdote, notice the social awareness and the give and take shown by three children during an episode of dramatic play.

OBSERVATION: *While I was in the kindergarten classroom, I observed three students playing together in the playhouse set up in the corner of the room. There were two girls and one boy. They were playing so well together, I was really impressed.*

"Let's cook something," one of the girls said.

"No, I don't want to cook, I want to build a fire," the boy said.

"Well, I want to cook too," said the other girl.

I was expecting some sort of fight to come about, but that didn't happen. "Okay, us girls will cook, and you can build a fire, then we can eat in front of the fire when everything is ready." That was settled. The girls went on with their cooking, and the boy built his fire in the corner.

"Let's make spaghetti, it's one of my favorite meals," said the first girl.

"Okay," said the other girl. "You get the pans out and I will get out the food. We have to measure the amount of water that goes in the pan, how much do you think we need?"

"I don't know, how about three cups, that should be good." The first girl pretended to fill the cup three times with water and then dumped it into the pan on top of the stove.

The second girl continued, "Next, we need to make the sauce, you dump this can into the other pan, and I will watch the water."

The first girl dumped the sauce into the pan and pretended to stir it up. The second girl said, "The water is boiling now, we can put in the noodles. How much do we make?"

"Put in two handfuls, here I'll do it for you."

"Thank you."

While the girls finished up with their meal, the boy was sitting over in the corner trying to build his fire. He was sitting there very quietly, trying to figure out how to stack the wood (some real firewood the teacher had brought in). He had only three big pieces and a bunch of little pieces. When he ran out of big pieces he got very frustrated because he needed more. Finally, after about five minutes, he decided to put the big pieces on the bottom and set some of the little pieces on the top. That way the big ones could hold the little ones on top.

"Look how I made our fire," he said with a big smile on his face.

"Are you ready to eat?" the girls asked.

"Yes, I just have to get the fire started now, then I'll be ready," he said. He pretended to crumple up paper and throw it under the wood, and then pretended to light it with a match. "Ready," he said.

The girls dished up three servings of spaghetti into bowls, and then went and sat in front of the fire with the boy. "This is good spaghetti," said the boy.

"Thank you," said the girls, "We worked hard on it." They all sat there eating their spaghetti and when they were all finished, the three decided to help clean up together.

"We made too many noodles," said one of the girls.

"That's okay, I can take them home and feed them to my dog," the boy said, "He really likes them a lot." He pretended to dish the rest of the noodles into the bowl, and then he left along with the two girls.

REFLECTION: *I was impressed with the way that they played together. They compromised when one didn't want to do something, and they all pitched in to do the tasks together. They didn't argue even once, and they had a good time together. They were figuring things out for themselves and using so many skills, math skills to mention one.*

I never realized how important play was in the child's academic life. It's amazing to me how much the teacher and even me as an observer can learn about the child during play. One of the most important goals in beginning reading instruction is oral language development. It gives children the chance to talk, explain, and persuade. Their communication skills were so good and they were all flexible and willing to work together to accomplish what they needed to. I have never seen three children play so well before, especially two girls and one boy. It was very interesting for me.

Because of the stereotyped gender roles the children followed, we might miss the value of the story. But this is life to these kids. They were expressing what they know. Besides, the boy helped with the dishes! And notice Colby's comment: "I have never seen three children play so well before, especially two girls and a boy." This says it all. If our classrooms are to be encouraging places, we want—maybe above all else—for boys and girls to get along together. The three showed us this in their own wonderful way.

In addition, to mirror Colby's reflections about the "academic" learning she observed, an item analysis of the preceding anecdote yields the following learning transactions: language development, pragmatic conversing, problem solving, role exploration, task analysis, task sequencing, task completion, functional numeracy, dramatic interplay, team functioning, and empathic reasoning, to name just a few. One could argue that this role situation is a textbook case illustrating an emotional intelligence building process in early childhood education (D. Goleman, *Emotional Intelligence,* New York: Bantam Books, 1995).

The following anecdote portrays the learning benefits of dramatic play as well, but this time at a preschool level. Note the engagement of these four boys in non-stereotypic gender role behavior.

OBSERVATION: *During choice time, four boys were playing in the house area. They each had a baby in their hands and they were talking to each other. Jacob said, "You stay home and I'll go buy groceries." Taylor and Jonathan agreed and stayed in the house area while Jacob and Bubba went shopping.*

A few minutes later they lined up four chairs and pretended they were driving somewhere. Again, they each had a doll in their hands! They played together with the babies for the rest of choice time.

REFLECTION: *I was very happy and surprised to see those four boys playing in the house area because they usually play with the blocks and toy animals. It was great to see them playing with dolls too. Since I've never seen them playing in the house area, I was afraid they were developing a stereotypical image of boys and girls. What I saw today showed me they are not developing one.*

They were, however, demonstrating the occurrence of significant learning in the developmentally appropriate environment of an encouraging Head Start classroom. Otherwise, they would not have felt the freedom to become so engaged.

Reducing the Need for Serious Mistaken Behavior

It isn't realistic to eliminate all mistaken behavior from our classrooms. We want to make the serious kinds unnecessary, of course, by helping kids cope with the strong needs underlying them. But a lot of the other stuff—spontaneous arguments over materials, territory, and privileges, for instance—children actually learn life lessons from. Children learn from resolving conflicts with words, just as they learn from all the other problem solving they do. A teacher shouldn't pose problems for children—at least ones we don't think they can solve; they face enough of that kind already. But neither do we provide them with a sanitary (sterile) environment. To unabashedly mix metaphors, kids have got to get down and dirty (or at least down and snowy) in order to swim with the sharks and fly with the eagles.

So we work hard to help kids reduce the really hurting behavior, and we use naturally occurring mistaken behaviors to teach them mutual appreciation. We guide kids to progress from level-three mistaken behavior to level-one mistaken behavior—the experimental behavior that happens when we encourage children to take the initiative and learn. If we think about the real meaning of chapter four, we see that children who move from level-three mistaken behavior toward level one are making important progress in life skills. With the help of Geena, their teacher, the two children in the anecdote that follows show this progress, as observed by Jennifer.

OBSERVATION: *With the beginning of February, winter becomes an increasing frustration for many Minnesotans. Recently a preschool child reminded me that if you look at it right, winter's fun: "Jennifer, we can roll on the ground in the snow and not get muddy or dirty."*

On this day, following a quick fifteen minutes outside on a pretty cold play-ground, the children hurriedly took snowsuits off and put their shoes on. The children were busy tying their shoes or getting other people to tie their shoes. I glanced over at Scott (recently turned four) who had already tied his own shoelaces and was anxiously tugging at Brandon's shoes. Brandon tried pulling his laces away, but Scott won and had them in hand. Scott then began tying Brandon's laces. Brandon began to cry and shouted out, "Stop it, Scottie," and kicked his feet around.

"You stop it, stop yelling at me!" said Scott. This is where Geena, the teacher, stepped in.

Geena: Brandon, I see you are upset about something, can you tell me what has upset you?

Scott: Brandon just yelled and kicked and yelled some more!

Geena: Scott, I'd like to hear your ideas after I speak to Brandon. Brandon?

Brandon: (crying) I just want to try!

Geena: Try what? Tying your shoes?

Brandon: (crying and raising his voice) Yes, I wanna try by myself! That's all.

Geena: I can understand wanting to try. Scott, did you hear his words, he would like to try to tie his laces by himself and perhaps if he'd like help, he could ask you for it.

Scott: But...but...but...I wanna sit by Brandon at lunch 'cause he's my best buddy and he always pokes so slow with his shoes. I wanna hurry him up so he can sit by me.

Brandon continued to cry.

Geena: Scott, do you remember how sometimes you like to try to squeeze your toothpaste onto your toothbrush all by yourself? But, sometimes it's a little harder than you think, and you decide later that you want help, and then I help you?

Scott: Uh-huh.

Geena: Well, we all like to try things for ourselves and even if we need to take more time, it is important to try, that is how we learn. So do you think you and I could have Brandon try all by himself? He will ask if he'd like help a little later. Is that okay with you, Scott?

Brandon had stopped crying and was concentrating on tying his shoe.

Geena: Brandon, will that be okay with you for Scott to wait for you and help only if you ask?

Brandon nodded his head. After a few minutes, the boys walked to lunch with four pairs of shoelaces neatly tied and two very happy smiles!

REFLECTION: *The observation was a good indication of Geena's ability to foster self-help skills as well as self-esteem in young children. She showed her confidence in Brandon by encouraging him to continue tying (even though she understood he wasn't able to tie yet). Geena also helped Scott understand the importance of trying, and this also helped him have the patience to wait while Brandon continued to try (which in its own subtle way is encouraging to Brandon as well).*

Geena showed her ability to intervene without taking 100 percent control of the situation. She led the children to their solution without telling them exactly what to do and how to do it. Children need to be involved in the problem solving process and she clearly emphasizes this in her practice. This is only one of many positive observations I have made in this classroom. The children are often asking one another, "Can I share your blocks?" "Would you like to sit by me?" With the help of their teachers, I am amazed at the caring and helping community these preschoolers have made for themselves.

Geena took a level-one mistaken behavior situation and made it into a learning opportunity for Brandon, Scott, and Jennifer (the student observer). She modeled the famous guidance line, "It's okay to make mistakes, we just need to learn from them." The everyday classroom conflicts that teachers run into provide effective opportunities to help children get control of their responses and learn to solve the problems they encounter. Both Brandon and Scott showed this learning through their episode of level-one mistaken behavior. When children show serious mistaken behavior in an encouraging classroom, they usually are experiencing multiple difficulties, which require a comprehensive response (Dan Gartrell, *A Guidance Approach for the Encouraging Classroom*, Albany, NY: Delmar/ITP Publishers, 1998). One point of difference that helps such children reduce the need for serious mistaken behavior is a teacher like Geena, who keeps her cool and uses guidance.

From Conflict to Consideration

The message of chapter five was that we want to nudge children in conflict from high-level mediation (the adult is a coach, like Geena was) to low-level mediation (the adult facilitates the children's own resolution), to negotiation, where the children work the problem out completely by themselves. Negotiation that actually heads off conflict is what our goal actually should be—we call this *cooperation*. Play situations and mealtimes provide wonderful observation opportunities for assessing children's progress toward cooperation.

> **OBSERVATION:** *I was watching Ramon and Kristopher play together in the block area. They were building a Lego car to go down a ramp. Kristopher said, "Put this wheel on top of that and it'll go faster!"*
>
> *Ramon replied, "No, I want the one I got there!" Kristopher pushed Ramon's hand out of the way to put the wheel on. Ramon said loudly, "Don't, Kristopher!" Ramon started to push Kristopher's hand back, but then just let Kristopher put the wheel on. After this incident, the two boys continued to play together.*

> **REFLECTION:** *I feel that maybe Ramon let Kristopher put the wheel on because he got impatient with the holdup and just let him do it. Or, maybe Ramon let Kristopher put the wheel on simply because he had thought it through and maybe it would "make it go faster." I liked how the two boys worked it out on their own. They did not get a teacher to help them; they took it upon themselves to find a solution. I feel that this solution came from Ramon. I think that Ramon's action is a good example of his maturity level. He is one of the older children in the class.*

Many times, to negotiate a solution to a conflict, one child's insight (or foresight) brings the other along. Still, however their development and experience differ, both children learn through the negotiation, Kristopher as well as Ramon. Teachers should smile when they see children actively de-escalating conflicts—changing strong negative emotions into mildly negative ones that can be settled. Ramon did this in the anecdote.

OBSERVATION: *We were at the tables eating our muffins for breakfast. Ziggy and Twilla were at a table with the assistant teacher and the other children. Ziggy was holding up her muffin, and Twilla accidentally bumped her arm and the muffin fell on the floor. Ziggy gave Twilla a nasty look, and before she could say anything, Twilla had chosen a new muffin for her, and was holding it up for Ziggy to take. Twilla reached for the butter and said, "I'm sorry, Ziggy." Ziggy looked quite surprised and gave Twilla a big smile without saying a word!*

REFLECTION: *This was quite interesting. Twilla has had better days than today. Just the same I think when Twilla bumped Ziggy, she realized what she did and was truly sorry for it. I think Twilla knew how Ziggy would react, so she tried to make up for her mistake before Ziggy would say anything. I was happy to see that Twilla knew how to fix the situation on her own without any intervention by a teacher. I believe these girls have had difficulties together before. I believe Twilla knows Ziggy's personality, by the way she responded to her.*

Teachers should smile when children take the initiative to prevent an impending conflict. Negotiation between children that heads off a conflict before it happens is in some ways the most important negotiation of all. Let's look at another example of cooperation at mealtime in a Head Start classroom.

OBSERVATION: *A group of children, the head teacher, and myself were sitting at a table eating lunch. Everyone had received at least one portion of each dish. A few children had also received seconds already. Savanna decided that she wanted more pears, but before she took some, she stopped and asked Joey if he wanted any. She said, "Joey, do you want more pears? You haven't had more yet." She waited for Joey to say no, then helped herself to the rest of the pears.*

REFLECTION: *What I thought was great about this observation was the way Savanna put someone else's needs in front of her own. She realized that Joey had not been able to have more pears, and everyone else did. Although she wanted more herself, she asked Joey first instead of just taking them for herself. Savanna is one of the older children, and she sees what is going on more than the younger children. I also believe that her actions may be partly the result of modeling, her family, and the teachers in her life.*

Consideration for others is a life skill that we all appreciate, whatever the person's age who shows it. We don't always expect this skill in young children, though, and may not look for it as much as we might. The children in these three anecdotes show us that young children are considerate of each other, when we nurture this quality in the encouraging classroom.

Let's conclude this section with a group anecdote. Many teachers notice that as the year goes on in encouraging classrooms, even fairly young preschoolers begin to play in expansive, complex, and cooperative ways. Conflicts in such play are minimal, and the imaginative arrangements and role play they conduct are outstanding. When children spontaneously develop these situations, I know teachers who shelve the schedule, participate if invited, and watch the apple seeds grow and bloom.

OBSERVATION: *Today was a great day in our child care classroom. Downstairs during active play, a couple of children asked me to help them set up for bowling. We don't have pins, so I asked them what we should use. Andy said, "Let's use the blocks." I told him that was a great idea, but what should we use for a bowling ball. Alex told me any ball would work. So together Andy, Alex, Cindy, and I set up a bowling lane.*

By the time five minutes had passed, three-fourths of the children were involved in this activity. Some of the kids became cheerleaders—cheering for everyone! One girl was handing out blocks as prizes. During this time, the children were all working together, taking turns bowling, and supporting each other. Everyone who wanted to got a chance to bowl. The bowling game went on for over half an hour.

REFLECTION: *I didn't plan this activity, but it turned out to be one of the best learning experiences for me. The first thing it taught me was to take advantage of "teaching moments." Although I didn't intervene too much, I was able to have the children work together and use their thinking skills.*

The next thing I learned was the children really enjoy the teacher interacting with them on their level. As soon as I got down on the floor to help set up the "pins"

I had at least three or four more children come over to me to see what was going on. After it got going, they no longer needed me to participate.

Overall, this was a truly great experience. This activity was self-selected, and the children would let everyone join in without any fuss. You could just feel the positive energy in the air.

At times like these the encouraging classroom really shines, with children and adults sharing together in the adventure of life. A special teacher in my life once said, "Education is not preparation for life; it is life itself."

Loss and Resiliency

F ew children live the idyllic life that some adults attribute to childhood. Teachers understand this reality more than most. We would like to think that the teacher's job needn't include helping young children cope with death of a loved one, disruption to the family, dislocation from the familiar, or loss of personal control. In the best of all worlds, families provide the support for children to cope with loss, and we teachers are "free to teach." But then, in the best of all worlds a leading cause of death among our youth would not be violence—often by guns. Teachers do not teach in the best of all possible worlds. In the real life of the classroom, the teacher helps children cope with loss, and with the angry and hurt feelings that result when children cannot cope and understand.

In the encouraging classroom, when children get the help they need, they show progress. Their grief, depression, and anger diminish and they begin to respond. With support, children move from grief to resiliency, as Sharon observes in the following anecdote.

OBSERVATION: *My two older children had left to visit their father for the summer in another state. My youngest son, age four, needed to be with me, so during the last week of school I brought him to visit my class. The children were excited to see him. They were very friendly, as I knew they would be. But by early afternoon, my son had received too much attention and needed to sit on my lap. As I held him, without thinking about it, I kissed the back of his head.*

187

June Bug, who had been watching intently, said, "You kiss us sometimes too, right teacher?"

I did, to no one's concern in this community, and said, "Yes, I do, June Bug."

And she said, "And you love us too, right?"

"Yes, I love you all, June Bug."

REFLECTION: *June Bug is from a family of nine children that can only be called badly dysfunctional. The parents have ongoing problems that result in either their, or some of their children, being out of the home for periods of time. Several children in the family have multiple problems that they show regularly in school.*

June Bug craves attention from me, but because of our relationship she hardly ever has problems in my class. She is making the very best of a very hard situation, being a caring big sister, at the age of five, for her younger siblings. She has come a long way this year in coping with her situation and finding a place in our classroom. She leaves kindergarten a courageous little kid, older than her years. She will be missed.

Because of children like June Bug, Sharon thought a lot about moving on with her class and teaching first grade. It was a hard decision for her to remain a kindergarten teacher, but she decided that the school, and the community, needed her where she was. From circumstances of multiple loss, June Bug, in Sharon's class, showed real recovery.

Permission to Wonder

When they trust their teachers, children initiate learning activities, learn life skills, and engage in wonder. The role of the teacher in encouraging wonder must not be underestimated. Through contact talks, which is when most wonder occurs, children explore their lives, and life beyond. The expression of thought through wonder builds self-confidence, curiosity, knowledge, communication skills, and a sense of steadfast relationships.

But what about a child who comes into our classroom completely out of sorts and stays that way for most of the morning? One choice is to be patient and give correction until he fits back into our schedule—or explodes. Another choice is to "be understanding" (N. Weber-Schwartz, "Patience or Understanding?" *Young Children* 42 [3], 1987, 52–54), and if the child needs the encouragement of a contact talk, we find a way to give it. In a morning that included Ricardo's refusing breakfast (even though he seemed hungry) and later his refusing to go outside with the group, Cleo decided not to force the child, but to stay inside with Ricardo and talk with him.

OBSERVATION: *We started out by having him pick a book (I don't remember the title) that looked interesting to him. Instead of my reading the book to Ricardo, we discussed things in the pictures.*

Me: Wow, look at that! They seem like they are having fun. They are making such a mess!

Ricardo: I don't think they want to eat their breakfast. But if they don't their mom will be mad at them because they will want a snack right away.

Me: Why do you think they don't want to eat their breakfast?

Ricardo: They don't like it. (pause) Sometimes when I don't like the cereal, I just play with it until my mom gets mad and dumps it in the sink. Then I get really hungry later.

Me: What do you think that is?

Ricardo: That's oatmeal.

Me: Why do you think it's oatmeal?

Ricardo: Because I've made it before. It comes in a round box like that, and you put milk and water in it. Then I put fish in it.

Me: You put fish in it! In the oatmeal?

Ricardo: Yes, I done that before. I went fishing with my dad. I was standing on the dock and I catched a baby tuna. My dad said I could take it home for a pet, so I did.

Me: Wow, it must be interesting having a pet tuna. How did you take care of it?

Ricardo: I put it in my fish tank and I feeded it minnows every day. And it growed and growed until it wouldn't fit anymore and it started getting green stuff all over it so I put in my oatmeal. (He turned the page.)

Me: Look at that airplane. What do you think it would be like to ride in one?

Ricardo: I done that already. Me and my dad and Mike went to California to see my uncle. My mom, her name is Jennifer, and Katie didn't go. Mom really, really missed me though because she called me every day and told me she missed me. Katie was too little to go.

Me: So tell me about your airplane trip.

Ricardo: We seed an alien out the window. I sitted with my brother. The alien wanted a ride home.

Me: (pausing to think about this)Was he lost?

Ricardo: Yes, he didn't know how to find his house. He lives in Alien Land. So we let him come on the plane. He sitted with my dad. He didn't want to sit with me and I didn't want to sit with him. He was nice to my dad, but he was kinda scary looking. He had to go to the bathroom, so my dad showed him where it was. The plane took him to Alien Land and he found his mom and dad.

Me: What was Alien Land like?

Ricardo: It just had a lot of space stuff. Kinda like the moon. I'm really into space stuff. I have these, these little stars and planets that light up in the dark in my room, up there (pointing to the ceiling). They are really cool. I want my whole room to be space stuff so I can pretend I'm in space.

Me: That would be neat. What else happened on your airplane trip?

Ricardo: Well, we got to see all kinds of neat stuff in California. My uncle took us everywhere. I like the ocean. I went swimming in it. It was really, really cold. Me and my brother found all kinds of shells. Then Mike found a starfish. I looked and looked, but I couldn't find my own. (pausing) I don't really want to talk about this anymore. Can I go outside and play with the other kids now?

Me: Sure, thanks for visiting with me, Ricardo.

Cleo arranged with the other adults to go outside while she stayed behind to have the contact talk with Ricardo. Ricardo clearly welcomed the chance to talk with her. Would you guess that the boy had had an argument with his mom over breakfast? In the encouraging classroom, the goals for the program can be carefully planned. But the actual curriculum is what goes on each day between adults and children. Cleo gave permission for Ricardo to wonder, and so to express thoughts and feelings that released him from the day's trials. In doing so Cleo kept a rough morning from possibly getting worse and helped the child reconnect with his classroom community. She affirmed the working of a creative mind, thereby also affirming the child himself. In the encouraging classroom, every member has a place, even when problems arise, and that place affirms the child's right to grow.

I learned for myself the importance of wonder, when I saw it in a Head Start child named Virgil. Due to extreme and repeated family disruption, it took Virgil months before he would say anything to anyone in our classroom, let alone wonder. As his life stabilized, Virgil found resiliency, and his natural intelligence came through. We end the book with Virgil's story.

RECOLLECTION: *On a warm and windy September day, I was pushing children on the swings. To get them to talk, I would ask how high they wanted me to push them. One child said, "Up to the roof!" Another said, "All the way to the clouds!" When I asked Virgil, he replied, "Push me up to God's house."*

At that moment I grinned and thought about Virgil. This was his second year in Head Start. Outside during the summer, also on a windy day, I had asked the kids what made the wind blow. Virgil looked at me like I was a real dummy and said, "Don't you know, Dan? The trees push the air." With my usual serious expression I asked him how the trees did that. He replied, "Why the leaves is fans of course."

The previous September, Virgil, age three, had come into our class, stood by the door, and didn't say a word. We took him orange slices, toast, and milk. He returned the next day, but would not come to the table to eat—until October. Neither would he say a word, to anyone, not in Ojibwe, not in English. By the time Virgil had started Head Start, he had been in five different foster homes. He had just moved in with grandparents; that made six. He may have thought that the classroom was placement number seven.

Over the following months, Virgil gradually showed an interest in books, blocks, and following the teachers around. By January, he would play with other children but still not talk to anyone. The children accepted Virgil and only once in a while asked why he didn't speak.

Over the winter, he got comfortable enough to look at books with me, almost silently. On occasion, I would point to a picture of an elephant and call it an alligator. Virgil would chuckle.

On a warm April day, the class was going for a picnic on a beach where the lake ice was still piled up. I was sitting next to Virgil on the bus, and he was looking out of the window. We went over a bridge and Virgil looked carefully at the water. He turned to me and said, "Hey Dan, look at those ducks." Those were Virgil's first words.

When children are comfortable in your classroom, they show progress in many ways. We need to appreciate that progress in whatever form it takes, but most of all, we need to appreciate it when they wonder.

Suggested Readings

Derman-Sparks, Louise. "Markers of Multicultural/Anti-Bias Education." *Young Children* 54, no. 5 (September 1999): 43.

Hosfield, Doris. "A Long Day in Care Need Not Seem Long." *Young Children* 53, no. 3 (May 1998): 24–27.

Hunt, Rhonda. "Making Positive Multicultural Early Childhood Education Happen." *Young Children* 54, no. 5 (September 1999): 39–42.

Lawhon, Tommie. "Encouraging Friendships among Children." *Childhood Education* 73, no. 4 (Summer 1997): 228–231.

Reinsberg, Judy. "Reflections on Quality Infant Care." *Young Children* 50, no. 6 (September 1995): 23–25.

Spangler, Carol. "The Sharing Circle: A Child-Centered Curriculum." *Young Children* 52, no. 5 (July 1997): 74–78.

Wittmer, Donna, and Alice Honig. "Encouraging Positive Social Development in Young Children." *Young Children* 49, no. 5 (July 1994): 4–12.

Discussion Activities

For reasons of professionalism, as you respond to these discussion activities, please respect the privacy of all children, adults, programs, and schools.

1. Think about a child you are familiar with who has made clear progress in separating from home and finding connection in the classroom. Describe words and actions that indicate progress.

2. Think about a child you are familiar with who has made clear progress in connecting life at home and life in the classroom. Describe words and actions that indicate progress.

3. Think about a child you are familiar with who has made clear progress in moving from a safety position to one of full engagement in the educational program. Describe words and actions that indicate progress.

4. Think about a child in a classroom that you are familiar with who has made clear progress in overcoming strong-needs mistaken behaviors in the classroom. Describe words and actions that indicate progress.

5. Think about a child in a classroom you are familiar with who has made clear progress in learning to negotiate conflicts on his or her own. Describe words and actions that indicate progress.

6. Think about a child in a classroom you are familiar with who has made clear progress in moving from grief to resiliency. Describe words and actions that indicate progress.

7. Think about a child in a classroom you are familiar with who has made clear progress in gaining the ability to wonder. Describe words and actions that indicate progress.

An Invitation

I am small.
I come from small beginnings.
I am quiet, shy, introspective.
Written language is my voice,
My dialog with myself, with others, with Father God.
It allows me to be the "other" me that my personality cannot release.
It lets my ideas soar, my feelings be free,
my being expand into the world of life.
It permits my small self to become BIG.

For many years my wife, "Dr. J.," and I have encouraged our teacher education students to write journals. We have found that some students and fellow teachers add meaning to their lives by recording their observations and reflections about significant events of the day. My "hip" mother is one of those folks who journals. She has kept a journal since she was fourteen. When she was in her seventies, her journals were collected by the Schlesinger Library at Radcliffe College, Cambridge, Massachusetts. At the age of 84 she published her first book, a memoir based on her journals. If you journal, or have thought about keeping a journal, stay with it; go for it. Whether or not you publish, over time you will relish what you have included, and perhaps regret what you have not—take it from my mom.

And, if you have some journal entries (anecdotes) about human differences in early childhood classrooms, how young children do and don't get along for gender, cultural, age difference, physical, and behavioral reasons—I'd like to invite you to e-mail them to me. Be sure to include a phone number and other contact information. They would help with a future project on "young children's perceptions of human differences in early childhood classrooms." Meegwich (Ojibwe for thank you).

My e-mail address: dgartrell@vax1.bemidji.msus.edu

Dan Gartrell ("Dr. Dan") has taught Head Start in northern Minnesota and sixth grade in Ohio. He is director of the Child Development Training Program and professor of Early Childhood Education at the State University in Bemidji, Minnesota. He is the author of *A Guidance Approach for the Encouraging Classroom* (Delmar Publishers, 1998, second edition). Dan and his wife belong to a blended family that includes five children and four grandchildren. (He's got photos.)

APPENDIX:
Beyond Discipline to Guidance

During April, a student teacher in a Head Start classroom recorded in her journal an anecdotal observation of two children, Charissa and Carlos.

OBSERVATION: *Charissa and Carlos were building with blocks. Charissa reached for a block and Carlos decided he wanted the same one. They both tugged on the block and then Carlos hit Charissa on the back. Charissa fought back tears and said, "Carlos, you're not s'posed to hit, you're s'posed to use the 'talking stick.'"*

Carlos said "yeah" and got the stick. I couldn't hear what they said, but they took turns holding the stick and talking while the other one listened. After only a minute, the two were playing again, and Charissa was using the block. Later I asked her what the talking stick helped them decide. She said, "That I use the block first this time. Carlos uses it next time."

REFLECTION: *I really got concerned when Carlos hit Charissa and I was just about to get involved. I couldn't believe when Charissa didn't hit back but told Carlos to get the talking stick, and he did! Then they solved the problem so quickly. DeeAnn [the teacher] told me she has been teaching the kids since September to solve their problems by using the talking stick. Usually she has to mediate, but this time they solved the problem on their own. It really worked!*

A version of this article appeared in Young Children, *September 1997.* © *Daniel J. Gartrell*

Clearly, the conventional wisdom is that preschoolers do not typically solve a problem like this on their own by using a prop like a talking stick. But DeeAnn had been working with the children all year to teach them this conflict-management skill. So that there was consistency, she also had persuaded the other adults in the room to use the talking stick. Utilizing the ideas of S. Wichert (*Keeping the Peace: Practicing Cooperation and Conflict Resolution with Preschoolers,* Philadelphia: New Society Publishers, 1989), the adults started by using a lot of coaching (high-level mediation), but over time encouraged the children to take the initiative to solve their problems themselves.

Conflict management—in this case through the technique of a decorated talking stick—is an important strategy in the overall approach to working with children called *guidance.* By now guidance is a familiar term in early childhood education, as is its companion term, *developmentally appropriate practice* (DAP). However, like the misinterpretations of DAP that have surfaced in recent years, some interpretations of "guidance" show a misunderstanding of what the approach is about. Erroneous interpretations have led to the misapplication of guidance ideas: teachers who think they are using guidance, but are not.

This article is an effort to amplify the concept of guidance. The sections that follow define guidance; trace the guidance tradition in early childhood education; examine the present trend toward guidance; explain what guidance is not; and illustrate key practices in classrooms where teachers use guidance. The ideas in this article build from my 1994 textbook, *A Guidance Approach to Discipline,* and the writings of many other early childhood educators and developmental psychologists over the years.

Guidance Defined

Teachers who practice guidance believe in the positive potential of children, manifest through a dynamic process of development (P. Greenberg, "Avoiding 'Me against You' Discipline," *Young Children,* 43 [1], 1998, 24–25). For this reason, teachers who use guidance think beyond conventional classroom discipline—the intent of which is to keep children (literally and figuratively) in line. Rather than simply reacting to crises, guidance involves developmentally appropriate, culturally responsive education to reduce the occurrence of classroom problems (D. J. Gartrell, *A Guidance Approach To Discipline,* Albany, NY: Delmar Publishers Inc., 1994). *Guidance* means creating a positive learning environment for each child in the group.

With respect for the course of development of each child, the purpose of guidance is to teach children the social skills they need as citizens of a democracy (D. S. Wittmer & A. S. Honig, "Encouraging Positive Social Development in Young Children," *Young Children* 49 [5], 1994, 61–75): respecting others and one's self, working together in groups, solving problems using words, expressing strong emotions in acceptable ways, and making decisions ethically and intelligently. Teachers who use guidance realize that it takes well into adulthood to master these skills, and that in learning them children, like all of us, make mistakes. Because children are just beginning their personal development, teachers regard behaviors traditionally considered *misbehaviors* as *mistaken behaviors* (D. J. Gartrell, "Misbehavior or Mistaken Behavior?" *Young Children* 50 [5], 1995, 27–34). The interventions teachers make to address mistaken behaviors are firm but friendly, instructive and solution-oriented but not punitive. The teacher helps children learn from their mistakes rather than punishing them for the mistakes they make; empowers children to solve problems rather than punishing them for having problems they cannot solve; helps the child accept consequences, but gives consequences that leave self-esteem intact.

Guidance teaching is character education in its truest, least political sense—guiding children to develop the empathy, self-esteem, and self-control needed for *autonomy,* Piaget's term for the capacity to make intelligent, ethical decisions (C. Kamii, "Autonomy: The Aim of Education Envisioned by Piaget," *Phi Delta Kappan* 65 [6], 1984, 410–15). In contrast to the notion that the teacher handles all problem situations alone, guidance involves teaming with professionals and partnerships with parents on behalf of the child (Gartrell, *A Guidance Approach*).

The Guidance Tradition

The overview of guidance above sounds like futuristic education practice, maybe in the year 2050. The only task harder than learning democratic living skills is teaching them to others. In actuality, however, guidance has always been practiced by the kind of teacher who, if we were fortunate, we had ourselves; who we would want our children to have; who we would be like. From time immemorial there probably have been "guidance teachers." For over 150 years, a rich guidance tradition has been documented in the early childhood field (Gartrell, *A Guidance Approach*).

The Pioneers

Progressive educators long have viewed children as being in a state of dynamic development, with effective education and guidance practices responding to the developmental patterns of the child (Gartrell, *A Guidance Approach*). During the nineteenth century, the European educators Herbart, Pestalozzi, and Froebel began fundamental educational reform, in no small part as a result of their views about the child's dynamic nature (D. K. Osborn, *Early Childhood Education in Historical Perspective*, Athens, GA: Education Associates, 1980). Herbart and Pestalozzi recognized that children learned best through activities they could tie to their own experiences rather than through the strictly enforced recitation of facts.

German-born Friedrich Froebel was the originator of the kindergarten, at that time intended for children ages three to six. Froebel innovated such practices as manipulatives-based instruction, circle time, home visits, "mothers' meetings," and the use of women teachers (I. M. Lilley, ed., *Friedrich Froebel: A Selection from His Writings*, London: Cambridge University Press, 1967). (In the 1870s, Froebel's kindergartens were barred in Germany for being "too democratic.") For Froebel the whole purpose of education was guidance so that the "innate impulses of the child" could be developed harmoniously through creative activity. As a part of his early developmental orientation, Froebel believed that the nature of the child was essentially good and that "faults" were the product of negative experiences, sometimes at the hand of the educator (Lilley).

Like Froebel, Maria Montessori maintained a developmental viewpoint, that "the child is in a continual state of growth and metamorphosis, whereas the adult has reached the norm of the species" (E. M. Standing, *Maria Montessori: Her Life and Work*, New York: The New American Library, 1962). Montessori's remarkable vision included not only the innovations of the "prepared environment" and a child-oriented teaching process, but also the idea that intelligence is greatly influenced by early experience. It is interesting to note that Montessori's theory of "sensitive periods" of learning has been supported in graphic fashion by the brain research of today.

Montessori—along with her American contemporary, John Dewey—abhorred the traditional schooling of the day, which failed to consider children's development. She criticized didactic teaching practices with children planted behind desks, expected to recite lessons of little meaning in their lives, and kept in line by systematic rewards and punishments (M. Montessori, *The Montessori Method,* New York: Schocken Books, 1964). Montessori's approach made the child an active agent in the education process; through this responsibility children would learn self-discipline.

Like Montessori, Dewey viewed discipline as differing in method depending on the curriculum followed. The "preprimary" level in Dewey's University of Chicago Laboratory School featured project-based learning activities, building from the everyday experience of the young learners. Dewey saw the connection between school and society, postulating that our democratic ideals needed to be sustained through the "microcosm" of the classroom. In the 1900 monograph, *School and Society* (Chicago: University of Chicago Press, reprinted 1969), Dewey stated:

> If you have the end in view of forty or fifty children learning certain set lessons, to be recited to the teacher, your discipline must be devoted to securing that result. But if the end in view is the development of a spirit of social cooperation and community life, discipline must grow out of and be relative to such an aim. There is a certain disorder in any busy workshop; there is not silence; persons are not engaged in maintaining certain fixed physical postures; their arms are not folded; they are not holding their books thus and so. They are doing a variety of things, and there is the confusion, the bustle that results from activity. Out of the occupation, out of doing things that are to produce results, and out of doing these in a social and cooperative way, there is born a discipline of its own kind and type. Our whole conception of discipline changes when we get this point of view (16–17).

Dewey, of course, was not just speaking of early childhood education, but of schooling at all levels. Almost 100 years later, Dewey's words still challenge America's educators and capture eloquently "the guidance difference."

Mid-Century Influences

In the first half of the twentieth century, progressive educators and psychologists increasingly viewed children not in traditional moralistic terms (good and bad), but in terms responsive to a positive developmental potential. The nursery school movement in Britain and the United states was imbued with these progressive ideas and influenced the writings of two mid-century early childhood educators, Katherine Read and James Hymes.

Katherine Read came directly out of the nursery school tradition. Her venerable text, *The Nursery School: A Human Relations Laboratory,* first appeared in 1950 and is currently in its ninth edition (W. B. Saunders Company, 1993). For Read, the classroom is a supportive environment where both children and adults can gain understanding in the challenging area of human relationships. Read speaks clearly of the child's need for understandable, consistent limits and of the use of authority to encourage self-control:

> Our goal is self-control, the only sound control. But self-control can be sound only when there is a stable mature self. Our responsibility is to help the child develop maturity through giving him the security of limits maintained by responsible adults while he is growing (233).

James Hymes distinguished himself as director of the noted Kaiser Day Care Centers during World War II and later as one of the guiding lights in the founding of Head Start. Hymes wrote frequently about early childhood education matters, including the landmark text, *Effective Home–School Relations* (Englewood Cliffs, NJ: Prentice Hall, 1953). His works *Discipline* (New York: Bureau of Publications, Columbia University, 1949) and *Behavior and Misbehavior* (Englewood Cliffs, NJ: Prentice Hall, 1955), stressed the importance of understanding the reasons for children's behavior. He argued that often the causes of problems were not in the child alone, but a result of the program placing inappropriate developmental expectations on the child. Hymes and Read both stressed the need for teachers to have high expectations of children—but expectations in line with each child's development. They articulated a key guidance premise, that the teacher must be willing to modify the daily program for the benefit of children, not just hold the program as a fixed commodity, against which the behavior of the child is to be judged.

Jean Piaget is often considered the preeminent developmental psychologist of the twentieth century. Though known as a psychologist rather than as an educator, Piaget discussed implications of his findings for the classroom in *The Moral Judgment of the Child* (Glencoe, IL: The Free Press, 1932, translated 1960). Piaget shared with Montessori the precept that children learn through constructing knowledge by acting upon the environment. Further, Piaget shared with Dewey and Read a high regard for the social context of learning—a belief that peer interaction is essential for healthy development. Piaget maintained that education must be an interactive endeavor and that discipline must respect and respond to this fact. Speaking directly about the uses of conventional classroom discipline, Piaget protests:

> ...If one thinks of the systematic resistance offered by pupils to the authoritarian method, and the admirable ingenuity employed by children the world over to evade disciplinary constraint, one cannot help regarding as defective a system which allows so much effort to be wasted instead of using it in cooperation (366–367).

To their lasting credit, these mid-century writers agreed with Dewey, that the classroom is a "laboratory" in which the practice of democracy is to be modeled, taught, and learned. For these educators, the means to social, personal, *and* intellectual development was guidance practiced in the classroom by the responsible adult.

The 1980s

T hrough the 1970s, the guidance tradition was sustained by writers such as Jeanette Galambos Stone (*A Guide to Discipline,* Washington, DC: NAEYC, rev. ed., 1978) and Rita Warren (*Caring: Supporting Children's Growth,* Washington, DC: NAEYC, 1977), who authored widely read monographs for the National Association for the Education of Young Children (NAEYC), along with many others. While guidance was becoming an important practice in preschool programs, however, a new trend in the public schools worked against a long-sought goal of early childhood educators, the upward percolation of guidance ideas. "Back to the basics" became the fad for public school educators, and curriculum and teaching methods grew more prescribed (Gartrell, *A Guidance Approach*). During this time, academic and disciplinary constraints were imposed even on kindergarten and preschool children. With disregard for young children's development, teachers were pressured to "get students ready" for the academics of the next level—a pressure still felt by early childhood teachers today.

During these years the interactive nature of the guidance approach did not fit the regimen of the academic classroom. New "obedience-driven" discipline systems, such as *assertive discipline,* came into widespread use at all levels of public education and even in some preschool programs (D. J. Gartrell, "Assertive Discipline: Unhealthy for Children and Other Living Things," *Young Children* 42 [2], 1987, 10–11; R. Hitz. "Assertive Discipline: A Response to Lee Canter," *Young Children* 43 [2], 1988, 24). In their text *Discipline with Dignity,* R. L. Curwin and A. N. Mendler (Alexandria, VA: Association for Supervision and Curriculum Development, 1988) say this about the widespread adoption of "obedience models of discipline" by public schools during the period:

It is ironic that the current mood of education is in some ways behind the past. The 1980s might someday be remembered as the decade when admiration was reserved for principals, cast as folk heroes, walking around schools with baseball bats, and for teachers and whole schools that systematically embarrassed students by writing their names on the chalkboard. But we do have hope that the pendulum will once again swing to the rational position of treating children as people with needs and feelings that are not that different from adults. Once we begin to understand how obedience is contrary to the goals of our culture and education, the momentum will begin to shift. Our view is that the highest virtue of education is to teach students to be self-responsible and fully functional. In all but extreme cases, obedience contradicts these goals (24).

The Guidance Trend

Throughout the 1980s, and up to the present, writers at the early childhood level maintained their independence from the obedience emphasis in conventional discipline. In 1987, NAEYC published its expanded *Developmentally Appropriate Practice in Early Childhood Programs Serving Children from Birth through Age Eight* (S. Bredekamp, ed.). Supported by 600 references, the position statement advocates interactive teaching practices responsive to the development of each child. In relation to behavior management, the document reflects the guidance approach and draws a sharp distinction with conventional classroom discipline. In appropriate teaching practice,

> Children are provided many opportunities to develop social skills such as cooperating, helping, negotiating, and talking with the person involved to solve interpersonal problems. Teachers facilitate the development of these positive social skills at all times (55).

According to the NAEYC document, inappropriate practices are those in which

> Teachers dominate the environment by talking to the whole group most of the time and telling children what to do. Teachers spend a great deal of time enforcing rules, punishing unacceptable behavior, demeaning children who misbehave, making children sit and be quiet, or refereeing [as opposed to mediating] disagreements (55).

At both the preprimary and primary grade levels, the NAEYC document illustrates the ambiguous distinction between conventional discipline techniques and the use of punishment. In fact, in recent years a growing number of early childhood professionals have become dissatisfied even with the very term *discipline* (Gartrell, *A Guidance Approach;* Eleanor Reynolds, *Guiding Young Children: A Child-Centered Approach,* 2d ed., Mountainview, CA: Mayfield Publishing Company, 1996). The reason is that teachers have a hard time telling where discipline ends and punishment begins. Some educators believe that *discipline* is a neutral term and does not have to mean *punishment* (M. Marion, *Guidance of Young Children,* 5th ed., Columbus: Merrill Publishing Company, 1995). The reality, though, is that when teachers use discipline, they tend to include acts of punishment. They mix up discipline and punishment out of anger or because they feel the child "deserves it." The very idea of "disciplining a child" suggests punishment, illustrating the easy semantic slide of the one into the other.

Teachers who go beyond discipline do so because of the baggage of punishment that discipline carries. These teachers reject punishment for what it is: the extraction of "pain, loss, or suffering for a crime or wrongdoing" *(Webster's New World Dictionary).* For many years, educators and psychologists have recognized the harmful effects of punishment on children (Dewey; Montessori; Piaget; W. W. Purkey, *Self Concept and School Achievement,* Englewood Cliffs, NJ: Prentice-Hall, 1970). Some of the effects of punishment are:

- low self-esteem (feeling like "a failure")
- negative self-concept (not liking one's self)
- angry feelings, sometimes under the surface, toward others
- a feeling of disengagement from school and the learning process

A teacher who uses guidance knows that children learn little when they frequently hear, "Don't do that," or "You're naughty," or "You know better than that." When discipline includes punishment, young children have difficulty understanding how to improve their behavior (Greenberg). Instead of being shamed into "being good," they are likely to internalize the negative personal message that punishment carries (Gartrell, "Misbehavior or Mistaken Behavior?").

Experts now recognize that through punishment children lose their trust in adults (A. S. Clewett, "Guidance and Discipline: Teaching Young Children Appropriate Behavior," *Young Children* 43 [4], 1988, 26–36). Over time young people come to see doing negative things and being punished for them as a natural part of life. The increasing use of conflict management (teaching children to solve their problems with words) keeps children's faith in social processes. Conflict management and other guidance methods are being used more now because they work better than punishment (Nancy Carlsson-Paige and D. E. Levin, "Making Peace in Violent Times: A Constructivist Approach to Conflict Resolution," *Young Children* 48 [1], 1992, 4–13). These methods teach children how to solve problems without violence and help children to feel good about themselves, the class, and the teacher (D. E. Levin, *Teaching Young Children in Violent Times,* Cambridge, MA: Educators for Social Responsibility, 1994). Young children need to learn how to know better and do better. The guidance approach is positive teaching, and the teacher has faith in the young child's ability to learn (Marion).

Guidance: What It Isn't

The term *discipline* remains in wide use at the elementary, middle-school, and secondary levels. Whether writers embrace the term *guidance* or attach a positive qualifier to *discipline,* new works on classroom management can be expected that claim the use of guidance principles. With the never-ending parade of new information, it is important for readers to recognize what guidance is not—in order to better understand what it is.

FIVE MISUNDERSTANDINGS ABOUT GUIDANCE

1. Guidance is not just reacting to problems. Many problems are caused when the teacher uses practices that are not appropriate for the age, stage, and needs of the individual child. Long group times, for instance, cause young children to become bored and restless. (They will sit in large groups more easily when they are older.) The teacher changes practices—such as reducing the number and length of group activities—in order to reduce the need for mistaken behavior (Gartrell, *A Guidance Approach*). Changes to other parts of the education program—including room layout, the daily schedule, and adult-to-child ratios—also help to reduce the need for mistaken behavior (Marion). Guidance prevents problems; it does not just react to them.

2. Guidance does not mean that the program won't be educational. When activities are developmentally appropriate, all children succeed at them, and all children are learning to be successful students. The three R's are a part of the education program, but they are integrated into the rest of the day and made meaningful so that children want to learn (Bredekamp). When teachers use guidance, however, the three R's are not all there is. Guidance means, in the words of Lillian Katz, that the teacher makes *relationships* "the first R" (cited in B. Kantrowitz and P. Wingert, "How Kids Learn," *Newsweek* [50–56], April 17, 1989). The social skills that are learned through positive relationships come first in the education program. Children need to know how to relate with others in all parts of their lives. Beginning to learn social skills in early childhood will help children in their years of school to come and in adult life after that (Wittmer & Honig). (Social skills, after all, are really social studies skills and language arts skills.)

3. Guidance is not "a sometime thing." Some teachers think that it is natural to use "guidance" in one set of circumstances and "discipline" in another. Yet non-punitive guidance techniques exist for all situations and once learned are effective (Carlsson-Paige & Levin; Gartrell, *A Guidance Approach;* Reynolds). For example, a common *discipline* technique is the time-out chair. The time-out chair usually results in embarrassment to the child, seldom teaches a positive lesson, and is almost always punishment (Clewett). The teacher can cut down on the use of this punishment by reducing the need for mistaken behavior and helping children use words to solve their problems. If a child does lose control and needs to be removed, the teacher can stay with the child for a cooling-down time (Gartrell, *A Guidance Approach*). The teacher then talks with the child about how the other child felt, teaches a positive alternative for next time, and sometimes helps the child decide on a way of helping the other child feel better (making restitution). Guidance encompasses a full spectrum of methods, from prevention, to conflict resolution, to crisis intervention, to long-term management strategies. Teamwork with parents and other adults is frequently part of the overall approach.

4. Guidance is not permissive discipline. Teachers who use guidance are active leaders who do not let situations get out of hand. They do not make children struggle vis-à-vis boundaries that may not be there (Gartrell, "Misbehavior or Mistaken Behavior?"). Guidance teachers tend to rely on guidelines—positive statements that remind about classroom conduct—rather than rules that are usually stated in the negative, as though the adult expects the child to break them. When they intervene, teachers direct their responses to the behavior and respect the personality of the child (H. Ginott, *Teacher and Child,* New York: Avon Books, 1972). They avoid embarrassment, which tends to leave lasting emotional scars (Gartrell, *A Guidance Approach*). They make sure that their responses are friendly as well as firm. The objective is to teach children to solve problems, rather than to punish children for having problems they cannot solve. The outcomes of guidance—the ability to get along with others, solve problems using words, and express strong feelings in acceptable ways—are the goals for its citizens of a democratic society. For this reason, guidance has a meaning that goes beyond traditional discipline. Guidance is not just keeping children in line; it is actively teaching them skills they will need for their entire lives (Wittmer & Honig).

5. Guidance is not reducible to a commercial program. The guidance tradition is part of the progressive educational practice of the last two centuries. Guidance is part of the movement toward developmentally appropriate and culturally responsive education. Teachers who use guidance rely on the teaching team (adults in the classroom working together), and positive parent–teacher relations (Gartrell, *A Guidance Approach*). Guidance involves more than a workshop or a program on paper; it requires reflective action by the teacher, teamwork by the staff, and cooperation with families and the community.

Six Key Guidance Practices

Teachers who use guidance have classrooms of a particular kind. In the words of one teacher, when guidance is present, children want to come to school even when they are sick, as opposed to not wanting to come when they are well. Both children and adults feel welcome there. An informed observer who visits such a classroom quickly sees that "guidance is practiced here." Six key guidance practices follow. When they are evident in a classroom, the teacher is using guidance.

1. The teacher realizes that social skills are not fully learned until adulthood. In the process of learning social skills, children, like all of us, make mistakes. For this reason, the teacher regards behaviors traditionally considered to be *misbehaviors* as *mistaken behaviors* (Gartrell, "Misbehavior or Mistaken Behavior?"). The teacher believes in the positive potential of each child. She recognizes that mistaken behaviors are caused by inexperience in social situations, the influence of others on the child, or by deep, unmet physical and emotional needs. Understanding why children show mistaken behavior permits the teacher to teach social skills with a minimum of moral judgment about the child. The teacher takes the attitude that "we all make mistakes; we just need to learn from them."

The teacher shows this understanding even when children demonstrate *strong-needs* (serious) mistaken behavior (Gartrell, "Misbehavior or Mistaken Behavior?"). Such children are sometimes regarded as "bad children," but the teacher using guidance knows that they are children with bad problems that they cannot solve on their own. In working with strong-needs mistaken behavior, the teacher takes a comprehensive approach. She seeks to understand the problem; modifies the child's program to reduce crises; intervenes consistently but non-punitively; builds the relationship with the child; involves the parents; teams with staff and other professionals; develops, implements, and monitors a long-term plan (Gartrell, *A Guidance Approach*).

2. The teacher reduces the need for mistaken behavior. One major cause of mistaken behavior is a poor match between the child and the educational program. (The program expects either too much or too little from the child.) The teacher improves the match by using teaching practices that are developmentally appropriate and culturally sensitive. She makes democratic life skills a priority and helps each child to experience acceptance and success. When children's development, learning styles, and family backgrounds become the main priorities of the program, children become positively involved, and feel less need to show mistaken behavior.

3. The teacher practices positive teacher–child relations. The teacher perhaps cannot love every child, but works to accept each child as a welcome member of the class. In order to prevent embarrassment and unnecessary competition, the teacher avoids singling out children either for criticism or for praise. Instead, she

uses private feedback with the individual, and group-focused encouragement with the class. Even if they are preschoolers, the teacher holds class meetings both for regular business and for problems that arise (J. A. Brewer, "Where Does It All Begin? Teaching the Principles of Democracy in the Early Years," *Young Children* 47 [3], 1992, 51–53). The teacher relies more on guidelines—positive statements of expected behaviors—than on rules, with their negative wording and implied threats. She models and teaches cooperation and empathy-building skills. She models and teaches acceptance of children who might be singled out negatively for physical, cultural, or behavioral reasons. She teaches that differing human qualities and circumstances are natural, to be appreciated and learned from. The teacher understands that children who feel accepted in the classroom have less need to show mistaken behavior.

4. The teacher uses intervention methods that are solution oriented. The teacher creates an environment in which problems can be solved peaceably. She intervenes by modeling and teaching conflict resolution. She avoids public embarrassment and uses removal (redirection and cooling-down times) and physical restraint rarely, only as methods of last resort. After intervention, the teacher helps the child regain composure, teaches more acceptable behaviors, and supports the child's efforts at making amends and reconciling with the group. The teacher recognizes that at times she too will show human frailties. The teacher learns even as she teaches. As a professional, the teacher models the effort to learn from mistakes.

5. The teacher builds partnerships with parents. The teacher recognizes that being a parent is a difficult job and that many parents, for personal and cultural reasons, feel uncomfortable meeting with educators. The teacher starts building partnerships at the beginning of the year. Through positive notes home, phone calls, visits, meetings, and conferences, she builds relationships with parents. It is the teacher's job to build relations even with hard-to-reach parents. When the invitations are sincere, many parents gradually do become involved. The teacher recognizes that mistaken behavior lessens when parents and teachers work together.

6. The teacher uses teamwork with adults. The teacher recognizes that it is a myth that she handles all situations alone. The teacher creates a teaching team, fellow staff and volunteers (especially parents), who work together in the classroom. She understands that children gain trust in their world when they see adults of differing backgrounds working together. When there is serious mistaken behavior, the teacher meets with parents and other adults to develop and use a coordinated plan. Through coordinated assistance, children can be helped to overcome serious problems. As well, they gain in self-esteem and social skills. The teacher knows that effective communication among adults builds a bridge between school and community. Through working with a team, teachers accomplish what they cannot alone.

In summary, guidance goes beyond the traditional goal of classroom discipline: to keep children in line. A guidance approach teaches children the life skills they need as citizens of a democracy: self-acceptance, appropriate self-expression, and self-control. A guidance approach helps children take pride in their developing personalities and cultural identities. Guidance teaches children to view differences in human qualities as sources of affirmation and learning.

Guidance involves creating a successful learning environment for each child. The teacher plans and implements an educational program that is developmentally appropriate and culturally responsive. She serves as leader in a classroom community and helps all children to find a place and to learn. The teacher uses non-punitive intervention techniques, in firm but friendly ways, to establish guidelines and guide children's behavior. She uses conflict resolution as a regular and important tool.

The guidance approach involves teamwork on the part of adults, especially in the face of serious mistaken behavior. Guidance links together teacher, parent, and child on a single team. Success in the use of guidance is measured not in test scores or obedience, but in positive attitudes toward living and learning on the part of all of those involved in the classroom community.

Other Resources
from Redleaf Press

So This is Normal Too? Teachers and Parents Working Out Developmental Issues in Young Children
By Deborah Hewitt
Makes the challenging behaviors of children a vehicle for cooperation among adults and stepping stones to learning for children.

Practical Solutions to Practically Every Problem: The Early Childhood Teacher's Manual
By Steffen Saifer
Over 300 proven developmentally appropriate solutions for all kinds of classroom problems.

Reflecting Children's Lives: A Handbook for Planning Child-Centered Curriculum
By Margie Carter & Deb Curtis
Shows how to put children's needs at the center of your curriculum while dealing with all aspects of young children's programs.

Big as Life: The Everyday Inclusive Curriculum, Volumes 1 & 2
By Stacey York
From the author of Roots and Wings, these two curriculum books explore the environment of a child's life and the connections that make life meaningful.

The Kindness Curriculum: Introducing Young Children to Loving Values
By Judith Anne Rice
Create opportunities for kids to practice kindness, empathy, conflict resolution, and respect.

Making It Better: Activities for Children Living in a Stressful World
By Barbara Oehlberg
Offers bold new information and activities to engage children in self-healing and empowerment.

Optimistic Classroom: Creative Ways to Give Children Hope
By Deborah Hewitt & Sandra Heidemann
Over 70 activities will develop 10 strengths that allow children to meet and cope with the challenges they face.

Infant and Toddler Experiences
By Fran Hast & Ann Hollyfield
Filled with experiences – not activities – that promote the healthiest development in infants and toddlers.

1-800-423-8309